CURRICULUM BY DESIGN

Curriculum by Design

INNOVATION AND THE LIBERAL ARTS CORE

Mary Thomas Crane
David Quigley
Andy Boynton
EDITORS

FORDHAM UNIVERSITY PRESS   NEW YORK   2023

Library of Congress Cataloging-in-Publication Data available online at https://catalog.loc.gov.

Printed in the United States of America

25 24 23   5 4 3 2 1

First edition

To the faculty and students of Boston College

Contents

Preface: Curriculum Revision and the Foundations of American Higher Education

David Quigley

On the occasion of Boston College's 150th anniversary, Harvard University's President Drew Gilpin Faust, the eminent historian of nineteenth-century America, traveled across town to speak in the Jesuit university's theater in October 2012. To an audience of faculty, students, and alumni, Faust noted her host's 1863 foundation and the remarkable act of faith in higher education's power suggested by the act of establishing a college in the midst of the American Civil War. She recounted some earlier moments of not-so-friendly interchange between her institution and her host, while recognizing that so much had changed across the previous century and a half. Throughout her remarks, Faust recounted the many ways that American higher education looks radically different across a span of a century and a half, with the nation's colleges and universities struggling in our modern age for a sense of proper and enduring foundations. Harvard's president took advantage of the occasion to push back against some contemporary critics of higher education and their overly economic analyses of the value of a college degree. As Faust put it:

> By focusing on education exclusively as an engine of material prosperity, we risk distorting and even undermining all a university should and must be. We cannot let our need to make a living overwhelm our aspiration to lead a life worth living. We must not lose sight of what President Kennedy, speaking at the Boston College Centennial, referred to as "the work of the university . . . the habit of open concern for truth in all its forms."[1]

Reflection on earlier moments of American history, Faust argued, suggests a more expansive understanding of the work that the nation's colleges and universities are called to do.

Especially striking was President Faust's exploration of one particular element of the curriculum of the nineteenth-century American college, a required course in moral philosophy. Often taught by an institution's president, the class sought to prepare young men for the world beyond the campus and to see ways of connecting their classical learning to the emerging modern society that they'd be expected to lead. In describing the course and the lost world in which it was taught, Faust struck a somewhat melancholy tone in noting what has been gained but also what has been lost across the generations. A seminar in moral philosophy for graduating seniors seemed to offer a centering element for the nineteenth-century curriculum and a moralizing force for the institution.

Faust's visit to Boston College coincided with the opening of what has evolved into a decade-long renewal of BC's undergraduate core curriculum. The very idea of a core suggests a center around which all else revolves. Such a claim for centrality or a foundation is tough to advance in any corner of contemporary American society, and our institutions of higher education are no exception. Their very excellence has emerged over the past few generations through increasing specialization and ever finer and more nuanced distinctions between and within disciplines. And yet generations of faculty and academic administrators endlessly revisit the curriculum in hopes of somehow realizing their hopes for their shared work. At their best, common curricula introduce students to the liberating dimensions of a liberal arts education, inviting them to engage in a conversation about first principles that spans space and time. A well-designed core aspires to strike a dynamic balance between structure and freedom while making claims that ultimately there is some wisdom to be acquired from the school's faculty and the authors of assigned texts. In contemporary America, the possibility of a common conversation with shared understandings of facts has certainly grown increasingly difficult. Yet the lure of a core on our campuses suggests an enduring desire to find ways to bridge our disciplinary and generational differences.

Faust is not the only American historian to find rich possibilities in the undergraduate curriculum for linking back to earlier moments of American higher education. Studying the evolution of individual institutions' approaches to core revision offers a clarifying lens onto broader processes of institutional and cultural change. While linking back to the past, advocates of core revision simultaneously suggest that a campus-wide conversation might serve to open up new possibilities for pedagogical innovation. For over a century, since the late-nineteenth-century emergence of the modern research university, leaders of American higher education and their critics have struggled to maintain an emphasis on undergraduate teaching and foundational questions. Each generation seems to discover within the core new possibilities for engaging the campus community, linking to local traditions while exploring possibilities for purposeful curricular change. At their best and most successful, projects of core curriculum revision have been particularly potent ways of giving fuller life and dimension to an individual college or university's mission.

A brief survey of the four-century history of higher education in America clarifies some of the central challenges all institutions face in trying to develop a more perfect core. From the founding of Harvard College in 1636 until the third quarter of the nineteenth century, the colonial and then early national colleges were devoted, above all else, to educating young men for the ministry. Down to the Civil War, American institutions sustained strongly denominational identities, and training in theology and moral philosophy were often central to the course of studies for all students. There was no need to talk of a "core curriculum" across the first three centuries of American higher education, since there was such a consensus—at least at the institutional level—as to what should be taught and what young men were being trained to do.[2]

That collective certainty would collapse as the nineteenth century gave way to the twentieth, and the last 125 years of curriculum debates on the nation's campuses emerge from that historic shift. Between the end of the Civil War and the era of the First World War, a series of transformations in higher education and in society more generally forced a profound rethinking of the undergraduate curriculum and led some Americans, for the first time, to start thinking about something that could be called a core. Lincoln's administration had, in some ways, set this process of cultural change in motion in 1862 with the enactment of the Morrill Act, launching the nation's expansive network of public land-grant institutions. The last four decades of the nineteenth century witnessed a historic wave of institution-building, and access to colleges and universities was substantially expanded. No longer were the nation's colleges primarily training young men for the ministry. New types of institutions with very different missions emerged, and a new generation of young women and men pursued their undergraduate studies in a wider range of practical fields and across the liberal arts.

As access to higher education expanded across these decades, many colleges and universities experienced a disruptive period of institutional redefinition. George M. Marsden's 1994 book captured some of this dynamic in the subtitle: "From Protestant Establishment to Established Nonbelief." The rise of the modern research university reoriented higher education toward graduate and professional training, with universities now elevating "research" as a defining value and in many cases abandoning an earlier faith-based sense of institutional self. The historian Julie Reuben writes that the era's "marginalization of morality" is an underappreciated dimension of the rise of the modern university. By the second decade of the twentieth century, a number of faculty members and university leaders came to voice concern about broader changes in the nation's colleges and universities and especially about the diminished place of undergraduate education.[3]

American academics have since the First World War regularly revisited the question of a shared undergraduate curriculum, with certain anxieties recurring even as different moments have led to distinct solutions. A hundred years of debating and revising the undergraduate core has revealed a range of recurring challenges, from the substantive—what subjects and texts count as foundational—to the logistical—how many courses to require, who should teach the core. Already in the late nineteenth century leaders of American higher education had expressed worries about a turn toward research and the emergence of new specializations. The Christian foundations of most private colleges were challenged by forces of Gilded Age and Progressive Era modernization. A first step toward secularization undermined long-established patterns of intellectual life at many institutions.

Columbia University's landmark Core Curriculum, emerging in the aftermath of American involvement in the First World War, marked an important development in the history of U.S. higher education. Columbia's faculty helped invent an American Core, one that made an explicit argument for Western civilization and that has helped to define a Columbia education for more than a century. It's worth noting that many other institutions opted not to pursue a common curriculum in the aftermath of the First World War, and the succeeding decades spurred the creation of general education requirements at many colleges and universities. Most schools' faculty and academic leadership adopted the more flexible and, some argued, less ambitious general education pathway. Future generations would continue to look to the Columbia model as an aspiration for many but also a warning in that it would prove difficult to staff and sustain faculty engagement over time as well as to reconcile with the culture of the emerging research university.

American universities experienced a historic era of expansion and prosperity roughly from the end of World War II through the 1960s. The G.I. Bill fueled a historic expansion in enrollments, and the Cold War brought about a sizable expansion of federal support for higher education. Postwar colleges and universities educated a wider swath of American society. We are now fifty years removed from the end of that immediate postwar golden age era. The recent history of higher education has been, in many ways, an ongoing series of reactions to that earlier era and attempts to move beyond its culture of consensus, in individual institutions but also across the sector as a whole. Higher education leaders and faculty continue to grapple with enduring questions, including the authority of college presidents and their public role; the intersections of race, class, and the democratic purposes of higher education; America's global responsibilities, and the role that colleges and universities play in international relations. A vast cluster of interrelated concerns have fueled recurring and deepening anxieties about higher education's future.

Various contemporary experiments with core curricula have attempted to grapple with the legacies of those earlier moments while responding to the challenges of this era. Some schools have opted to internationalize their core requirements. Others have opted to emphasize opportunities for service learning and community engagements. Whether inter-, trans-, or post- is the preferred prefix, many institutions are questioning just how disciplinary their core should be. A shift away from the nation-state as the primary unit of study has accompanied a broader questioning of the civilizational claims of earlier cores.

Financial pressures and declining enrollments have spurred some campus conversations about the core and about liberal education more generally. Many public colleges and universities have experienced declining state support (as a percentage of institutional budgets), with legislators in some cases pressing for a radical remaking of undergraduate education to respond to labor market needs. The liberal arts, for generations a central element of the democratization of higher education in America, has on some campuses in recent years been understood to be a tool of elitism and privilege. Core revision in the third decade of the twenty-first century must account for this shifting context in articulating new arguments for the enduring and liberating power of undergraduate liberal arts education.

The history of Boston College, a Jesuit, Catholic university and thus idiosyncratic, still reveals certain important aspects of the broader history of American higher education. For its first hundred years, most undergraduates would have followed a course of study that had its roots in the Ratio Studiorum, the 1599 Jesuit document that provided a template for curricula for centuries of Jesuit schools around the globe.[4] Most graduates as late as the early 1960s would have primarily focused on a series of philosophy courses, and the move toward a more modern curriculum came late in Boston College's history. Fr. Michael Walsh, S.J., served as president from 1958 to 1968 and led the transformation of the undergraduate curriculum along with many other aspects of the institution. He looked to educational leaders beyond campus and even beyond the network of Jesuit colleges and universities, developing a surprising collaboration with Victor Butterfield, the president of Wesleyan University, around the remaking of Boston College's curriculum.[5] The 1960s and succeeding decades generated anxieties within faith-based institutions about the relationship between religious belief and pluralism, yet Walsh's leadership reflected an optimistic openness to the possibilities of modernization. Students could pursue a curriculum organized around majors, expanding electives, and the beginnings of a core curriculum for the first time in Boston College's history. A remarkable generation of curricular innovation resulted with the PULSE program, which features a theology and philosophy course linked with a service learning component, and the great-book-organized Perspectives program emerging by the early 1970s, programs that continue to thrive. The next campus-wide conversation about the core curriculum would not occur until the late 1980s when a more fractious campus culture produced a resulting set of documents that allowed for some limited innovation but largely sought to defend the idea of the core from critics. Less experimentation resulted in the last years of the twentieth century, and the 1991 compromise would be the core that remained in place at the start of the last decade when the ongoing process of core renewal began.

Here, some autobiographical reflections may help. I arrived at Boston College as an assistant professor of history in the summer of 1998 and quickly became interested in the university's distinctive undergraduate program. Every student was expected to take two semesters of history as part of a core curriculum that often took up more than a third of a student's total coursework over four years. (See Appendix 3 for a list of current requirements.) As someone who had graduated from Amherst College a decade earlier, a place that had all of one four-credit course as a general education requirement, Boston College's institutional commitment to a shared educational experience for all undergraduates was bracingly distinct. At the same time, I was struck by the seemingly low level of engagement with the core displayed by some of my students and faculty colleagues. Our core seemed too often to be something that needed to be gotten out of the way or, for faculty, something that was taught grudgingly between specialty seminars and upper-division electives organized around one's own research. As a historian, I grew interested in how we had arrived at the core state of affairs at the turn of the millennium, with a set of still-to-be-realized possibilities. Not even a decade had passed since the last bout of core revision on campus in 1991 when I arrived, but it seemed like decades earlier. It would take more than a decade, until 2012, to reopen a campus-wide conversation about the core. Nine years later, this collection speaks to what we've achieved and the work that remains ahead. The collected essays are written in the hope that this might assist others in thinking about how to advance local conversations about meaningful curricular revision. When our renewal experience began, nearly a decade ago, it had been a quarter century since the last revision of the university's core curriculum. While there was some dissatisfaction with particular elements of the curriculum, there had been a general unwillingness to revisit the core.

Early conversations about the core between 2011 and 2013 revealed some excitement that we were willing to put fundamental questions on the table. In pointing to some peer schools doing interesting work and in noting some lingering dissatisfactions with the 1991 revision, other campus voices emerged pointing to new hopes for what a revised core could do. Santa Clara University, among our Jesuit peers, had recently developed an innovative approach to their core. Columbia University continued to invest in its core, suggesting opportunities for addressing some modern critiques of the idea of a single set of required courses. Across town, Harvard University had recently attempted a once-in-a-generation review of its general education requirements, offering both a model and a warning for different members of our community. Over time, as imagining gave way to designing and eventually to implementing a Renewed Core, new collaborations between schools and departments began to take place across campus. Enduring Question and Complex Problem courses generated creative new approaches to engaging students, faculty, and the university's distinctive mission. Lessons still being learned by all involved in renewal relate to the inescapable politics of the process, the need to attend to details, the willingness to change one's own thinking, and the critical importance of persistence by a few key academic and faculty leaders. The success of ongoing and substantive renewal depends ultimately on the proper allocation of resources in support of the curriculum and its teaching. New courses and new programming are only possible when an institution aligns its budgetary priorities with its commitment to transformative undergraduate education.

Recent successes have driven home some of those learnings while also teaching about the complexities of implementing and sustaining meaningful curricular change. Those of us involved from the beginning agree that it remains gratifying to see the ways in which hundreds of colleagues have through their own work and commitment brought the Renewed Core to life. The engagement of university faculty, across fields, generations, and schools, and as evident in the pages that follow, has been perhaps the most inspiring outcome. Core renewal stands as a model for other innovations on campus, and as an invitation to a deeper conversation about what makes Boston College distinctive and what we value in common as members of the university community. The pages that follow are written in the hope of sharing some of one university's experience with curriculum renewal and in the spirit of a common conversation about core values and aspirations that, in our best moments, has defined American higher education.

Boston College is not immune to contemporary higher education's continual search for the remedy to what seems to ail us. A certain faddishness has long characterized higher education as a whole. Global partnerships, the latest technology, transdisciplinarity—recent decades have been marked by pronounced anxieties about the purposes of higher education and an at times desperate pursuit of a series of novel responses. Yet through it all, at colleges large and small, brand-name universities and recent upstarts, the centering work at many institutions remains the project of transmitting an agreed-upon curriculum to each cohort of new undergraduates. At once an inescapable responsibility and reassuring routine, the classes that make up a core curriculum or a set of general education requirements consume a substantial part of any institution's human, physical, and financial resources. Several years working on curricular renewal reinforces our sense that the core provides an unparalleled link back to institutional history and mission. Working together with faculty colleagues across campus opens up new opportunities to think imaginatively and collectively about an institution's current state and future prospects. The work certainly has its frustrations and demands persistence over time. We've learned that it is critical to take seriously the concerns of critics and to attempt to pitch a big tent. It is necessary to remember that the work of renewal never ends but extends across generations and connects the current cohort of faculty colleagues to future generations. Core renewal ultimately is animated by a powerful faith in the intellectual and cultural resources of the institution and in its future students and faculty. A decade into the work of core renewal, I'm more convinced than ever that the work of curricular revision is the most important work that we are called to do as college faculty and academic administrators. The following essays document one institution's recent attempt to deliver on the promise of a transformative undergraduate education for all students.

Notes

1. "Medalist," *Boston College Magazine*, Fall 2012.

2. This and the next several paragraphs are drawn from David V. Quigley, "The Making of the Modern Core: Some Reflections on the History of the Liberal Arts in Catholic Higher Education in the United States," *Integritas* 2, no. 3 (2013): 1–12.

3. George M. Marsden, *The Soul of the American University: From Protestant Establishment to Established Nonbelief* (New York: Oxford University Press, 1994); Julie A. Reuben, *The Making of the Modern University: Intellectual Transformation and the Marginalization of Morality* (Chicago: University of Chicago Press, 1992).

4. John O'Malley, S.J., "How the First Jesuits Became Involved in Education," in *The Jesuit Ratio Studiorum: 400th Anniversary Perspectives*, ed. Vincent J. Duminuco, S.J. (New York: Fordham University Press, 2000), 56–74.

5. Charles F. Donovan, S.J., David R. Dunigan, S.J., and Paul A. FitzGerald, S.J., *History of Boston College: From the Beginnings to 1990* (Chestnut Hill, Mass.: University Press of Boston College, 1990), 297.

CURRICULUM BY DESIGN

PART I
Innovation and the Liberal Arts Core

This first group of essays explains how and why Boston College worked with Continuum, a human-centered design consulting firm, to engage university stakeholders in a renewal of our liberal arts core curriculum. Journalist Bill Bole was embedded with the BC and Continuum team during the two-semester renewal process, and his chapter provides a narrative account of how it worked. Toby Bottorf is a vice president of Service Experience and Design at EPAM Continuum whose chapter explains some of the challenges of working in higher education from the perspective of the design firm. Andy Boynton, John and Linda Powers Family Dean of the Carroll School of Management at Boston College, explains why human-centered design is a useful tool for curriculum revision.

This section also includes essays that describe the challenges we encountered and successes we achieved as we implemented the new curriculum, first as a pilot and then after the program was officially approved. Mary Thomas Crane provides a narrative account of the development and assessment of the Complex Problem and Enduring Question courses through the pilot phase, and Stacy Grooters, executive director of the Boston College Center for Teaching Excellence, explains how the pedagogy workshops (renamed course design workshops) were developed and improved over time.

Next, this section includes essays by Gregory Kalscheur, S.J., Dean of the Morrissey College of Arts and Sciences, and Jack Butler, S.J., Haub Vice President for the Division of Mission and Ministry, that explain the link between traditions of Jesuit pedagogy and spirituality and the new courses we created. Finally, an essay by faculty member Brian Robinette reflects on what he experienced through the process of Core renewal.

1

Choreographing the Conversation

How Designers Helped Clear an Academic Logjam

William Bole

In November 2012, Boston College began holding town-hall-style meetings in hopes of enlisting faculty and others in a difficult conversation about the university's undergraduate Core curriculum, which had not seen a revision since 1991 (in other words, since before most of the undergraduates in 2012 were born). As a fine arts professor said during the second of two meetings that month, "Core avoidance here is like tax avoidance. It's become an art form." Standing at the front of a large lecture hall were people with stellar campus credentials, including the dean of arts and sciences, the dean of the management school, and the director of the university's influential Institute for the Liberal Arts. They and others, however, had little to show for their efforts over months and years to cultivate true dialogue—which explained the presence of someone else at the late-afternoon gathering, a man wearing thick black eyeglasses and a gray sporty blazer with a white open-collar shirt.

That was Anthony Pannozzo, then senior vice president of Continuum, a leading design and innovation consultancy. Boston College had hired the firm to choreograph conversations about renewing the Core curriculum, which students had generally come to see as something to get through, not something likely to challenge or inspire them.

At the first gathering, Mary Crane, director of the Institute for the Liberal Arts, did not wait for the professors to express their wariness of bringing in design consultants to help solve an academic problem. "If I had gotten the letter that you got a couple of weeks ago, I'd have a lot of questions," she admitted to about seventy-five faculty members, alluding to a letter informing them that Boston College had brought Continuum on board to spearhead the dialogue. "Initially, we went in with total skepticism," she recounted (referring to most university leaders, one exception being the Boston College Carroll School of Management's dean, Andy Boynton, who had floated the idea). "Never! Never! How can these people ever help us with our Core?" She explained that senior academic officers gradually warmed to the notion during discussions with more than one consultancy.

After initial remarks at the second town hall, the faculty interrogated Pannozzo on Continuum's experience with universities, which was sparse. He mostly deflected the questions, before Crane interjected, "As far as we know, nobody has tried this approach to revising the curriculum. So we're taking a risk." (Later she upped the ante to say "huge risk.") To which David Quigley, then dean of arts and sciences, now provost, pointed out that other universities aiming to reinvigorate core studies have taken risks and failed—on their own, without design consultation. There was no need to name names, including that of a preeminent institution across the Charles River: The academic graveyard is full of praiseworthy plans to revise core curricula that went nowhere.

So began the public portion of the Core Renewal process at Boston College. At the start of the 2012–2013 academic year, a team of university notables led by Quigley, Crane, and Boynton had begun meeting or otherwise collaborating day and night on the project, as Continuum quietly conducted "stakeholder interviews" with faculty, students, administrators, and alumni, not initially about the Core but about their broader visions and hopes for the institution and the academic enterprise. The process would at times seem foreign to faculty members, or a vocal number who balked at the "vision first" approach and were well armed for debate over the minutiae of curriculum proposals.

Ultimately, there would be a proposed framework for deepening and enlivening Core studies at Boston College. The process that began as a risky venture would end fittingly and bracingly at the end of the academic year—with a call on each school and department to give the proposal a thumbs up or down.

In the spring of 2012, Crane, Quigley, and Boynton began meeting at a diner about a mile and a half from campus, and it was at one of those meetings, over breakfast, that Boynton broached the idea of using a design firm. Crane was underwhelmed by the notion, relating her impression of management consultants as "people in suits who tell you things you could have figured out yourself." (Obligingly but not very enthusiastically, she leafed through books on management and design provided by Boynton—which now round out a shelf of design volumes in her campus office.) Quigley was more open to the suggestion. He and Crane agreed to talk with consultants at the Cambridge offices of IDEO, a premier international design firm headquartered in Palo Alto, California.

Hearing how the consultants go about designing conversations, all three members of this breakfast club began to think that such a process might help break through some of the barriers at Boston College, barriers that stood in the way of productive conversations about the Core curriculum. Forces were indeed at work, having generally to do with inertia as well as with the turf protection all too familiar in academe (some departments feared losing favorite courses in the curricular makeover). Positions were entrenched, for many on campus. The three principals of the effort realized that if the undertaking at Boston College had any chance of success, it would have to involve a far-reaching, many-sided dialogue with multiple stakeholders, and they wondered how they would be able to pull that off, logistically as well as politically, given the hard-held views and resistance to change. There was a pressing need for empathetic listening, which goes to the heart of the creative problem-solving approach known as "human-centered design." Most of all, there was need of a shared vision.

After transitions at IDEO scattered the firm's Cambridge team, the Boynton-Crane-Quigley trio had similar discussions with Boston-based Continuum, and the three were similarly impressed. They began trying to sell the idea to some key faculty members who supported Core revision, but even this natural constituency was initially dubious. Crane recalls a meeting in which she told sociology professor Juliet Schor and biology chair Thomas Chiles (now vice provost), "They are not like other consultants. What they do is different. They're not going to come in and advise us. They're going to talk to people. It's a process." The two professors became sympathetic to the idea, which raised hope that a critical mass of others would do the same.

In October 2012, the letter announcing the Core Renewal initiative, and Continuum's role, went out to all faculty and was soon followed by the first pair of town hall meetings. Continuum is known primarily for innovations in product design, including its spawning of the Swiffer mop and the iconic Reebok Pump, so there was natural skepticism about ushering the firm not simply into higher education, but into the sanctum sanctorum of a Jesuit liberal arts university—the Core curriculum. A newly constituted, eight-member Core Renewal team had to make it clear to the faculty—as well as to Continuum itself—that while Boston College was looking to the designers to foster an environment in which conversations about the Core would flourish, no one was asking them to fashion a renewed curriculum. There would be no need for them to evolve from Swiffer to Socrates; the task of developing a final product and proposals would fall notably to the clients. Skepticism lingered, but the faculty as a whole would, at the very least, quickly come to tolerate the presence of design consultants on campus.

Continuum builds an initial phase of learning and observation into all of its projects, whether conducted for a university, a bank, or a luxury carmaker. At Boston College, the Continuum team (with five day-to-day members and others who pitched in at times) sat in on Core courses, slipped into student government meetings, took suppers in dining halls, lounged in lobbies, and found their way to other campus haunts. Two youngish members of the team latched onto an admissions tour before realizing they were at an awkward age for such an outing, not quite blending in with either the high school seniors or the parents. Among Continuum's early observations was that the sense of community among students is palpable.

At the same time, the consultants were beginning to meet with small groups of stakeholders, bringing a level of empathy to those conversations that others had found hard to muster. For example, as leaders of the initiative acknowledged, it was always tempting for faculty members and advisors to roll their eyes when hearing students say they'd like to take courses that are more challenging but are reluctant to do so because of possibly injurious effects on their GPAs. "But the Continuum people are interested" in this dilemma, Crane noted in an interview at the time. "They're not rolling their eyes. They're asking: 'How can we change this?'"

Likewise, Continuum's Pannozzo made a point that might not have passed inspection in an epistemology course but illustrated the desire to nurture safe spaces for dialogue. "Everything we're hearing has to be taken as true, because it's truth according to the individuals who said it," he remarked during the fall of 2012. He added in an interview, "We're complete outsiders. When faculty talk to us, they can't assume we know anything. The faculty member becomes more open and introspective, and that introspection gets us to an interesting conversation." Another aspect of those conversations during the early weeks and months of the consulting project was the "vision first" approach, in which Continuum seeks (in all kinds of projects) to understand "what motivates you, what your aspirations are, what frustrates you," in Pannozzo's words.

By mid to late November, a broadly inclusive conversation about the future of the Core was in full sail, both publicly with the town hall meetings and behind closed doors. The Boston College and Continuum teams were coming together several times a week, both on campus and at Continuum's headquarters (then in Newton, Massachusetts, before the company moved to Boston's Seaport District). Pannozzo reported frequently on what the consultants had learned from various stakeholders, including alumni who gave a vigorous A+ to their alma mater, and yet something below a B specifically to the Core, for the familiar reasons (not interesting or challenging enough, perhaps overly weighted with prerequisites and distribution requirements). "We were also really struck by how embedded Jesuit values are in the student culture," he related, mentioning the often-heard "persons for others" as an example. "Those values really do hold and make an impact."

For their part, the Core Renewal team (co-chaired by Boynton, Crane, and Quigley) was hashing out concerns such as the need to keep up with the growing caliber of Boston College students and challenge them upon arrival in freshman year. The committee also began wrestling with the fact that the Core occupied a sprawling share of the undergraduate curriculum (some 40-odd percent, according to informal estimates by members of the committee at that time). "How do you make it remarkable?" Juliet Schor ventured at one of those meetings. She had joined the team after her initial skepticism about bringing in design consultants, as did Chiles.

Meanwhile, Continuum was making the ideas visible and tangible in a dedicated room on campus. Black gator boards and other props were popping up in the project room in Gasson Hall, the collegiate-gothic centerpiece of the main campus. At the top of one board was the heading, "Stakeholder Interviews." Below were tacked black-and-white photos of key stakeholders (among them, University President Fr. William P. Leahy, S.J., and two students identified simply as "Nick and Siobhan"). Alongside the photos were yellow and pink Post-its highlighting quotes from the interviews, such as "Help people decide how to live," with an added scrawl from the Continuum team—"Good!!!" Continuum consultant Daniel Sobol noted that the tall, rectangular boards and their contents serve as "our communal brain."

At the start of the spring semester of 2013, the Core committee gathered in a cavernous conference room with high ceilings and whiteboard walls at Continuum's offices in Newton, roughly four miles from campus. There, they spent three and a half hours reviewing the first draft of a "vision statement" along with feedback from University President Leahy. Key members of the renewal process, including both Boston College and Continuum team members, had met with the president and were generally upbeat about his reactions. He had affirmed the process, observing that progress toward renewing the Core "would have been impossible" without outside help (in Boynton's telling), although he was more guarded about the content.

The statement, produced jointly by Continuum and the Boston College people, included a preamble that emphasized:

> It is important, at this point in our work, to remember that we have endeavored upon this journey because we all share a belief that we can design a Renewed Core fully rooted in our University's values, that more

powerfully engages students and faculty. Rather than focus on the current
Core itself and problem diagnosis, we took a step back to understand
how the Core fits into the bigger picture at Boston College and what
goals students, faculty, alumni, and . . . [Jesuits] are trying to accomplish.

The sixteen-page document took the form of a PowerPoint presentation with
tables, graphics, and brief descriptions. For instance, one page was titled "Develop the Whole Person," and it included a stick figure with a thought bubble
displaying seven dimensions of the person: "Thinking/Knowing/Discover-
ing/Reflecting/Impacting/Relating/Working." The document also identified
three basic priorities for Boston College's Core: to inspire intellectual engagement, chart a purposeful journey, and build a foundation for future learning
and personal development.

The next day, January 25, an influential group of twenty faculty and administrators convened on campus to register their opinions. To an extent, the reactions by that group—organized as the Core Advisory Committee—had to
be gratifying to the BC and Continuum teams. Pannozzo started off the meeting by inviting withering criticism of the vision statement—"It's a draft. It's a
straw man." But there were some strongly affirming comments, like this one
by a faculty member actively involved in promoting the university's Jesuit and
Catholic mission: "It [the document] gives me hope that change is possible."
The utterance was a refreshing break from the fatalism that had clouded
conversations about the Core in the past, the feeling that nothing would
change, even with the best of plans and intentions.

All the same, the meeting served up early signs of impatience with the low-
content approach to jump-starting a conversation about the Core. "What
you've presented here is very incomplete," said an administrator. He said no
document of this kind could be complete "without a statement on what you'll
teach" in a core curriculum, even if in a very general sense. Making a tactical
point, Quigley replied that in other efforts to renew core studies at other universities, "The third rail has been leading with content," or specific proposals
rather than a shared vision. Later on, after one faculty member called it a "terrific document," the administrator added: "I don't think it's a terrific document, but it's a ball that's moving forward."

Nearing the close of that meeting, the university librarian hit a high note
when he said, "This is what BC is. We could have this conversation in a civil
and productive way." No one needed to point out that they were having the
conversation thanks in no small part to a design and innovation process.

Then came another pair of town hall meetings that drew more than a hundred faculty members, including many who flinched at the style and broader

tone of the document. Some were repulsed by what they saw as the absence of a coherent narrative in the document, and the reliance on charts, lists, and bullet points. As expected, faculty members also pushed for a focus on content in both the document and the wider discussions underway. One thing had become clear: the Core Renewal process was catching interest at all levels of the university. Boynton joked at the time, referring to staff at the campus recreation complex—"I think that even people at the RecPlex want input."

On January 31, immediately after a reception following the town hall meeting, the Core committee held a hastily planned session over dinner to start working with possible frameworks of a renewed Core. With Boynton at the whiteboard in a campus meeting room, the discussion centered on the possibility of freshman courses built around "Wicked Problems" such as global poverty. While committee members had become fond of this motif, suggested by Schor during sessions in December, there was some general apprehension. A Continuum vice president who attended that meeting cautioned, "We should explore one or two other ideas, because it's a little dangerous to fall in love with one idea at this point."

The next two months brought the Boston College team through the meadows and into the weeds of curricular renewal, in discussions facilitated by the design consultants. "It's starting to get complicated," Boynton said during an all-day meeting at Continuum on a Saturday in mid-February.

The team grappled with a number of realities, including that while many, in theory, were in favor of trimming the Core's hefty footprint, few were willing to pare it down in their own departments. As the group explored a plan for interdisciplinary courses taught by a pairing of professors, with breakout sections perhaps led by graduate students or part-time faculty, Boynton leaned over to Quigley and whispered, "We haven't even gotten to grading issues." During a lunch break, while others spilled into the hallway to grab their boxes of portabella mushroom sandwiches and other fare arrayed on a table, Quigley crouched at a whiteboard wall and with a blue marker began jotting down thoughts under the heading, "Mechanism," adding this question about the renewed Core—"Who's going to be keeping their eyes on it?" With a dwindling amount of unmarked space on the whiteboards, Daniel Sobol retrieved a rolling ladder so he could continue writing at the upper reaches of the walls. He held his red marker as Quigley thought out loud, "We should not allow the AP students to place out, but place up."

Gravitating to the center of discussions was the broader idea of structuring courses for a renewed Core around what the team was now calling "the Ps and Qs," problems and questions. "It's a nice way of signaling what BC is all about," Quigley said at one gathering. That too required drilling down into such questions as whether there were enough big lecture halls for large collections of students who would come together once a week under the tentative plans, or enough faculty resources to sustain smaller discussion formats that were equally part of those plans.

In late March of 2013, the team began circulating versions of a detailed document titled "Toward a Renewed Core," which put a tight focus on creating challenging and topical courses for first-year students.[1] By then, the Ps and Qs had evolved into "Complex Problem" and "Enduring Question" courses. The problems courses (each one dealing with a contemporary global challenge such as climate change) would be team-taught by professors from diverging disciplines, and include three-times-a-week lectures, small-group lab sessions for project work, and weekly one-hour evening sessions that promote reflection and further learning. The courses looking at a perennial question such as justice and the good life would come in pairs: They would be smaller, seminar-style classes in which faculty from different departments would teach separate though linked courses with overlying topics to a shared group of students. The two approaches, looking at a "Complex Problem" or an "Enduring Question," would hardly replace the existing Core. Instead, the new courses would offer alternatives to first-year students who might otherwise take less challenging introductory classes.

Continuum held another round of small-group conversations (including "village visits" to departments and schools, and "co-creation" sessions with students and faculty), before setting up the final and most pivotal sessions in the Core Renewal process. These latter sessions would form a tale of two town hall meetings—gatherings that could not have been more unlike each other, from the standpoint of faculty responses to the proposals.

At the first of those larger meetings, on April 3, some faculty members took sharp exception to the whole idea of gearing the new courses to first-year students. "Why the first year?" asked one professor, arguing that students need a foundation in their disciplines before taking on interdisciplinary "questions" and "problems" courses. "I don't see how they could begin with complex problems." Committee co-chair Crane acknowledged, "Some departments feel strongly that students need a two-semester foundation before taking other courses," but after rattling off other ways of thinking about what constitutes a foundations course, she stressed: "The most important thing is to do something powerful in the freshman year for students." Crane gave the example of students creating a problem-solving proposal for the United Nations, which opened the way to another faculty member's retort—"I can guarantee you that the UN won't give a damn. . . . If we want real depth" in student projects taking on such complex topics, "it should be done at the end rather than the beginning" of the four years.

There was also some trepidation about team-taught classes: "We're going to have to find dancing partners with faculty of other departments. Is that workable?" Some felt the process was moving too quickly (one political science professor complained that the March 27 document was circulated "just before Easter," which fell three days before the town hall).

The reactions led Crane to underscore a practical point about Core Renewal and the highly participatory thrust of this process. "If the faculty hate it, it won't work. We can't offer the courses unless people want to offer them. . . . Honestly, it would be stupid to go ahead with this if a big chunk of departments don't want to be involved in it." At that point, an English professor stood up to say, "The only way to know is to ask people what they really think"—a suggestion he fine-tuned by using the word "vote."

That meeting is what prompted the Core Renewal committee to pursue the idea of consulting with each department and school to get an up-or-down consensus on the revised Core. Three weeks later, the final town hall meeting delivered a vastly different impression of faculty sentiment. The meeting began in a large, tiered lecture room with the usual greetings by Crane, who also made the passing comment, "Trust across departments is not something we're accustomed to." She added, "We've learned some things from Continuum about innovation," particularly the need for "meetings like this," taking notes, bringing together the Core committee almost immediately after the wider gatherings, "making changes" in the curricular design, and so forth.

This time, few disagreed with either the broad vision or the main content of the proposal. There was one echo of the criticism leveled on April 3, with a professor questioning whether students could adequately absorb the material in classes that look at complex problems and questions "before they have the tools to do so," tools gathered in foundational discipline-based courses. That professor, however, quickly added that he "could see the value" of offering the more challenging and topical courses to freshmen as a way of stirring intellectual curiosity. After that, the conversation veered mostly into details and possible ways of tweaking the plan.

"There's a moment now, a constellation of forces," said an English professor, referring to the renewal process with Continuum that would soon end. "I don't think reverting to the status quo is an alternative." A management professor added, "I hope we don't deliberate this too long. Try it. Experiment. Make corrections." She called on her colleagues to resist the "sleepiness" of a conventional academic process that, to cite one example, took Harvard University three years to unveil a far less substantive revision of its general studies. Chiles shared his excitement about the prospects of team-teaching a course with a political scientist or maybe even a fine-arts professor. "I don't know what it is, but I have a bunch of crazy ideas," the biologist said. "The possibilities are limitless."

Five years later, it is difficult to say with certainty what accounted for this tale of two reactions. Was it the somewhat rushed and fairly modest revision of "Toward a Renewed Core" prepared after the April 3 meeting? Or the randomness of faculty turnout at each event? Or perhaps the accumulating sense that the Core committee had forged a genuinely responsive and democratic process of curricular change? Likely, it was all of the above.

In any case, what mattered ultimately was the department-by-department consultation that took place over several days in early May 2013. In the Morrissey College of Arts and Sciences, thirteen departments lined up behind the proposed framework, six turned against it, one was evenly split, and three abstained. Meanwhile, the management and nursing schools went unanimously for Core Renewal, with the education school adding to the predominant "yes" column.

The Continuum team broke down its project room and cleared out of campus. For some time afterward, the university would further evaluate the Core Renewal ideas, with a view toward planting them more deeply in the ground of Boston College's Catholic, Jesuit mission. Father Leahy established the Core Foundations Task Force to continue the work, and the highpoint of that process was the creation of a document in 2014 titled "The Vision Animating the Boston College Core Curriculum," drafted under the direction of Gregory Kalscheur, S.J., now dean of the Morrissey College of Arts and Sciences (see Appendix A). That statement underscored a key role of core studies at a Jesuit institution, which is to nurture personal as well as academic exploration among students, and to help invite them into "a conversation about questions that have long concerned reflective people and . . . into a dialogue of faith and reason in pursuit of truth." In 2015, Boston College piloted its new Core courses (see the essay "Ambitious Plans" by Mary Crane for an account of what came after the work with Continuum).

By all available accounts, the collaboration with Continuum still represents the lone example of a university calling on a design and innovation firm to help set in motion a major curricular breakthrough. In that sense, the designers are batting a thousand.

Note

1. "Toward a Renewed Core," Fordham Research Commons, https://research.library.fordham.edu/education/7/.

What Do We Know?

Or, The Perils of Expertise

Toby Bottorf

The work described in this book is truly groundbreaking. By that I mean: Nobody involved had ever redesigned a core curriculum, together or independently. And nobody's done it since. As William Bole concludes in his narrative of the project, this approach has a 100 percent success rate in curriculum redesign, based on this one and only known attempt.

This track record reflects how we do our best work at Continuum (now EPAM Continuum): We embrace problems that are new to us because we want to create something that is new to the world, and we're dogged and resourceful in getting our ideas out into the world. In this essay I want to share a perspective that is different from those of all the other contributors. I'm representing the designers and strategists who were brought in as outside consultants to work on this daunting project that everyone knew was necessary, but few were enthusiastic to tackle, or even thought likely to succeed. For readers looking to apply lessons from this project to their own distinct challenges, I'll share details on how we work, the value of this approach to higher education, and the way we identified and overcame the obstacles we encountered.

One difficulty we met immediately and persistently was a gap in understanding and addressing the problem. When we began working with Boston College, we did not have a shared language or a common understanding of what good process or good decisions look like. We did not agree on what elements were necessary to begin. Our designers recognize and are comfortable with the fact that innovation is always the work you do with incomplete information. Often, as was true here, we are quite alone in that comfort. Often, we answer anxious questions about a project's direction with a calm "We don't know yet." We expect our confidence to be infectious, but it can have the opposite effect. Our own comfort with ambiguity sometimes unsettles rather than reassures. On this project, it may have suggested to BC that we were clueless, or naïve. We were.

I believe that comfort with uncertainty is not a sign not of our (limited) command, but of our high ambition: If you haven't become disoriented at some point in an innovation project, you probably aren't solving the whole problem or solving it completely. Disorientation leads to reorientation, often with a suddenly clear understanding of the problem. With that, assumptions, preconceptions, and conventional wisdom are revealed as mental constructs, as useful shortcuts for making sense that can, however, obscure new evidence. Getting to this new understanding by reframing the original problem is an essential part of any transformative work. It requires that you begin before you know where you're ultimately going to end up. For that to work you need to trust the process.

Yet we were similarly misaligned in our expectations for how confidence and credibility should arise out of the process. For us, the design process is a journey of increasing clarity and conviction as we conduct research and analysis and start to model a new reality. However, we could have anticipated better how this process and the underlying mind-set might look to educators and administrators. We learned two important lessons that we've applied to all the other work we've since done with educators.

The first is to avoid words that mean different things to different parties. Most obviously, what we mean by "research." We claim that we have a rigorous method for conducting research, and we do, according to our needs. But our needs and our standards are different from those of an academic researcher or scientist. We're not looking for proof, or repeatability of results. We are learning not to reach conclusions, but to find the smartest possible beginnings. We conduct our "research" for generative reasons, in order to understand the needs, values, and motivations of the people for whom we're designing. Our goal is to understand what we're solving for, for people—emotionally, functionally, and socially.

Our second lesson was to acknowledge the tension in how we value and depend on expertise. For any educator hoping to apply human-centered design or design thinking processes to their own innovation challenges, this issue is crucially important. We're not experts in our client's domain. We expect our methods and outlook to be complementary to deep educational expertise. Andy Boynton's essay recounts the skepticism our presence generated: "What do design and innovation consultants know about higher education, let alone the academic heart of a university?"

The question "What do we know?" is especially pointed coming from a university. Universities exist to create and spread knowledge. Knowledge and expertise are their essential currency. For us to reply by saying that "knowing too much can blind you to other possibilities" is to challenge a deeply entrenched and cherished cultural norm.

And yet. One of *our* cherished beliefs is that great insights and ideas are hiding in plain sight. Seeing what is right in front of you is very hard, and is made harder by deep expertise. Somebody, but apparently not Mark Twain,[1] put it like this: "It ain't what you don't know that gets you into trouble. It's what you know for sure that just ain't so."

Our work requires that we reveal and challenge the assumptions behind a stated problem that are so generally shared and seemingly resolved that they have become invisible. We practice naïveté, questioning what everybody agrees on, and why things are the way they are. Designers are inherently restless and optimistic people, on the lookout for the ways things could be better. Tacit assumptions bug us, because they seem like threats that nobody is responding to. They often contain an organization's received wisdom about what can't be done and shouldn't even be tried. They create blind spots.

All our strategists—I almost said "researchers"—are trained to "study people like you're from Mars." We actively cultivate our "beginner's mind," to borrow a phrase from Zen Buddhism. We strive to keep our minds unclouded by assumptions and expectations. It's crucial that we bring our clients to this same vantage point, and we do this through a process of reframing problems, which I'll discuss in more detail shortly.

For something as intricately assembled as a curriculum, that moment of breakthrough clarity was always going to be elusive. Educators and administrators recognize each part and how well or badly it fits into other parts. They want to jump right into those details. Or, from our perspective, to skip an important step. So, to avoid premature arguments about the myriad details and see the curriculum as a whole, we stepped way back. We chose to ignore for a while all the minutiae of how a solution might or might never work. All the logistical, financial, and pedagogical details could easily have caused us to lose the plot. We needed to create space for meta thinking and reflection, and to foster conversations that could lead to a shared vision. This reframing was an exercise in consensus building, in simplification and abstraction to key principles. We made progress possible by not diving right in on all that was contested or unclear. Instead, first we drafted a vision statement and socialized it with a diverse group of stakeholders, each offering feedback based on their own priorities and investments in different aspects of the outcome.

Our role was not to redesign individual courses or the details of the new curriculum. As complementary partners, we wanted to leverage all the resident expertise and stimulate passionate engagement with the new curriculum. We were setting the conditions for innovative work to be done by Boston College, not by us, often through shuttle diplomacy among the varied constituents.

To succeed, we needed to legitimize our unfamiliar and unproven process, our way of framing and solving ambiguous challenges. This approach is often called human-centered design, or more recently, design thinking. Other writers in this book use either term.

Human-centered thinking is generalist, but it's not generic. It's a flexible practice without a predetermined domain. It offers a clear process and a few governing principles, which are sustaining during the murky middle when we may *still* not know what we're making. These are, first: Design for people. And second: Make and test things in order to learn. Together, these governing principles require a mind-set that is experimental, empathetic, and optimistic, and which can be applied to almost any problem. Indeed, it is best suited to unfamiliar or ill-defined problems. With this way of approaching each new and different challenge, the focus is always on the unique particulars of that challenge, because the human needs, values, and aspirations that we're designing for are so particular.

Our credibility rested on the assumed credibility of our approach—which is to say, we had very little at the start. Human-centered design is the process we have subscribed to at Continuum for over thirty-five years. Its history and greatest success have been in humanizing products and technologies. Our Greatest Hits include the Swiffer, the Insulet Omnipod (an insulin delivery device), and UCAR, a premium ride hailing service in China. More recently, this approach has become more broadly understood as design thinking, which is a simplified and more portable evolution of our way of working. We think it has been oversimplified and overgeneralized. Anyone can now buy a book or take a course that will help you design your life. The book is filed under self-help. Given that reality, early distrust of the idea that our way of working could bring success to this project was totally justified. We had much to prove. On the one hand, human-centered design is clearly a great way to develop certain things, mainly new products and services. On the other, design thinking seems to be a practical philosophy about pretty much anything. Neither alternative is reassuring. Some members of the faculty found it hard to swallow at times. How could the same approach that led to the invention of the Swiffer help redesign a core curriculum? We heard loud and clear from one, "I'm not a mop!" Skepticism was a reasonable response.

It was easy for us to empathize with that reaction, because that "beginner's mind" I referred to earlier includes a general skepticism, an acceptance of our limited understanding. In reality, we needed to apply our approach in a way that found the sweet spot: neither a forced application of a methodology from other domains nor a vague translation of things that have no domain whatsoever. We needed to collaborate and build trust by modeling an approach that we believe in deeply, one that can tackle all sorts of challenges and that is broadly applicable outside the traditional esthetic domain of design. Design entails the ingenious framing of problems worth solving, and the elegant crafting of their solutions. This way of working is particularly effective in an environment of complex systems with messy stakeholder ecology, constrained by bureaucracy or regulation and threatened by disruptive business models.

I want to highlight three ways I think our approach was useful, and even essential to the success of this work: It helped the team get unstuck on a fraught and unappealing challenge; it synthesized varied perspectives to build a shared model of the goal, one that could be owned by all parties; and it offered a safe and steady way to build and test ideas.

Reframing Intractable Problems

The decision-making process in higher education can be politically intricate and procedurally opaque. In this environment, even a great idea must be socialized in the right way or it will be rejected. The insistence on right process can lead to locked-in orthodoxies, or lower expectations about what is possible. This leads to teams utterly unprepared to take on unfamiliar challenges. They are stuck at the outset when asked to confront problems that everybody agrees are essential to address, but nobody believes are possible to resolve. Pessimism becomes self-fulfilling.

There are many kinds of intractable problem. Most commonly, we see these three: those based on zero-sum assumptions that create false choices; those with circular (chicken and egg) dynamics, where every individual factor must be addressed first or last; and those with unclear governance that are everybody's-yet-nobody's problems. We saw elements of all three in this work.

Intractable challenges like these require the jolt of a fundamental re-frame. Reframing helps to defamiliarize and then reorient in new ways. It makes visible all the stuff that was right there all along. It leads to innovative work that seems obvious after the fact, which is a hallmark of great design.

Reframing itself was a difficult model to get people to embrace. We succeeded in getting people to subscribe to a vision statement that would then direct the details of the new curriculum. But we had less success in reframing this work "as experience."

The idea that experiences can be "designed" takes some getting used to. My background is in designing services and experiences: things like digital apps, financial service "products," or interactions you have with the people who work in service jobs in shops and restaurants. We often point out that "you may not have designed this experience, but your customers are having one. So maybe it should be designed." Even when we're designing physical products, we think in terms of the best experience of use. We get people to first articulate and agree on what is desired as an experience. With this reframe, the focus is not on the thing, not on what you are making or offering; it's on what people do and feel as a result. *What's the desired impact on a student's life and learning?* Thinking this way is a big shift. Reframing, especially around experience, can help get diverse and even combative groups all looking at the same problem in objective and compatible ways.

This outside-in reframing, or looking at things from the customer's perspective, ran into some resistance. The humanist perspective—designing for people, meeting them where they are—was easy to embrace, because it is very aligned with Jesuit ways of being in the world. But the idea that students were "customers" was deeply problematic. There was no way a purely "customer-centered" model would be embraced. In reality, we did not need one. We were trying to build a dynamic system, and our end users were not only students, but faculty also. Steering clear of the word and the question of who was the "customer," we still were able to define a model of the right student outcomes, described as how we aimed to "develop the whole person," and put it at the heart of the vision statement.

Synthesizing Diverse and Passionately Held Viewpoints

Design thinking projects often require that we bring together the diverse perspectives of passionate experts. Building consensus in a fiercely independent stakeholder ecosystem is a crucial prerequisite. The way in which we conducted empathetic interviews and the range of people we listened to helped reconcile perspectives that at first glance appear to be in conflict. We heard students say they wanted more challenging courses. We heard professors say they didn't really, not if it meant their grades could suffer. We treated both perspectives as subjectively true and tried to find a frame that made sense of both subjective realities.

When we finish learning, we conduct a review of what we heard. We do not interpret (yet) or judge. This work, and the way it was documented and socialized, led to very productive conversations and the beginning of belief in common ground.

This was crucial progress, given how much ground we needed to make up in proving the validity of our approach. We started with very little inherent legitimacy. The first signs of any kind of consensus had been that we were outside consultants, not to be trusted, and that this whole thing was not likely to work. For the sake of staying optimistic and showing positive energy, we saw that in the best possible light: At least our varied and stakeholders had found common cause about *something*.

Higher education can be a highly political and territorial environment. We became facilitators and mediators in an environment where diverse constituencies had very different needs. We knew we could not impose change on people as independent as university faculty members. We generally never expect to be able to force change on people, as a part of our outside-in mind-set, so we were well prepared. We expect that any change must be activated by self-interest (based on personal needs or values) and grounded in intrinsic motivation and belief.

In all our work, we apply two simple rules, which we think of as the customer experience bill of rights. Whatever we are designing, we have to work with these two inescapable truths from the customer's—or end user's—vantage point: First, "You can't make me!" And second, "I'm not doing it wrong." This is especially true when designing for tenured faculty.

Making Progress Possible

We follow a deliberate innovation process through projects, which is especially valuable for projects with uncertain or open outcomes. This orients us to where we are in the journey and what we should do next. It helps us sequence work in the right way, such as by postponing questions about the details of implementation that can gum up progress if asked too early. Generally, we move through a succession of four questions with a sense of increasing momentum. We go from asking "What do we know?" to "What does it mean?" to "What should we do?"—that is, defining the strategy—and then on to the visible and material phase of design, figuring out "What does that look and feel like?" In that last phase, we design and test in fast iterations to make sure it works.

At the end of each phase, we build consensus around our current decisions and capture the implications that frame and drive the next phase. Each phase has a rhythm of divergent thinking, where we ensure everyone is appropriately heard and engaged, and convergent thinking, where we drive toward decisions and consensus. This way of working can *look* unstructured, and has space for improvisation, but it is always rigorous and evidence-based.

So, while those are three reasons for educators to adopt this way of working, ultimately this is just a process. The only real reason to engage in this human-centered work is because of a meaningful challenge centered on people. We have helped institutions of higher learning develop a framework for a more inclusive campus climate; we have defined a student-centered vision of services to direct large technology investments across nine offices (such as admissions, registrar, academic, and career advising); we have even rewritten a university's mission. We were trusted to do all this work and more because we had previously worked with Boston College. On all these projects, each done with greater domain expertise than the last one, we started with our carefully cultivated beginner's mind. But, of course, we *are* experts, only in things that seem inexpert. It takes ongoing effort and a true method to strip away preconceptions, to imagine what's possible out of a true and empathetic understanding of people, their context and social dynamics.

We brought our particular set of skills to bear, which as I've described, mostly consists of knowing *how*, not *what*. We helped to reveal important things that were hiding in plain sight, to cultivate belief and momentum on work people were not excited about, to reorient around a shared vision, and to communicate a clear, inspiring, and plausible story. Storytelling is core to what we do.

Our leap of faith is not to claim: *Just because we've never done this before doesn't mean we don't know how.* It's to say, *When you're trying to do something new, it helps to have never done it before. Or at least to act as though you never have.*

We were sustained throughout by just how familiar the challenge seemed to us, in a strange way. We understood that we were trying to help realize the promise of a great liberal arts education. And we recognized in that objective some of our own priorities as designers, including the belief that knowing facts and concepts is not enough, and that building durable, resilient ways to confront any new question is the greater goal.

Note

1. The movie *The Big Short* opens with this epigraph and, like many others, attributes it to Mark Twain. It sounds like Twain, but scholars at the Center for Mark Twain Studies of Elmira College have found no citation.

Innovation

Andy Boynton

More and more, higher-education leaders are acknowledging the need to innovate—to forge new ways of responding to challenges such as retaining or attracting students and bolstering revenue. One survey released by *The Chronicle of Higher Education* in late 2017 concluded that these leaders "now regard innovation as a major task that requires fresh thinking." College and university officers are responding in part to their own assessments (they're less likely than in the past to say U.S. higher education is the best in the world). They're also mindful of public opinion: Only a quarter of Americans agree that our system is just fine the way it is. In the *Chronicle* survey, clear majorities of senior academic leaders went further to say that students—more than any other group, such as politicians, trustees, and faculty—should be the driving forces behind innovation. Faculty, however, should have the greatest input into decisions about how to address student concerns, according to the respondents. At the same time, the leaders were far less sure about next steps. How to carry out a process of innovation? Experts who reviewed the survey results noted that these officials at times also seemed to confuse innovation with technology or with rebranding to better sell their programs.[1]

At Boston College, where I serve as dean of the Carroll School of Management, we face our share of challenges—one of which has been to renew and enliven the university's large undergraduate Core Curriculum. As already told in these chapters, we decided to seek out a design and innovation firm to facilitate much-needed discussions about the Core and help bring about the "fresh thinking" that would spark a new approach to our Core studies. Needless to say, the decision raised questions as well as more than a few eyebrows. What do design and innovation consultants know about higher education, let alone the academic heart of a university? Put another way, more neutrally: Can principles of innovation travel well from management to higher education, especially when it comes to matters related to coursework? Probably the best way for me to begin answering these and similar questions is to hark back to the summer of 2011, when I broached the possibly crazy idea of inviting design consultants to help tackle our problems with the Core curriculum.

By then, academic deans had engaged in numerous conversations about the future of our Core studies, which affect not only arts and sciences students but those from the professional schools as well. The Core had last been updated in 1991. It was not adequately engaging the passions and intellects of our students—or, to be frank, our faculty. We were not challenging our increasingly capable students as much as we should. We wanted to make our Core curriculum more forward-looking, with ways of thinking and learning that draw in part on multidisciplinary approaches. I felt a special stake in the outcome of these discussions, as an alumnus of Boston College and the dean of a business school that has integrated the liberal arts into management learning, with a view toward helping our future leaders think critically, analytically, broadly, and creatively.

The Core was not working as well as it could, and conversations about the Core—among the larger ranks of faculty and administrators (including myself)—had become stale and predictable. They were going nowhere. Against this backdrop, we decided that we needed a fresh approach to innovation, one that called for people from outside our immediate circles to help foster discussions and unleash ideas.

Here, let me inject a very simple principle of management and innovation: All organizations are good at some things and not others. Institutions of higher learning, and especially national research universities, are good at creating and imparting knowledge. When it comes to change and innovation—not so much. You could write dissertations on why this is the case. My sense is that the reason would have something to do with two characteristics of a university, both of which are laudable and essential—deep expertise and a strong culture. I would say that both of those organizational traits combine to make universities change-resistant. Our cultures are, in a sense, too rich, too closed; this reality has a number of advantages, but it's a prescription for business-as-usual over the long run.

What we definitely did not need was expertise in higher education: We were overflowing with knowledge of that variety. Rather, we needed help from people who were experts in nothing more or less than change and innovation. In this context, it's worth drawing a distinction that some management theorists have made between the stock of knowledge and the flow of knowledge or ideas. At Boston College and other major universities, the stock is considerable, and it mainly involves a rich collection of faculty who are experts in their fields. These institutions also store a vast amount of knowledge about a university's tradition and values (in our case, the tradition of Jesuit Catholic liberal arts education) as well as about its students.

A store of knowledge is wonderful, but with regard to the Core at Boston College, it was not helping us move our ideas among faculty or students. We had a stock of knowledge about learning in general and core studies in particular, but we had a great deal of trouble using it; we couldn't leverage that repository of expertise. What was missing was a vibrant flow of ideas—capturing concerns, synthesizing, feeding back, testing ideas, setting out a vision, going back and forth with iterations, and otherwise engaging in the art of idea flow.

All of that was needed because of the logjam of conversations about the Core at Boston College. We did not need or want people externally who would come up with specific solutions to our core problems. We needed people who would listen sympathetically to any and all sides of the issue at Boston College and pull people together in conversation. We needed process, not content (certainly not in the early stages of this innovation project).

But why a design firm in particular? There are straightforward answers to that question, but first, I want to say that we should not be too fixated on the difference between design thinking and some other innovation processes. In recent years the lines between design thinking and innovation have blurred considerably. That is largely because of the growing influence of design, which has gone far beyond its familiar roots in physical product design and has extended to services, organizational processes, and user experiences (including digital interactions). Empathizing with users, becoming absorbed in their experiences, rapid prototyping, and a healthy appetite for failure (that is, failing early to succeed sooner)—these are indicia of design thinking that have swept the broader innovation world. To my way of thinking, the sweeping is far from complete, and industries of all kinds have a long way to go before embracing design thinking in practice, not just in principle or aspiration.

Still, to answer the "why design?" question a little more directly: It has to do with hierarchy, or the lack of it. We might think of our institutions as hierarchical, and we all know there's enough of that in higher education. In a practical sense, however, top-down approaches don't go over well, especially with regard to curriculum and teaching. We cannot fire most of our regular faculty, nor would we want to take such drastic action. We cannot make them teach something or teach in a way that goes against their sense of how they should impart knowledge and inspire learning. As teachers, they have a craft, which we need to respect and approach with great care.

Design thinking is a good model for working in such an environment because it is fundamentally nonhierarchical. It is human-centered, which is key to any effort that seeks to engage students and faculty. Most companies using design strategies will speak of "the customer" and his or her experiences, frustrations, and aspirations. Our students are not customers, but they are end users, and so are, in a sense, the faculty. They're teaching or learning in a setting where we seek to innovate. Human-centered design forces us to understand that whether we're talking about a project to create a new and improved mop or a richer, livelier curriculum, there's a person at the center of it.

In the remainder of this essay, I look more closely at some other design/innovation principles that could help with the fresh thinking urgently needed in our institutions of higher education. Along the way, I'll illustrate those principles with examples from innovation projects at major companies as well as our own experience at Boston College. Some of these examples are based on interviews I've conducted with designers, including those at Continuum.

Bridging Distant Worlds

Melding ideas from disparate realms is one of the pressing tasks of innovation in almost any project. Andrew Hargadon of the University of California, Davis, has driven home this point in his historical studies of innovators such as Thomas Edison. A noted expert in technology management, Hargadon points out that people in Edison's New Jersey laboratory took their knowledge of electromagnetic power from the telegraph industry, where most of them had worked, and transferred it to products they developed for other industries, such as mining and railways. Occupying such a spectrum of spaces, the technicians in Edison's legendary "invention factory" picked up knowledge they couldn't have gained by working in a single industry. They "bridged distant worlds," as Hargadon puts it.[2]

One aspect of this bridging is that the innovators aren't necessarily striving for dazzling originality. "Edison's inventions were not wholly original," Hargadon points out. "Like most creative acts and products, they were extensions and blends of existing knowledge."[3]

To get the off-the-beaten-path ideas you have to venture into less-familiar idea spaces. The sociologist Ronald S. Burt has studied this process and has consistently found that standout ideas come from managers who forge conversations with people outside their immediate circles. These people span what Burt refers to as "structural holes," gaps between different groups of people. Those who stand near the structural holes are "at higher risk of having good ideas," as Burt styles it. "This is not creativity born of genius. It is creativity as an import-export business."[4]

In one of his first studies on the subject, in 2000, Burt worked with several hundred supply-chain managers at the military contractor Raytheon. He had them jot down ideas for improving the company's supply chain—ideas later evaluated by senior executives with long experience in that arena. The managers were also asked if they had talked about the ideas with others in the company, and with whom they had the most detailed conversations. In the end, the most highly rated ideas came from managers who had stepped into the unfamiliar spaces, sharing their notions with people beyond their teams and specialties.[5]

One reason for the breakthroughs in our Core Renewal project is that we bridged the distant worlds and positioned ourselves near the structural holes. To begin with, we did so by seeking out the design consultants, bringing together that world and higher education (specifically, Boston College's search for a better way of resolving the problems with our undergraduate Core curriculum). As noted, the design world gave us not so much the content for much-needed curricular change, but a process that seemed unfamiliar to us in many ways (including Continuum's emphasis on reaching a shared vision, first, before addressing the specific content of proposals, which is what curriculum experts immediately want to do).

Once the process was underway, we also began drawing bits and pieces of ideas from different realms—for example, reaching deep into the Jesuit humanities tradition to come up with our plan for courses revolving around perennial questions, while drawing on the natural and social sciences for ideas about what we initially called "Wicked Problems." These two disparate sources of insight came together to create the centerpiece of our core-renewal approach, which pivoted on courses in "Enduring Questions" and "Complex Problems."

Note also that we weren't looking to be creative for its own sake and come up with pure originality—a first-of-its-kind innovation in liberal arts education. We were extending and blending "existing knowledge," in Hargadon's words, and arriving at a solution that was creative and original *for us*.

Deep Discovery

There are a number of problems with the way many organizations go about innovating, and if I had to elevate one above all the others, it would be the tendency to believe we know more than what we actually do, at the outset of projects. It's easy to think we have a clear understanding of the situation and that we know what the problems are; as a result, we go straight to the solutions. What this leaves out is the need to explore problems and realities in the initial phase and engage in a process of deep discovery, together with end users.

Consider one of the more illustrious projects undertaken by Continuum: the development of the Swiffer cleaning tool. Back in the 1990s, Procter & Gamble knew it wanted to make floor-mopping a better experience, if not a pleasurable one, but there was so much that the consumer products giant did not know. Most of all, the P&G executives did not realize just how odious a task it was to mop a floor. The company also didn't quite grasp the fact that its own product—the time-honored mop—was contributing to the misery. Mops were doing so, for example, by unhappily blending water and dust, which produces dirt and leads a consumer to spend as much time rinsing mops as they do cleaning the floors. Hardly anyone understood that the mop had to go.

For P&G, one of the roads to innovation ran right through the homes of a relatively small number of typical consumers. The design team fanned out to eighteen homes in Boston and Cincinnati to observe people and their mopping rituals. That's when the team noticed that most people swept the floors before they mopped (because mops aren't good at getting rid of dust) before engaging in the ritual of mop rinsing (otherwise, during the next mopping they'd return dirt to the floor). It was dirty work, so people wore old clothes. In the end, P&G unveiled Swiffer Sweeper, a cleaning tool that was half-broom, half-mop, and mess-free, using dry disposable cloths. First introduced in 2001, the Swiffer line of products (including wet cloths as well) is now the greatest-ever success in the storied history of P&G.[6]

This methodology was not unique to the Swiffer project. A decade before that, Reebok Corporation was altogether certain that it had a solution to its recent competitive woes. An upstart company named Nike had begun eating Reebok's lunch with its sensational new athletic shoe, the Air Jordan. Reebok was reeling, and the best it could come up with was a me-too idea: It wanted to produce a knock-off version of the Air Jordan line. But, as with P&G, there was much that Reebok didn't know (and, at that moment, didn't care to know). The company wasn't looking to step back and question its assumptions. It wasn't ready to dig deeply into the possibilities of what customers might want to see in a running shoe. It wanted certainty.

During the initial stage of discovery, Reebok soon realized that the knock-off was a dead end—for one thing, there was only one Michael Jordan who could singularly market such an athletic shoe. The company also learned well from a bunch of high school basketball players who had been recruited by Continuum to try out a crude prototype (a "Frankenstein model") of a new sneaker that used inflatable air to provide better support and a more comfortable fit. In focus groups, prior to this experiment, the kids and other consumers had dismissed as ludicrous the idea of inflatable shoes. Many projects would have ended right there—and Reebok almost put a stop to it, but an enlightened

CEO let it go further. The next scene: high school kids in Newton, Massachusetts, trying out the makeshift shoes, not in a conference room, but in their own environment, on the basketball court. They liked it, and the iconic Reebok Pump was born.[7]

At Boston College, we used this process of deep discovery as part of our efforts to renew the Core curriculum. We went into the project with no assumptions about how to solve the problems with the Core, or even about what the problems were, other than a general lack of engagement on the part of students and faculty. We had no proposals or solutions in mind, so we dug deeply into the experiences of various stakeholders and created a feedback loop in which ideas bounced between the different parties, the Continuum team, and our Core Renewal team. During the early phases of the project, most of these ideas revolved around a developing vision of core studies in the context of a Jesuit liberal arts education. We eventually used a so-called "back-casting" approach to figure out how we could get to that vision, through our designs of a renewed curriculum.

Experiential Modeling

Many people think of prototyping as something done at the end of an innovation process, after coming up with an exact and final idea of the product or service that is needed. Design methodology, however, often calls for a different approach in which the experimentation starts early, during the stage of deep discovery, as indicated in the example of the Reebok Pump. In this way, many designers (not all) practice what Continuum refers to as "experiential modeling" rather than full prototyping, which happens later in the innovation process.

One example of this modeling from the not-for-profit world was a project that Continuum conducted for the Department of Homeland Security, which in recent years has been exploring the future of emergency response management. To start with, teams of design consultants and others began traveling with emergency responders on their calls, and they learned, among many other things, that paramedics usually do not wear the bulky bullet-proof vests they are given to protect against attacks on them (which sadly have become frequent in recent years). That is because they have little or no time to put them on during an emergency, and they prefer not to wear the awkward gear during their non-emergency hours.

After gaining this insight, the designers did some experiential modeling. They asked EMTs to try on ordinary paintball vests—a crude prototype ordered through Amazon via two-day mail. The technicians were able to picture themselves wearing the vests all day. That simple exercise made it possible for the design team to envision a vest made of extremely light-weight fabric strong enough to repel bullets (material for such fabric is on the horizon). It was but one insight in a much larger, ongoing project.[8]

During the Core project, we borrowed from these techniques—for example, by circulating early-phase documents that laid out possible visions of core studies along with basic priorities, and were intended primarily to stoke conversation. We also used computational models that allowed us to get an early handle on logistical questions, including the resources (physical space, for example) necessary for introducing curricular innovations, as well as how new courses (with added sessions such as labs and evenings of reflection) would fit into existing student schedules. It's best to start modeling those plans before settling on them.

Compatibility

One much-overlooked aspect of innovation is the need to make sure that the new idea is compatible with the organization—its systems and processes. Popular themes such as "disruption" are more glamorous, but a high degree of compatibility is necessary—and needs to be a major factor in the design.

The story of Thomas Edison and the introduction of electrical service is instructive in this regard. Edison did not make the first incandescent bulb, but he did create the first system to distribute power for electric lights on a large scale. More to the point, the Edison electric system prevailed because he understood that to introduce electricity into homes, the idea would have to be compatible with what customers already knew and with how utilities operated at the time. So, Edison started with electric lights and went to extraordinary lengths to make the first lamps as similar as possible to the gas lighting that people had been using for half a century. Consumers saw that electric lights would fit easily into their homes and would provide the same function as gas, but without the smoke, flickering, and fire risk. Likewise, Edison did not try to invent a whole new infrastructure; instead, he ran the electricity through the pipes, fixtures, and meters already in customers' homes. One general lesson: It is extremely hard to scale up an innovation without doing what Edison did to achieve compatibility.[9]

I do not mean to pit compatibility against significant change. There is, in fact, a dynamic relationship between compatibility and disruption—between the old and the new, between "the way we do business around here" and the adoption of trailblazing ideas. Big ideas must be sufficiently robust to break new ground, but must also be implementable and economically viable. If the idea can't be implemented by the organization, then by definition it's a bad idea and a poor investment.

We grappled with compatibility all through the Core project and continued to do so as we fielded pilots and worked steadily to improve the offerings. Seeing to it that these offerings align with Boston College's mission and identity has been one critical part of the task. We have also learned that compatibility will often require compromise, given the reality that resources (funds, faculty availability, physical space, etc.) are not infinite, in any organization. For one thing, we ended up with a wonderful, multifaceted curriculum, but one that was limited largely to first-year students, not to the entire undergraduate population. To do otherwise would have been incompatible with our existing capacity.

In this essay, I have addressed the "Why design?" question, but I am closing with a few words about another question, closer to my sphere of higher education—"Why a business school?" Why would a school of management and its dean play such an active role in renewing an undergraduate liberal arts curriculum? In the context of Boston College, it is an easy question to answer: Our programs at the Carroll School of Management are deeply interwoven with the university and its Jesuit liberal arts mission. But that aside, why should any business school actively engage in an effort of this kind?

In my mind, the answer has much to do with the bridge between liberal arts and management that many are trying to build. Arts and sciences schools increasingly see the value of integrating their programs with professional education and experiences as part of their approach to contemporary liberal arts learning. For their part, a growing number of business schools want to teach their students to think deeply, broadly, creatively, analytically—to seek out new ideas every day and to become lifelong learners. At some schools like ours, we also want to produce leaders who are engaged with urgent social and ethical challenges in contemporary business and society. Helping our students pursue their passions in the liberal arts is one way of accomplishing those aims.

I think, again, of Thomas Edison. He placed a high value on broadly diverse learning, according to his biographers Sarah Miller Caldicott (his great-grandniece) and Michael Gelb, writing in their book *Innovate Like Edison*. All of Edison's prospective employees had to take a written test of 150 questions, among them: What is the first line in the *Aeneid*? Who composed *Il Trovatore*? What voltage is used on streetcars? Edison demanded scores of 90 percent or better for those who would be initiated into his invention factory in Menlo Park, New Jersey.[10] In many ways, we are just catching up with the Wizard of Menlo Park.

Notes

1. "Making Way for Innovation: Crafting New Strategies for the Future of Higher Ed," *Chronicle of Higher Education*, https://futuresinitiative.org/rethinkhighered/wp-content/uploads/sites/193/2017/07/Making-Way-for-Innovation-.pdf. Unfortunately, the article is no longer available online.

2. Andrew Hargadon, *How Breakthroughs Happen: The Surprising Truth about How Companies Innovate* (Boston: Harvard Business School, 2003), 49.

3. Andrew Hargadon and Robert Sutton, "Technology Brokering and Innovation in a Product Development Firm," *Administrative Science Quarterly* 42, no. 4 (1997): 1.

4. Ronald S. Burt, "Structural Holes and Good Ideas," *American Journal of Sociology* 110, no. 2 (2004): 349, 388.

5. Burt, "Structural Holes and Good Ideas," 349–399; Michael Erard, "Where to Get a Good Idea: Steal It Outside Your Group," *New York Times*, March 22, 2004, https://www.nytimes.com/2004/05/22/arts/think-tank-where-to-get-a-good-idea-steal-it-outside-your-group.html.

6. Andy Boynton, "The One Thing Companies Get Wrong When Trying to Innovate," Forbes, September 15, 2014, https://www.forbes.com/sites/andyboynton/2014/09/15/the-one-thing-most-companies-get-wrong-when-trying-to-innovate/?sh=2963a4ba378b.

7. Andy Boynton and Bill Fischer, *The Idea Hunter: How to Find the Best Ideas and Make Them Happen* (San Francisco, Calif.: Wiley, 2011), 60–61.

8. Andy Boynton, "When a Prototype Isn't Enough, Use Theatrical Tricks to Sell Your Idea," *Harvard Business Review*, June 16, 2017, https://hbr.org/2017/06/when-a-prototype-isnt-enough-use-theatrical-tricks-to-sell-your-idea.

9. Hargadon, *How Breakthroughs Happen*, 6–7. "Edison's Electric Lighting System," Thomas A. Edison Papers, https://edison.rutgers.edu/life-of-edison/innovation-series/lighting/conceiving-the-system.

10. Michael J. Gelb and Sarah M. Caldecott, *Innovate Like Edison: The Success System of America's Greatest Inventor* (New York: Dutton, 2007), 146. "Could You Work for Thomas Edison?" Edison Muckers, https://www.edisonmuckers.org/tag/edison-test/.

Ambitious Plans Meet Reality

How We Made the Renewed Core Work

Mary Thomas Crane

In May 2013, after a slim majority of departments and schools approved of the proposal for a renewed Core (see "Toward a Renewed Core,") and Continuum left campus, the three of us (David Quigley, Andy Boynton, and Mary Crane) who had led the renewal process were elated, relieved, and eager to move on to implementing our ambitious plan.[1] We felt we had gained enough support to set up a new system of governance for the Boston College Core and to completely transform the first-year curriculum, assigning all incoming students to large "Communities of Inquiry" in which they would take a Complex Problem course (a team-taught, interdisciplinary course addressing a contemporary social problem) and a pair of Enduring Question courses (two separate but linked courses addressing a perennial human question from two disciplinary perspectives). Together these courses would constitute 12 credits of their first-year load. How we would actually manage to do this: Find enough faculty (and teaching fellows) to offer 7,500 seats in completely new collaboratively taught courses, develop labs and reflection sessions using novel pedagogies, find classroom space to offer multiple 225-person lecture courses, was not entirely clear at the time. We had hopeful ideas, but no detailed plans. This new requirement and these new courses would have to be phased in gradually, we figured, but we were confident that we could make it work.

Fortunately, William P. Leahy, S.J., the president of Boston College, approached the renewal of the Core with more wisdom and a healthier dose of caution than the three of us. When departments and schools weighed in on the plan, they wrote reports that detailed both their enthusiasm and their concerns. Father Leahy read all of these reports carefully and took faculty concerns seriously, wanting more consensus than we had garnered before allowing us to move forward. We spent the summer of 2013 meeting with the president and attempting to respond to these concerns, some of which, in retrospect, I now see were well-founded.

Many faculty members believed that requiring all first-year students to complete 12 Core credits would be unworkable for STEM students who needed to take a number of prerequisites early on in their college career. Others believed that the large size of the proposed Complex Problem courses (225 students) would be alienating for first-year students. Another set of concerns focused on the interdisciplinary nature of the courses, with some arguing that first-year students would not be ready to undertake such work before mastering any disciplines at the college level. The philosophy and theology departments were especially concerned that students who had not studied either of these subjects in high school would need a foundation in their disciplines before moving on to interdisciplinary study. Some felt that it was a mistake to separate out reflection from regular classroom practice, since they found it integral to their own teaching, while others felt that reflection had no place in a rigorous academic course. Many were sure that there simply would not be very many faculty members who were willing to take on interdisciplinary team-teaching, never mind project- or problem-based learning. Others questioned whether these new courses would be rigorous and whether the Complex Problem courses could possibly be worth 6 credits.

The president also felt that the Vision section of "Toward a Renewed Core" had moved too far from the Jesuit mission of the university. In an effort to appeal to the broadest possible range of faculty members we had tried to translate principles of Ignatian pedagogy into secular language, but it was important to university leadership that the vision for the Core articulate an explicit and distinctively Jesuit rationale for our liberal arts Core.

Summer turned into fall, the 2013–2014 school year began, and in January 2014, in response to all of these questions and concerns, Father Leahy appointed a new task force to draft a new mission statement for the Core and eventually to work toward a small-scale pilot of the Complex Problem and Enduring Question courses. This group was chaired by then associate dean of Arts and Sciences Gregory Kalscheur, S.J. Professor Julian Bourg of the History Department joined the task force and took a central role under the leadership of Father Kalscheur in the work of crafting a new vision that combined aspects of the existing 1991 Boston College Core, the Core Renewal proposal ("Toward a Renewed Core"), and the tenets of Jesuit education. By May 2014, the task force had a new vision ("The Vision Animating the Boston College Core Curriculum," see Appendix A and the essay by Father Kalscheur) and a charge to pilot a few Complex Problem and Enduring Question courses in the 2015–2016 academic year.

Julian Bourg and I were appointed as project managers in charge of developing a three-year pilot of Complex Problem and Enduring Question courses, beginning on a very small scale with only three Complex Problem courses and six Enduring Question pairs. Since the ambitious goal of grouping all freshmen into large learning communities for these courses and common reflection experiences was no longer on the table, we made a series of pragmatic decisions about the size and structure of the courses. Because we no longer needed to accommodate the whole first-year class, we scaled back the size of Complex Problem courses to 76 students (based on the size of widely available classrooms) and the Enduring Question courses to 19 (below the *US News and World Report* small-class threshold). In order to accrue classroom time that would equal 6 credits, CP courses had to have at least three 50-minute lectures, a 75-minute lab, and a 110-minute reflection session each week. Teaching a CP would "count" as two courses of the teaching load of each faculty member involved. Because Enduring Question faculty were each teaching a regular 3-credit course, we felt we could only require EQ faculty and students to attend four evening reflection sessions in the course of the semester.

That just left us with the problems of figuring out what reflection actually was, what labs in non-STEM fields should be like, finding faculty willing to develop and teach completely new courses and pairing them with each other, and persuading departments to assign graduate teaching fellows (out of their regular TF pool) to run the labs in the CP courses. We also had to find classroom space for class sessions, labs, and reflection. We needed to figure out how the divisions of Mission and Ministry and Student Affairs could contribute to the reflection portion of the courses and persuade them to become involved. We also needed to find ways to inspire and encourage faculty to develop new modes of active pedagogy and to develop courses that met the learning goals laid out in "Toward a Renewed Core" and the new Vision. We were daunted by the amount of work that getting these courses up and running would involve, especially since we were doing it on a volunteer basis. I made a strategic visit to the provost early in the fall to suggest that we couldn't take on a task of this magnitude without compensation, which he agreed to provide.

Fortunately, Boston College was also committed in other ways to providing the resources necessary to successfully implement this new curriculum. Boston College had undergone a change in academic leadership and it was especially important that the new provost (Quigley) and new dean of Arts and Sciences (Kalscheur) had been involved in developing the courses and the vision and were invested in their success. A crucial early decision to offer a $10,000 stipend to each faculty member willing to develop new Complex Problem or Enduring Question courses made recruitment easier and allowed us to require faculty to attend a pedagogy workshop over several months in the spring and to require submission of a syllabus that met course guidelines before they could receive a check.[2] In addition, each Complex Problem course was provided with a budget of $2,000 to fund lab and reflection activities, including refreshments, outside speakers, and field trips. Each Enduring Question pair received $1,000 for these kinds of expenses. The Core office would eventually provide help with ordering food and scheduling transportation.

For the three years of the pilot phase and beyond, matching faculty to develop and teach these courses was a huge challenge, both time-consuming and difficult. Eventually, after five years or so of offering Complex Problem and Enduring Question courses, we had a cohort of faculty willing to regularly repeat their courses, and this relieved the pressure of needing to match faculty to create enough new courses to provide the 1,000 seats per year that became our goal. At first, though, we tried a range of strategies for bringing people together.

From the start, a number of faculty were willing to participate, some because of the stipend, some because of interest in interdisciplinary team teaching, some motivated by a bit of both. But they had to be matched up with teaching partners, had to find common ground with that partner and identify a topic, and then had to come up with ideas for courses that would meet the criteria for EQ and CP courses and appeal to students. Over the next few years we tried a bunch of different methods for matching faculty with each other: an online wiki site where people could post topics they were interested in (not successful), keeping a spreadsheet of faculty and topics (helpful), social/matchmaking events (somewhat successful), one at a time introductions via email (labor intensive but the most successful method). We returned to Continuum at one point with a group of administrators and faculty members to brainstorm approaches to matchmaking, but nothing proved to be a silver bullet that would shorten this process or make it less difficult until we accumulated a sufficient backlog of repeated courses that reduced the number of new courses we needed to recruit for each year (see Appendix C, "Complex Problem and Enduring Question Courses, 2015–2021" for a list of every CP and EQ offered since the beginning of the pilot to the spring semester of 2021).

Some faculty members had friends or spouses in other departments and were able to find a common topic and matched themselves. Others would write to us with a general topic, and we would simply start emailing everyone who might plausibly be interested in co-developing a course in that area. There were many highly successful matches made in this way as well as episodes of faculty ghosting potential partners, leaving them at the altar to pair with someone else, and other misunderstandings. To my surprise, given the highly hierarchical nature of the academy, many of the most successful pairings extended across significant status divides, with tenured full professors working happily with full-time non-tenure-line professors of the practice. Most professors of the practice in the Morrissey College of Arts and Sciences at BC are hired and promoted based on excellence in teaching, so in many cases they took the lead in developing effective pedagogies for the course. To my knowledge, almost all of these across-status pairings have been successful and in some cases inspired tenure-line faculty to change their approach to teaching across the board.

In order to make the Complex Problem and Enduring Question courses distinctive, ensuring that they involved active learning and that they incorporated some aspect of the Jesuit emphasis on integrating course material with life beyond the course, we had mandated that the Complex Problem courses include weekly labs, and that both EQ and CP courses featured separate evening sessions for reflection. Weekly labs were supposed to reinforce course material through projects, experiments, exercises, and other active learning techniques. Reflection sessions were supposed to help students learn how to reflect on what they were learning, and to ask students to connect course material to the world, or to their own lives.

We worried that CP faculty would not be willing to develop and be present for three lectures and a lengthy evening reflection session each week. We had hoped that the divisions of Mission and Ministry and Student Affairs could help with developing and leading reflection sessions in some way. Julian and I had a series of meetings with the leadership of those divisions and soon discovered something we should have already known: The professional staff working in those areas already had full-time jobs and could not be expected to take over responsibility for aspects of courses. Nor could they be expected to assist with courses under the direction of faculty. Working together with the leadership of those divisions, we identified some ways in which faculty could tap into programming those offices already offered. Representatives from the career center, library, women's center, office of health promotion, institutional diversity, and elsewhere had always been available for class visits and outreach to students. Mission and Ministry helped to develop and train students for the POD (Purposeful Ongoing Discussion) model of peer mentorship developed by Brian and Tara Gareau in their CP on climate change and now used in a number of Complex Problem courses (see Gareau essay). But for the most part, faculty were creative and came up with their own ideas for reflection sessions (which include exercises, films, guest speakers, discussions, and field trips). We began to compile lists of successful reflection ideas, which we made available to faculty as they developed their courses. A number of the faculty essays in this volume reveal how crucial the reflection session has ended up being in ensuring the distinctiveness and success of these courses.

In November 2014 we received proposals for the first set of Complex Problem and Enduring Question courses to be offered in the 2015–2016 academic year. We went back and forth with faculty, providing feedback to help shape proposals to reflect the new guidelines for these courses, making sure that they engaged meaningful problems and questions, seemed engaging to students, and were explicitly interdisciplinary. We tried out titles and course descriptions on a focus group of undergraduates and began learning that what seemed fascinating to a middle-aged academic was often incomprehensible to an eighteen-year-old student. Faculty willingly rewrote titles and reshaped descriptions in response to this feedback. We were able to approve three CP courses and six EQ pairs, meeting the goal that we had set out to offer, and began working with the Center for Teaching Excellence to plan the required pedagogy workshop. We also began meeting with student services to identify classrooms and schedule the classes, labs, and reflection sessions. The pedagogy workshops took place as planned in second semester. As Stacy Grooters's essay in this volume explains, they got off to a somewhat rocky start and became more successful over time.

We also went to department chairs and requested teaching fellows to assist in the large Complex Problem courses, primarily by running the labs. We had assumed that since these Complex Problem courses replaced other departmental Core courses, graduate students could just be shifted from regular Core courses to these new ones. In fact, virtually no departments had extra teaching fellows that they could assign to these courses. Coming up with teaching fellows was another annual struggle until 2017, when the Provost's Office provided funding for a Core Fellows program that brought in postdoctoral visiting assistant professors to co-develop and run labs and teach Enduring Question courses. This added a significant expense to the program, one that we had not anticipated during the Core renewal process; however, it also improved the quality of the labs. In recent years, current Core Associate Dean Brian Gareau and Assistant Dean Elizabeth Shlala have improved the Core Fellows program so that it provides crucial support and mentoring to the Fellows while they are at BC.

Boston College was also willing to provide ample resources to help us promote these new courses to incoming students. The Office of University Communications filmed short videos that featured each faculty pair discussing their course. Glossy brochures were printed and mailed to all families of incoming students. Letters were sent to parents. Julian and I met with summer advisors and student orientation leaders, plugging the courses to them. This flood of videos and brochures did attract students to the courses and, I believe, helped set an expectation that they were new, exciting, and special. Some of those involved with existing Core and first-year programs questioned the intensive and expensive promotion that these new courses received.

In the summer of 2015, Julian Bourg was named the first associate dean for the Core and a new University Core Renewal Committee was formed with both elected and appointed members. I have been an appointed member of the committee since its formation and continued to work with Julian on developing the CP and EQ courses, and then with the new associate dean, Brian Gareau, who replaced Julian in June 2018. As the first set of courses began to run, Julian also had to reorganize the process for approval of regular Core courses, revamp the website, continue to approve regular courses, while matching faculty, finding classrooms, scheduling classes, soliciting proposals, designing a pedagogy workshop, and finding teaching fellows for even more courses to be offered in 2016–2017. This was too much work for a single person to do. Eventually the Core office gained an assistant director (Charles Keenan, then Elizabeth Shlala), a graduate assistant, and under Brian Gareau a staff assistant to help with this work, but the full complement of staff was not in place until 2018.

We were all anxious and excited when the first Complex Problem and Enduring Question courses began in the fall of 2015. When I ran into faculty who were teaching these courses that fall in elevators and in the halls, I eagerly stopped to ask how their courses were going. Almost immediately I started to get anecdotal evidence that faculty found teaching these courses to be a lot of work but highly rewarding. We began to hear that students found them engaging and transformative. A group of students from the EQ "Truth-telling in History" and "Truth-telling in Literature" courses approached the Core office with a proposal to create a new undergraduate concentration in truth-telling, so enthralled were they with the courses. Julian and I were invited to visit a joint final class session of "Inquiring about Humans and Nature," and "Imagining Humans and Nature." We listened as the students talked about how the course had been eye-opening for them. They commented on the importance during their first year of the community formed in the course, getting to know and appreciate people from different backgrounds whom they would most likely not otherwise have gotten to know. When asked about their favorite reading from the courses, they spoke enthusiastically about Sophocles' *Antigone*, Thoreau's *Walden,* and the papal encyclical on the environment, *Laudato Si'.* They talked about how much they enjoyed talking about those books in class and how they often continued the conversation outside of class. They talked about how the course stretched their thinking and helped them see both humans and nature in new ways. I have to admit that I had tears in my eyes as I listened to these first signs that the new courses did at least some of what we hoped they would do to revitalize liberal arts education at Boston College.

However, anecdotal evidence was not enough. We needed a comprehensive assessment plan for these courses so that we could figure out what worked and what didn't work and revise them as needed. We needed to make informed decisions about whether the courses should continue, and at what scale, after the end of the three-year pilot. We worked closely with the Boston College Office of Institutional Research, Planning, and Assessment (then under the direction of Kelli Armstrong), which devoted considerable time and effort over several years to evaluating these courses (another sign of BC's commitment of resources). IRPA also collected information about the Core as a whole, to be included in an annual "State of the Core" report that the associate dean was required to prepare each year for the steering committee of deans and vice presidents. IRPA had access to information about the students who enrolled in the pilot courses and those who were in regular core courses based on admissions data. They also had the results from the Higher Education Research Institute's *The Freshman Survey*, regular course evaluations, and a special survey that they administered to students enrolled in Complex Problem and Enduring Question courses. In addition, IRPA conducted focus groups to gather reactions from faculty and teaching fellows who taught the pilot courses.

Assessment of the first year of CP and EQ courses (2015) showed that they were for the most part very successful. Demographic data showed that more women than men enrolled in these new courses (63.4 percent female, 36.6 percent male). Most of the students (76.4 percent) were from the Morrissey College of Arts and Sciences (with only 5.7 percent from Nursing, 12.2 percent from Management, and 5.7 percent from Education). Correlation with *The Freshman Survey* data revealed that students who enrolled in the pilots scored significantly higher on civic engagement, pluralistic orientation, social agency, and likelihood of college involvement, but significantly lower on academic self-concept and college reputation orientation. In other words, the students choosing to take these courses were more open-minded, adventurous, and engaged, but less confident about their academic ability. On the survey administered by IRPA to EQ and CP students in the fall (with an 84 percent response rate), they strongly agreed that they gained knowledge of two different disciplines and developed habits of reflection. Students slightly disagreed that they had considered the role of religious faith in their courses. They found these courses to require somewhat more effort than other core courses (mean of 3.6, with 4 as more effort and 5 much more effort). Results in the spring were similar. Student comments in both fall and spring were "overwhelmingly positive" (in IRPA's characterization) and reflected high levels of engagement and enthusiasm: "The most valuable thing about my Core Pilot course experience was that I actually wanted to go to class and learn about the subject." "I now continuously think about the issues and topics brought up in class on a daily basis, unlike some of my other core classes where it is easy to sit in on lectures and leave without ever thinking or reflecting about what you learned."

"The small size of the class and the knowledge and passion of these professors created amazing dialogues about issues that really matter." "The whole class was eye-opening, and it made me more aware of everything around me, all the cause and effects in society due to climate change, namely social justice." "I see how the course material is present in my everyday life outside of the classroom, from the decisions I make to the formation of my personal beliefs." "This course, as cheesy as this may sound, changed my life."

These surveys also revealed areas that needed improvement. In addition to the usual complaints about work load, students felt that the lab portion of the Complex Problem courses were not always helpful: "The lab I got was far more work than others." "The topics in the labs were engaging, but there wasn't enough time to fully immerse yourself in them. Each week there was a new lab with a new topic assigned, with little to no discussion about the lab from the previous week." Some students did not get much out of the reflection sessions: "Some reflections seemed to be a repetition of what was said in lectures which felt boring and a waste of time." "The least valuable aspect to these Core Pilot classes was the formality of needing an evening discussion (Reflection). While they were enjoyable, they did not add a great deal to the quality of the course." With Enduring Question pairs, students sometimes felt that the two classes were not as coordinated as they might have been: "Both courses were individually valuable and of interest to me, but there were times when I found it difficult to find relationships between the two." Based on these comments, we worked to improve the pedagogy workshops (renamed as course development workshops) to emphasize better integration of labs, reflection sessions, and the two connected Enduring Question courses.

At the end of the first pilot year, then, we had a clear sense of problems that needed continuing work. Over the course of the next two years we steadily increased the number of seats offered in Enduring Question and Complex Problem courses as we worked on all these issues. Faculty felt that the course development workshops improved. We began to learn how to make labs and reflection sessions more effective, and instructors from previous years shared their knowledge with faculty enrolled in the workshops. Along the way we tried some experiments, offering some larger (150-seat) Complex Problem courses, some smaller writing intensive Enduring Question courses, some courses that were opened up to sophomores and juniors as well as freshmen, and experiments with the POD model of peer mentorship for the reflection sessions. We were able to develop a new "maker space" classroom to be used for labs and began to bring in postdoctoral Core fellows to replace graduate student TFs. The Core Renewal Committee also began to develop direct assessment of student work from CP and EQ courses in an attempt to get a clearer sense of whether learning goals were being met.

The accumulated evidence was ultimately enough to continue offering Enduring Question and Complex Problem courses after the three-year pilot period ended. We settled on a goal of offering around 1,000 seats per year in these courses, a number that seemed to meet student demand without eating into enrollment in PULSE and Perspectives, the long-standing and very popular interdisciplinary Core courses offered by the philosophy and theology departments. We offered 1,022 seats in the 2018–2019 academic year, and saw 85 percent of those seats filled (866 total students). In 2019–2020 we offered 971 seats and filled 89 percent (861 students).[3] Some departments began to renew their own departmental Core offerings along the lines of these courses, including theology, history, and English. Julian Bourg and Brian Gareau in turn brought together groups of faculty to revise the dated Cultural Diversity requirement, implementing new courses on "Difference, Justice, and the Common Good" in America, and on "Engaging Difference and Justice" throughout the world.

The 2021 academic year marked the sixth year of Enduring Question and Complex Problem courses. A number of faculty regularly repeat their EQ and CP courses, but we have also had a steady stream of new courses, including courses involving faculty from the Law School, Lynch School of Education and Human Development, School of Social Work, as well as the Morrissey College of Arts and Sciences (see appendix, Master List of Complex Problem and Enduring Question Courses). Most of these courses have been successful, and those that have been less so seem naturally to fall by the wayside. Faculty still reliably describe these courses as their "hardest and most rewarding" teaching roles. Students continue to comment that they help them develop an intellectual community, recognize the difference between high school and college thinking, connect school work to life, and foster habits of self-reflection. Some Boston College faculty members still regard our collaboration with Continuum as problematic, but almost everyone now views the courses that were developed as a resounding success.

Notes

1. For the text of "Toward a Renewed Core," see https://research.library.fordham.edu/education/7/.

2. After a few years, it became clear that Complex Problem courses were more work to develop and teach than Enduring Question courses, and we had some trouble recruiting faculty willing to take on this work. We made a decision to raise the CP stipend to $12,500 and reduce the EQ stipend to $7,500.

3. *State of the Core*, 2020, Report by Associate Dean for the Core Brian Gareau, Boston College, table 6, page 27.

Slowing Down and Opening Up

Preparing Faculty to Co-design a General Education Course

Stacy Grooters

A key element of implementing the Renewed Core was the requirement that all faculty teaching in the program participate in a series of workshops the spring prior to launching their courses. Initially called "pedagogy workshops" and later renamed as "course design workshops," these sessions were intended to invite faculty to think more intentionally about their pedagogical practices and to support them as they developed their course plans and syllabi. The Renewed Core administrators approached the then newly created Center for Teaching Excellence (CTE) with an invitation to partner on planning and facilitating those workshops. The CTE had been established in 2014 by consolidating a handful of existing instructional development programs offered through the school's student learning center with a well-established educational technology unit that had a strong history of supporting faculty via instructional design and project-management services. Under its new mission, the CTE was meant to continue its support of educational technology, but now as part of a larger emphasis on teaching and pedagogical innovation, broadly defined.

Getting faculty to recognize that the CTE's mission now extended beyond educational technology was sometimes a challenge in the center's early days, and so the invitation to partner on the Renewed Core workshops was an excellent opportunity for us to connect with a group of highly motivated and talented faculty in conversations well aligned with the CTE's new mission. This was our chance to show these faculty what the "new CTE" was really about. That said, the Renewed Core workshops also posed a challenge for us since the CTE, like most teaching centers, was designed to be a resource that instructors seek out *voluntarily*; its programs and services are nearly always optional—and, in many instances, even confidential. The fact that for many of these faculty their first interaction with the CTE would be through a required program raised the stakes for us. We knew that participants would base much of their perception of the CTE and its usefulness on their experience in these required workshops—workshops about which at least some of the Renewed Core faculty harbored clear reservations.

Educational developers are well versed in the various flavors of skepticism that faculty can bring to teaching center workshops and other programs. Most common are concerns that workshop facilitators will take a "one size fits all" approach to teaching—ignoring the variations that emerge across different disciplinary and course contexts—or that facilitators will disregard faculty's hard-earned pedagogical expertise developed over years of classroom experience. Other faculty find teaching a fairly straightforward enterprise and so don't see the value of spending hours reflecting on their practice with colleagues; or, in the words of one Renewed Core instructor, they simply believe that "pedagogy is boring." Luckily, educational developers also have a lot of practice in overcoming faculty skepticism, and we were pleased over the years to hear from faculty participants in the Renewed Core workshops—either informally or through anonymous feedback surveys—that they had come into the workshops with low expectations but typically left finding them worth their time. These comments ranged from a friendly "that wasn't as bad as I thought it would be" as someone walked out of the room to feedback a year later from a faculty member who now found himself applying ideas learned in the workshops across all his courses.

In order to head off possible instructor skepticism, we sought to design the workshops to center faculty members' own expertise and disciplinary contexts as well as their perceived needs as they prepared to teach in the Renewed Core. Identifying what those needs were took some time. We experimented over the years with different areas of focus—negotiating "difficult dialogues" in the classroom, facilitating more effective group projects, taking more project-based approaches to instruction, minimizing plagiarism—but discovered that while some faculty found those conversations useful, there was too much variation across the group to narrow in on any one pedagogical question that the majority of the group considered relevant. Instead, it became clear that we could best engage the largest number of participants by focusing on what was unique about the Renewed Core: its expectation that faculty co-design their courses. Whether they were collaborating to design a single interdisciplinary course, as in the case of the Complex Problem courses, or designing two distinct but intentionally interrelated Enduring Question courses, almost all Renewed Core faculty found themselves in course design territory they'd never navigated before.

In the end we settled on a few basic elements as essential for the success of these workshops:

1. *Focus on course design collaborations:* Our primary goal in the workshops was to facilitate more productive planning conversations among the teaching partners. We highlighted the challenge of co-designing and co-teaching as central to the work of the Renewed Core and were explicit about our goal that the workshops help faculty be better collaborators.

2. *Honor faculty expertise:* By making room for experienced faculty voices in the workshops and also by setting aside time in each session for faculty to share their developing plans with each other, we demonstrated our respect for the collective expertise and pedagogical wisdom of the group. This also signaled our hope that the workshops could serve as nascent communities of practice that the faculty could continue drawing on once the semester began.

3. *Leave plenty of time for collaborative work:* The most consistent feedback we got over the years was that faculty most valued dedicated time to work with their partners, and so we worked to minimize the amount of "presenting" in the workshop so that we could maximize their time for collaboration.

These touchstones informed our approach to the required workshops, described in more detail in the following section.

Workshop 1: Ignatian Pedagogy and the Core Curriculum

The initial workshop in the series was meant to orient faculty to the values underlying the Core Curriculum and how those aligned with Ignatian pedagogical principles. During this session, the associate dean for the Core welcomed the new Renewed Core instructors and provided an overview of Core Curriculum goals as well as important logistical details faculty needed to be aware of. The faculty teaching teams also had the opportunity to introduce themselves and describe the courses they'd be teaching. This seemingly routine exercise often sparked a heightened sense of energy in the room as faculty got a chance to hear the creative visions of their colleagues and see how their own course(s) fit into the larger work of the Core. That initial session also included a presentation on the tradition of Ignatian pedagogy by the dean of the Morrissey College of Arts and Sciences. Explained in more detail in an earlier chapter, the dean's presentation focused on the Ignatian pedagogical paradigm's attention to context, experience, reflection, action, and evaluation, and how those elements informed an overarching commitment to education as a transformational enterprise.

Workshop 2: Backwards Design and Aligning Course Goals

The second workshop introduced faculty to the idea of "backwards design" and drew largely on Dee Fink's work in *Creating Significant Learning Experiences*.[1] Fink argues that taking a "backwards" approach to course design—working first to identify course learning goals rather than starting with decisions about course content—encourages greater alignment of course elements to course goals and so leads to improved student learning. In the Renewed Core workshops, we spoke not only of the learning benefits of backwards design but also its usefulness as a tool to facilitate better coordination and communication between course partners. We explained that it wasn't unusual for faculty to have strong convictions about the course design practices that work for them—practices often learned through trial and error or inherited from mentors or colleagues—without ever articulating to themselves how and why those practices work. And so when faced with having to negotiate a common approach with their teaching partners, faculty sometimes struggled to explain their teaching rationales. The backwards design process could be a tool, then, to help faculty slow down and reflect on the beliefs about teaching and learning underlying their choices. Our goal was that, as course partners worked together through the backwards design process, they would begin surfacing their common teaching values as well as important differences in how they viewed learning and the classroom, allowing them to discover those differences early on in their partnership (rather than discovering them once the course was already well underway).

In the workshop, we simplified Fink's multistage process into a three-step formulation: First, define course learning goals; then design assessments to measure whether students are meeting those goals; and finally plan the day-to-day activities and assignments that will help students learn and progress toward those goals. We represented this process in three questions—(1) What do I want my students to learn?; (2) How will I (and my students) know if they've learned it?; and (3) How will I help them learn it?—all considered within the context of what Fink calls "situational factors." These contextual factors, such as student population, curricular requirements, instructor strengths and values, as well as larger social and political happenings, can serve to shape a course's development and its ability to meet students' needs.

As a starting point for discussion in the workshop, we gave faculty a series of prompts about their course's situational factors to first discuss with their course partners and then to share with the larger group. In those discussions of course context, most faculty tended to highlight two areas as most pressing to them. First, they raised concerns about the particular challenges of teaching first-year students in a general education setting. Many of these faculty had either never taught first-year students before or at least hadn't taught them in a while (and some had only taught graduate students previously), and so they spent quite a bit of time reflecting on how they might need to adjust their expectations to meet their Renewed Core students where they were. The second area of concern had to do with faculty members' pedagogical comfort zones and how well those meshed with those of their partners. For some faculty, the very structure of the Renewed Core courses posed a new challenge: For example, a faculty member who'd primarily taught large lecture courses was now having to imagine herself into a small, discussion-based seminar. Others realized differences in how they preferred to organize course time or design major assessments.

This surfacing of pedagogical differences usually served as a useful transition into the next stage of the workshop, which focused on how faculty members' different disciplinary contexts may also pose challenges to their collaborations. We introduced the notions of "unconscious competence" and "expert blind spots"—the idea that as we gain expertise in a field we can lose track of how we came to learn that knowledge in the first place—and how those gaps could pose a challenge, not only as they sought to build a course that would be meaningful to first-year students who were likely novices in the field, but also as they tried to collaborate with their partners across disciplinary differences.[2] The notion of "threshold concepts" and "disciplinary bottlenecks" (Middendorf and Shopkow) also proved useful; inviting faculty to identify the conceptual stumbling blocks students typically experienced in their courses was often a helpful jumping-off point for conversation among course partners about how their disciplines could intersect.[3] Sometimes it was through the work of unpacking such disciplinary concepts that faculty found the most interesting areas for interrogation. In one instance, a faculty member from economics working with a colleague from philosophy realized that their understanding of "choice" and how it worked were remarkably different, and so they ended up designing one of their central assignments to encourage students to interrogate those cross-disciplinary meanings of "choice."

All of these discussions of course context and disciplinary differences set the stage for the activity that took up the bulk of our time in that second workshop, which was an exercise meant to facilitate faculty conversations about their common course learning goals. For those teaching Complex Problem courses, this exercise was meant to help them come to consensus about the central goals for their co-taught course; for the Enduring Question courses, it was about identifying areas of overlap between the goals defined for each of the paired courses. The exercise was inspired by a similar approach developed by Emily Lardner, formerly of the Washington Center at Evergreen State College, a national leader on learning community course design. Faculty were first asked to work independently to brainstorm their responses to a prompt: "What do you want your students to know and be able to do as a result of their participation in your course?" They were encouraged to generate as many ideas as they could and were asked to write each distinct response on a separate sticky note. To help spur their thinking, faculty were given visual representations of Bloom's Taxonomy as well as Fink's Taxonomy of Significant Learning, and they were also encouraged to consider the long-term impact they hoped to see: "In five to seven years, how do you hope your course is still relevant to your students' intellectual, professional, personal, spiritual, civic lives, etc.?"

After taking about ten minutes to reflect individually on their learning goals, faculty pairs were then asked to compare their responses and look for areas of synergy. Having only one goal per sticky note allowed faculty to experiment with different ways of grouping ideas and to discover novel approaches to defining their course goals. We tried to leave at least thirty to forty-five minutes for faculty to work through this activity, and it was not unusual that faculty pairs moved on from their work with the sticky notes to more formal course planning during that time. We concluded that workshop with a brief moment for faculty to share what they had discussed, so they could see how others had approached the puzzle of integrating their course goals.

Workshop 3: Reflection Sessions and Integrated Learning

The third workshop focused primarily on designing the reflection sessions for each course. Faculty were typically divided by course type for this workshop: those teaching Enduring Question courses in one group and Complex Problem faculty in the other. The session for the Complex Problems faculty also incorporated some discussion of their lab sections—which in earlier years were actually the subject of an additional fourth workshop for the Complex Problems faculty—but as the visiting Core Fellows took more and more responsibility for designing those labs, there was less emphasis placed on them in the spring workshops. Our approach to this workshop also changed as faculty's understanding of the reflection sessions and the role they played evolved. In the early years of the Renewed Core, most faculty understood the reflection sessions to be co-curricular elements of the course, opportunities for students' formative self-reflection and personal growth, but not necessarily a space where much learning happened relevant to the course content. However, over time, faculty came to see that it was in those reflective spaces, which asked students to connect what they were learning to their own lives and commitments, where students did some of their deepest thinking about course content. And, in particular, faculty observed students using those spaces to do the work of integration, of exploring the interplay between the two disciplines being studied.

As that connection between the reflection sessions and student learning became more evident, we placed more and more emphasis in the workshop on the importance of designing those reflection sessions to align with course learning goals, with a particular emphasis on the goals related to cross-disciplinary comparison and dialogue. We typically kicked off that workshop with a call back to the earlier session on backwards design and reminded faculty of the work they had done to identify joint learning goals for their course(s). We reminded them about the three basic questions of backwards design and the benefit of aligning course learning activities with course learning goals. We then walked the faculty through a "taxonomy" of common reflection sessions types—such as field trips, guest speakers, writing exercises, or "on campus yet out-of-the-classroom" activities—and provided specific examples from past faculty to help participants think through their own ideas. After time for questions and discussion, we gave faculty the rest of the workshop time to work on designing their own reflection sessions with their partners. With about fifteen minutes to go at the end of the workshop, we again asked faculty to share what they had developed so far. Getting to hear the creative ideas of their colleagues sometimes served to spur new approaches for others in the room.

Workshop 4: Assessment, Assignment Design, and Power in Faculty Partnerships

The final Course Design workshop went through the most changes over the years, largely because the Renewed Core's approach to program assessment also went through significant changes during that time. The expectations regarding program assessment were loosely defined in early years, and so those first workshops tended to focus more on *learning* assessment rather than *program* assessment: helping faculty identify the learning goals they were most interested in assessing in their own courses and thinking with them about effective ways to design assignments that might generate useful evidence regarding students' progress toward those goals. In later years, the program shifted to a more centralized approach that sought to assess a single Core Curriculum goal across all courses each year, beginning with the Core's goals regarding disciplinary integration: the ability "to identify and articulate the strengths and limitations of the disciplines and the relationship of the disciplines to one another" and "to apply more than one disciplinary perspective to the same enduring question or complex contemporary problem." The program developed a rubric to assess this goal, and all Renewed Core faculty were asked to design one assignment (whether low-stakes or high-stakes) that could be appropriately evaluated by that rubric. We spent a good part of that final workshop reviewing the rubric and discussing a sample assignment meant to illustrate what the program was asking of faculty.

Building on that conversation about specific assessment expectations within the Core, we then shifted to a more general discussion of effective assignment design before giving the pairs time to start working on the assignment they'd be submitting for assessment. Again returning to the overarching framework of backwards design, we talked about strategies for designing assignments that better align with desired course outcomes. In particular, we focused on the findings of the Transparency in Learning and Teaching (TILT) project spearheaded by Mary-Ann Winkelmes, which shows that increased transparency in assignment design—particularly when defining an assignment's purpose, task, and criteria—positively affects students' learning experiences in a course, with an even greater benefit for traditionally underserved students.[4] In the workshop we also presented the TILT recommendations for increasing transparency as yet another tool for unpacking the different assumptions teaching pairs were bringing to their work.

After faculty worked on their assignments and shared out their plans, we concluded that final session by returning to one of the animating questions of the seminars: how to more effectively collaborate in designing and teaching these courses. This return was spurred, in part, by recent feedback we had heard from an experienced Core instructor that revealed that we had not done enough in past years to highlight how power can play a part in these partnerships. This faculty member had faced challenges in negotiating expectations with a teaching partner that were clearly exacerbated by the differences in their rank and institutional position. We decided to allude to this recent situation in the workshop and then shared some resources for faculty's further reflection, both on co-teaching recommendations more broadly and also on the particularities of collaborating across differences in social and institutional privilege. Our final message to the group was to encourage them to continue talking about their partnerships, their teaching values and assumptions, and to remind them that it would be an ongoing project to build a successful teaching team.

Notes

1. L. Dee Fink, *Creating Significant Learning Experiences: An Integrated Approach to Designing College Courses* (San Francisco, Calif.: Jossey-Bass, 2013).

2. Susan Ambrose et al., *How Learning Works: Seven Research-Based Principles for Smart Teaching* (San Francisco, Calif.: Jossey-Bass, 2010).

3. Joan Middendorf and Leah Shopkow, *Overcoming Student Learning Bottlenecks: Decode the Critical Thinking of Your Discipline* (Sterling, Va.: Stylus Publishing, 2018).

4. Mary-Ann Winkelmes et al., eds., *Transparent Design in Higher Education Teaching and Leadership: A Guide to Implementing the Transparency Framework Institution-Wide to Improve Learning and Retention* (Sterling, Va.: Stylus Publishing, 2019).

Core Renewal as Creative Fidelity

Gregory Kalscheur, S.J.

During the Fall 2013 semester, our Core Renewal process produced a proposal for a renewed Core curriculum at Boston College. The proposal, *Toward a Renewed Core*, placed special emphasis on creating an intensive, rigorous, interdisciplinary learning experience in the first year. This experience was grounded in two new types of core courses based on Enduring Questions and Complex Problems. These courses were intentionally designed to enable students to make integrative connections between disciplines, to foster active, engaged, problem-based learning, and to enhance student reflection on what is being learned in the classroom. The proposal highlighted reflection as an important component of courses within a renewed Core curriculum—not just in the new first-year courses, but throughout the Core. The proposal described reflection as the effort (1) to appropriate the meaning, significance, and value of the work of the disciplines, (2) to consider the purposes of a liberal arts education at a Jesuit, Catholic university, and (3) to integrate the various intellectual experiences of the Core and the major, building habits of discernment that would enable students to develop as "men and women for others" with an orientation toward service and enabling each student to chart a purposeful journey for their lives.

Drawing on the university's commitment to prepare students to live lives of meaning and impact by integrating the intellectual, the social, and the spiritual dimensions of their lives, the proposal articulated the following vision for the Renewed Core: "At the heart of the Boston College experience, the Core will unify and inspire the Boston College community in a shared intellectual endeavor. It will play a central role in each student's education as a whole person, preparing them for citizenship, service, and leadership in a global society. The Core will inspire intellectual engagement, establish an enduring foundation, and chart a purposeful journey."

Before moving ahead with the implementation of pilot Enduring Question and Complex Problem courses, we faced the challenge of demonstrating how the objectives of these courses and the vision of the Core Renewal proposal more broadly were grounded in the history, tradition, and apostolic aims of Jesuit education. The 2014 document, "The Vision Animating the Boston College Core Curriculum" (see Appendix A), reflects our effort to ground the aspirations of Core Renewal in the tradition of Jesuit education. I believe this effort can be understood as an exercise in creative fidelity.

In an address to a gathering of Jesuit major superiors at Loyola, Spain, in September 2000, then-Superior General Peter-Hans Kolvenbach, S.J., challenged the Society of Jesus to discern how best to pursue its contemporary mission with a commitment to "creative fidelity." For Fr. Kolvenbach, discerning the way forward calls for "a new point of departure, a fidelity to the experience of Ignatius which is at the same time creative."[1] Fidelity to the apostolic mission of the Society of Jesus is lived out "by examining the experience of Ignatius and the first companions, by discerning how to make fruitful today our rich spiritual heritage, nourished incessantly by the Spiritual Exercises, our long, many-faceted apostolic tradition, and our particular way of proceeding which launched and sustains the dynamism of our apostolic religious life." Creative fidelity calls us "to imbibe, as it were, the Ignatian charism. Not to repeat it mechanically, but to re-create it here and now at the service of the Church and the world."[2]

Commitment to a core curriculum is a distinctive aspect of Jesuit education. This commitment finds its roots in the *Ratio studiorum*, the plan for studies in Jesuit schools whose definitive edition was promulgated in 1599.[3] In modern terms, the *Ratio* might be described as a "combination of core curriculum guidelines, faculty handbook, and pedagogical manual."[4] As Fr. Kolvenbach suggests, our challenge today is not to repeat mechanically the methods of the *Ratio*, but to design and implement a core curriculum that is faithful to the history, tradition, and apostolic aims of Jesuit education while creatively engaging the present experience of students and faculty members. In that sense, our Core Renewal process can be understood as an initiative striving to enact the sort of creative fidelity to which Fr. Kolvenbach called us.

Apostolic Aims—Why Did the First Jesuits Get Involved in Education?

The apostolic aims of the Society of Jesus set out in its foundational document, the *Formula of the Institute*, are quite broad. The document states that the Society was founded

> chiefly for this purpose: to strive especially for the defense and propagation of the faith and for the progress of souls in Christian life and doctrine, by means of public preaching, lectures, any other ministration whatsoever of the word of God, and further by means of the Spiritual Exercises, the education of children and unlettered persons in Christianity, and the spiritual consolation of Christ's faithful. . . . [Jesuits should be ready] to perform any other works of charity, according to what will seem expedient for the glory of God and the common good.[5]

These aims do not explicitly include the establishment of colleges and universities. When the first Jesuits took up the invitation to begin schools in the late 1540s, they seemed to have quickly recognized that the schools could provide an environment in which students could grow in their understanding of Christian life and doctrine. More broadly, Saint Ignatius and the early Jesuits understood educating students as a work of charity that helped people by contributing to the common good of society.[6]

In a letter written to his fellow Jesuits in 1551, Juan Polanco set out fifteen reasons justifying Jesuit involvement in schools. The final reason highlights the benefits to society flowing from the sort of people the students will become:

> From among those who are at present only students, various persons will in time emerge—some for preaching and the care of souls, others for the government of the land and the administration of justice, and others for other responsibilities. In short, since young people turn into adults, their good formation in life and learning will benefit many others, with fruit expanding more widely every day.[7]

The early Jesuits thus took up the work of operating schools "because of the type of person they promised to produce."[8] They hoped to form "good citizens and leaders for the city."[9]

Jesuit Education as Formation, Not Just Information

The early Jesuits put the *studia humanitatis*, the study of humane letters, at the heart of this formative educational project.[10] Jesuit education emerged in the midst of a world marked by two competing educational ideals: the intellectual rigor and disciplinary professionalism of the university and the desire of humanistic schools to form students' characters for meaningful lives oriented toward service of the common good. The early Jesuits saw these two ideals as complementary and hoped to integrate them in their schools. The first Jesuits had been educated at the University of Paris, and "they esteemed the intellectual rigor of the scholastic system and the power of detached analysis it provided, and they believed in its goal of training highly skilled graduates in the sciences and in the professions."[11] At the same time, they were attracted to the humanist educational project and the potential that the humanistic study of literature, drama, and history helped "to foster *pietas*—that is, good character."[12] As John O'Malley has explained, the Jesuits were attracted to a curriculum with the study of the humanities at its heart because the *studia humanitatis* explored fundamental, enduring human questions and "the ambiguities of human decision-making" in a humane way—"not so much through abstract principles but through stories and historical examples that illuminated moral alternatives and, supposedly, inspired students to make choices leading to a satisfying human life."[13]

This sort of educational project hoped to cultivate in students the virtue of prudence—"good judgment, the wisdom that characterizes ideal leaders. . . . Prudence is the virtue of making appropriate and human decisions, the virtue of the wise person."[14] For the early Jesuits, the intellectual talent "that was most valued in the mature student was good judgment; education should concentrate its efforts in the cultivation of that faculty."[15] If the measure of our schools as Jesuit schools is who our students become as people,[16] prudence oriented toward the common good is central to the character of the sort of person Jesuit schools hope to produce: the person of wisdom and discernment, well prepared to put their gifts and talents at the service of the common good.

Thus, the course of studies in the tradition of Jesuit education is understood to be formative, not simply informative.[17] One commentator has described the Jesuit Order's *raison d'être* as a teaching body as the education of students' minds and desires so as to produce well-educated people "who by reason of their intellectual fitness will be able to face and solve, for themselves and others, the composite problems of life, social, civic, moral, and religious—who, in short, may contribute through influence, service, and example to the up-building of the kingdom of God in the heart of humanity."[18] In the early Jesuit schools, "Every Jesuit knew that the focus of the school was on the students, [and] [e]veryone knew that the first goal of an education was to form the upright character of a learned man who was to fulfill tasks for the common good."[19]

In addition to integrating intellectual rigor and formation of character, the tradition of Jesuit education has also sought to help students develop an integrative habit of mind. As Gerald McCool, S.J., notes, "from its beginning, the aim of Jesuit education has been the systematic development" of a distinctive habit of mind (what he calls "a cultivated Catholic mind"):

> a mind whose range was broad enough to embrace the realm of human knowledge as an articulated whole, yet sufficiently familiar with the diverse branches of knowledge to unify the multitude of disciplines without confusing them. That ideal of perspective, discipline of mind and imagination, analytic skill, and ability to see things as a whole was the integrative habit of mind.[20]

The motivation for cultivating in students this integrative habit of mind is ultimately religious. The Catholic intellectual tradition and the Jesuit commitment to education as a ministry of the word of God can be grounded in the essential conviction, "based on both faith and reason, that the world makes sense and that the human mind has the power to understand it."[21] As McCool explains:

> That understanding can be brought about if the liberal arts, science, and philosophy are united by a sound and believing mind under the light of faith. Once human knowledge has been integrated by a coherent education, it will enable the believing mind to understand God's revealed word. More than that, it can lead a prayerful and reflective mind through the meaning which it finds in God's creation to knowledge and love of God himself. Inspired by that tradition, in its sixteenth- and seventeenth-century form, my own intellectual ancestors, the old Jesuit schoolmasters, could cheerfully spend their life in the classroom. For what they were doing was forming minds which, in the beautiful Ignatian formula, "could find God in all things."[22]

Movement toward the "Jesuit ideal of an integrative whole in knowledge" is, therefore, a central goal of a liberal education in a Jesuit university, grounded in the conviction that our "creating and redeeming God" is present and at work in our world and "the human person has a divine call to wholeness."[23] In an academic world often defined by "a narrow professionalism" and by disciplines vying with one another to secure a place for themselves in the undergraduate curriculum,[24] interdepartmental cooperation and an interdisciplinary style of teaching help promote the integration of knowledge that is a traditional aim of Jesuit education.[25]

Early Jesuit educators drew on their experience of the *Spiritual Exercises* to bring into the educational apostolate an identifiably Jesuit emphasis on interiority, reflection, and growth in freedom. The *Spiritual Exercises* embody what John O'Malley has described as a "call to interiority" that provided a Jesuit point of contact with the humanist educators' goal of forming an inner-directed leader capable of discerning and choosing what will best promote the common good.[26] The *Exercises* emerge out of Ignatius's experience of God teaching him in a personal and direct way "through his experience of joy and sadness, of hope and despair, of desire and revulsion, of enlightenment and confusion."[27] Ignatius was convinced that, through these experiences, God was guiding his life and his choices.

John O'Malley suggests that the aims of Jesuit education can in part be grounded in a conclusion drawn from the experience of Ignatius as embodied in the *Exercises*: "[I]t is of the utmost importance for every human being to attain personal, inward freedom, so as to be able to follow the movements toward light and life that God puts within us, or, if you prefer a less religious formulation, to allow us to live in ways that satisfy the deepest yearnings of our hearts."[28] Jesuit pedagogy thus hopes to inculcate habits of attention and reflection that will allow students to become people who discern in freedom how to make choices that will respond to God's call as experienced in the movements and deepest yearnings of their hearts.[29]

Sharon J. Korth describes the reflective dimension of Jesuit pedagogy in this way:

> Reflection and discernment were integral parts of Ignatius's learning process. Reflection is a thoughtful reconsideration of some subject matter, experience, idea, purpose, or spontaneous reaction, in order to grasp its significance more fully. Thus, reflection is the process by which meaning surfaces in human experience by understanding the truth being studied more clearly; understanding the sources of one's sensations or reactions in the consideration; deepening one's understanding of the implications for oneself and others; achieving personal insights into events, ideas, truths, or the distortion of truth; coming to an understanding of who I am . . . and who I might be in relation to others. Reflection is a formative and liberating process that forms the conscience of learners in such a manner that they are led to move beyond knowing to undertake action. Faculty lay the foundations for "learning how to learn" by engaging students in the skills and techniques of reflection. A major challenge to faculty is to formulate questions that will broaden students' awareness and impel them to consider viewpoints of others.[30]

As that description of reflection makes clear, the tradition of Jesuit education expects the teacher to play a distinctive role in the formative educational process. A teacher in a Jesuit school does not just convey information. Every Jesuit teacher in the early schools knew that "he was above all an educator, a 'formator,' one who helped along the growth and maturation of souls."[31] The early Jesuits shared the humanists' goal of teaching literature and history in an authentically humanistic way—in a way that helped students understand these subjects as pertinent to the way that they might live their lives in the world.[32] As John O'Malley explains, if a liberal education is to be truly liberating, we must be attentive to the way in which a text or a subject is taught and the goals we have in teaching that text or subject:

> If the subjects we know as "the humanities" are taught as professional disciplines, as if they were introductory courses for somebody contemplating a professional career in them, they hardly deserve the designation humanistic. They lose their humanistic value and become—well, a form of professional or pre-professional training. Unfortunately, that is the pattern into which all of us trained in graduate school tend unthinkingly to fall. We teach as we have been taught. "Liberal Arts"—no subject is in itself liberating. It all depends on how it is taught.[33]

Formative teaching in the early Jesuit schools was aided by personal interest in and contact with the student: "[A]s a means of guaranteeing the harmonious development of mind and spirit, the Jesuit schools make much of human contact between teacher and student. The student knows that the Jesuit teacher is interested in and concerned about his peculiar problems and his progress, with the result that their reciprocal relations are generally cordial, intimate, and helpful."[34] The teacher was expected to be a model of integration and good character, who taught by personal example and through personal presence, not only through their words.[35] The early Jesuits stressed the importance of loving their students and "cultivat[ing] a respectful *familiaritas* with them."[36] In the words of Benet Perera, an early Jesuit philosopher and teacher,

> The teacher should be the sort of person whom the student trusts because of his learning and practice, understands because of his skillful fluency in teaching, loves for his enthusiasm and diligence, respects for the integrity of his life, and, when the occasion arises, feels he can approach freely for advice because of his humanity and personal warmth.[37]

The *Ratio Studiorum* clearly "placed exacting demands on the vocational *ethos* of the teacher. . . . The teacher was in a real sense the center and spirit of the *Ratio* system since it was largely through his initiative and directive influence that the *Ratio* goal of formation rather than mere information would result."[38] As Gerald McCool explains, "Teaching in the ideal of Ignatius means stimulating self-activity and conveying through personal influence the intellectual and moral values which have become the teacher's own. In the tradition of St. Ignatius, there is something sacred about the work of teaching; it is a vocation, and a lofty one at that."[39]

Creative Fidelity and the Challenge Ahead

For the early Jesuits, education was an apostolate oriented toward forming students to become people of wisdom and good judgment who are well prepared to put their gifts and talents at the service of the common good. Their characteristic approach to education as a mission of formation gave a central place to the study of the humanities, strove to integrate intellectual rigor with character formation, expected students to develop an integrative habit of mind and a sense for the wholeness of truth, encouraged students to deepen their capacity for reflection and discernment, and called on teachers to carry out a distinctive role that embodied the reflective formative pedagogy that gave life to the Jesuit school.

Our 2014 document, *The Vision Animating the Boston College Core Curriculum*, hopes to guide the ongoing work of Core Renewal as an initiative enacting creative fidelity to the apostolic aims and characteristic pedagogical approaches that are part of the history and tradition of Jesuit education. The integration of intellectual rigor and formation of character oriented toward service of the common good; the development of an integrative habit of mind through interdisciplinary conversation, a focus on enduring human questions and complex global problems, and a pedagogy that strives to deepen students' capacity to engage in discerning reflection; and focused attention to the special role of faculty members who teach in the Core constitute the heart of this vision.

I believe our initial efforts to implement this vision have borne significant fruit.[40] The long-term success of Core Renewal, however, will require sustained attention to helping faculty members understand and more broadly embrace the distinctive vision and pedagogical aims of the Jesuit educational tradition that we hope to embody with creative fidelity in the contemporary Boston College Core Curriculum. Given the distinctive formative role that this pedagogical vision expects faculty members to play, effective Core Renewal will require much more than creating innovative courses and new curricular structures. Faculty members need "to develop a *Ratio-Studiorum*-like vision, and that cannot be done in a single year or even in a single decade."[41] Ongoing faculty formation for a shared educational aim and distinctive pedagogical approach will need to be a sustained priority for teachers across the Core, not just those preparing to teach Enduring Question and Complex Problem courses for the first time. In the words of John O'Malley, efforts to realize the integrative ideal of the Jesuit educational tradition "will be meaningless unless faculty strive for it in their own persons."[42] Helping faculty members to know, understand, and embody "in their own persons" the Jesuit educational vision animating the Core Curriculum remains the fundamental challenge of Core Renewal as creative fidelity.

Notes

1. Peter-Hans Kolvenbach, S.J., "Creative Fidelity in Mission," *Review of Ignatian Spirituality* 31, no. 95 (2000): 27.

2. Ibid., 29.

3. See Cristiano Casalini and Claude Pavur, S.J., eds., *Jesuit Pedagogy, 1540–1615: A Reader* (Chestnut Hill, Mass.: Institute of Jesuit Sources, 2016), 17; see also Dennis C. Smolarski, S.J., "Jesuits on the Moon: Seeking God in All Things . . . even Mathematics!" *Studies in the Spirituality of Jesuits* 37 (Spring 2005): 5 (describing the *Ratio Studiorum* as "the first guidelines for a 'core curriculum' for Jesuit schools"); Association of Jesuit Colleges and Universities, *Some Characteristics of Jesuit Colleges and Universities: A Self-Evaluation Instrument* (Washington, D.C.: Association of Jesuit Colleges and Universities), 9 (noting that the core curriculum should be "reflective of the institution's commitment to faith and justice and key values of the institution").

4. Smolarski, "Jesuits on the Moon," 13.

5. John W. Padberg, S.J., general ed., *The Constitutions of the Society of Jesus and Their Complementary Norms: A Complete English Translation of the Official Latin Texts* (Chestnut Hill, Mass.: Institute of Jesuit Sources, 1996), 4 (Formula of the Institute, 1550).

6. John W. O'Malley, S.J., "How the First Jesuits Became Involved in Education," in *The Jesuit* Ratio Studiorum: *400th Anniversary Perspectives*, ed. Vincent J. Duminuco, S.J. (New York: Fordham University Press, 2000), 64.

7. Paul F. Grendler, "The Culture of the Jesuit Teacher 1548–1773," *Journal of Jesuit Studies* 3 (2016): 31–32.

8. John O'Malley, S.J., Foreword to *Traditions of Eloquence: The Jesuits and Modern Rhetorical Studies*, ed. Cinthia Gannett and John C. Brereton (New York: Fordham University Press, 2016), xii.

9. John W. O'Malley, S.J., "From the *Ratio Studiorum* to Civic Spirituality," *Fundamental Questions* (Fall 2004): 20; see also Grendler, "The Culture of the Jesuit Teacher," 32–34.

10. See John W. O'Malley, S.J., "Jesuit Schools and the Humanities: Yesterday and Today," *Studies in the Spirituality of Jesuits* 47, no. 1 (2015).

11. O'Malley, "How the First Jesuits Became Involved in Education," 68. See also John W. O'Malley, S.J., "From the 1599 *Ratio Studiorum* to the Present: A Humanist Tradition?" in *The Jesuit* Ratio Studiorum: *400th Anniversary Perspectives*, ed.

Vincent J. Duminuco, S.J. (New York: Fordham University Press, 2000), 144 (The Jesuit humanistic tradition "is not a uniform or easily defined tradition. It was humanistic, but it also had a deep concern for science. It believed passionately that education was about the formation of more fully human persons, but it also recognized the importance of professional training and esteemed it").

12. O'Malley, "How the First Jesuits Became Involved in Education," 68; see also Casalini and Pavur, *Jesuit Pedagogy*, 17 (The *Ratio* "assumes without comment that the Renaissance humanist pedagogical program and the intellectual goals of contemporary universities were good and worth pursuing").

13. John O'Malley, S.J., Foreword to *Traditions of Eloquence*, x.

14. Ibid., xi.

15. John W. O'Malley, *The First Jesuits* (Cambridge, Mass.: Harvard University Press, 1993), 214.

16. See Peter-Hans Kolvenbach, S.J., "The Service of Faith and the Promotion of Justice in American Jesuit Higher Education," *Studies in the Spirituality of Jesuits* 33, no. 1 (2001): 23–24.

17. Allan P. Farrell, S.J., *The Jesuit Code of Liberal Education: Development and Scope of the "Ratio Studiorum"* (Milwaukee: Bruce Publishing, 1938), 408; see also O'Malley, *The First Jesuits*, 214 ("[T]he Jesuits looked more to formation of mind and character, to *Bildung*, than to the acquisition of ever more information or the advancement of the disciplines").

18. Farrell, *The Jesuit Code of Liberal Education*, 408. See also Eugene J. Devlin, S.J., "Character Formation in the *Ratio Studiorum*," *Jesuit Educational Quarterly* (March 1953): 213 (a characteristic animating principle of the *Ratio* "is that mind and will be trained in one relation. The *Ratio* considered development of intellectual capacity inadequate and unrealistic unless the will was at the same time strengthened in good. The end product of training in such a system was not only an educated [person] but a [person] of virtue and character as well").

19. Casalini and Pavur, *Jesuit Pedagogy*, 29.

20. Gerald A. McCool, "The Jesuit Ideal of a Teacher: A Complex and Developing Tradition," in *Examining the Catholic Intellectual Tradition*, vol. 2, *Issues and Perspectives*, ed. Anthony J. Cernera and Oliver J. Morgan (Fairfield, Conn.: Sacred Heart University Press, 2002), 138.

21. Gerald A. McCool, "Spirituality and Philosophy: The Ideal of the Catholic Mind," in *Continuity and Plurality in Catholic Theology: Essays in Honor of Gerald A. McCool, S.J.*, ed. Anthony J. Cernera (Fairfield, Conn.: Sacred Heart University Press, 1998), 217.

22. Ibid. See also Michael Buckley, S.J., *The Catholic University as Promise and Project* (Washington, D.C.: Georgetown University Press, 1998), 84 ("Nothing is finally profane. Precisely because of the divine origin of all things and the quality of divine presence in all things, every aspect of nature is to be revered and treasured, every science and human development is in its integrity gift, sacred, providential, and of God. Everything, then, becomes a way to God because everything is descending from God").

23. McCool, "The Jesuit Ideal of a Teacher," 147.

24. Ibid., 139.

25. See also ibid., 147 ("The Jesuit ideal of an integrative whole in knowledge as the goal of a liberal education, even if we take it as an asymptote, preserves education from a number of distortions. Faith in the presence in the world of a creating and redeeming God is a protection against a narrow, this-worldly secularism or a despairing resignation to an unintelligible universe. Conviction that the human person has a divine call to wholeness is a defense against a narrow professionalism in education or the tyranny of a single discipline. Interdisciplinary cooperation is neither a sacrilege nor an imposition. Fidelity to an old and coherent tradition frees the educator from slavery to the present or to the immediate future").

26. O'Malley, "From the 1599 *Ratio Studiorum* to the Present: A Humanistic Tradition?" 136. See also O'Malley, "Jesuit Schools and the Humanities," 17–18 ("The quintessence of the Spiritual Exercises is, to use an old-fashioned expression, the development of the inner-directed person, a human being who acts not from superficial conformity to ethical standards but out of a sincere, heartfelt, and discerning appropriation of them. In other words, like the humanistic educational program, the Exercises want to produce a certain kind of *person*").

27. O'Malley, "How the First Jesuits Became Involved in Education," 61.

28. Ibid.

29. See also Robert R. Newton, *Reflections on the Educational Principles of the Spiritual Exercises* (Washington, D.C.: Jesuit Secondary Education Association, 1977).

30. Sharon J. Korth, Précis of *Ignatian Pedagogy: A Practical Approach*, in *A Jesuit Education Reader*, ed. George Traub (Chicago: Loyola Press, 2008), 282–283.

31. Casalini and Pavur, *Jesuit Pedagogy*, 29.

32. O'Malley, "Jesuit Schools and the Humanities," 10–13, 27.

33. O'Malley, "Jesuit Schools and the Humanities," 27. "If we teach Shakespeare, for instance, as if the students before us are mini-doctoral candidates, we are not teaching them in a humanistic mode. We are creating them in our own professional image and likeness. . . . [N]o subject, . . . no text, is automatically liberating. It all depends on how it's taught. It all depends upon what our goals are in teaching it. Let me go further. Almost any subject can be liberating, depending on how it's taught." John O'Malley, "Boston College Dean's Colloquium" (unpublished text) (March 18, 2014), 24–25; see also McCool, "The Jesuit Ideal of a Teacher," 146 (noting the importance placed on *the way* in which a teacher teaches the arts and sciences).

34. Farrell, *The Jesuit Code of Liberal Education*, 408–409.

35. McCool, "The Jesuit Ideal of a Teacher," 143 ("Knowing [the students] well, he could then guide their intellectual, moral, and religious development by his own personal example. Education, in the ideal of the *Ratio*, was a dynamic process carried on through the personal interaction of students and their professors").

36. O'Malley, "Jesuit Schools and the Humanities," 21.

37. Casalini and Pavur, *Jesuit Pedagogy*, 31.

38. Devlin, "Character Formation in the *Ratio*," 222. See also Paul Shore, "Celebrating the *Ratio Studiorum* at St. Louis University," *Conversations on Jesuit Higher Education* 16, no. 1 (Fall 1999): 48 ("Central to the execution of the program outlined in the *Ratio* was the instructor, and without a grasp of the duties and expectations of this instructor the *Ratio* cannot be understood. The teacher of the curriculum outlined in the *Ratio* was a Jesuit. This meant, among other things, that the instructor would approach the content to be taught from a fully integrated perspective of one who saw spirituality and academic formation as completely intertwined").

39. McCool, "The Jesuit Ideal of a Teacher," 148; see also McCool, "Spirituality and Philosophy: The Ideal of the Catholic Mind," 223 ("To teach is to share in the work of the Interior Master, the Divine Pedagogue. . . . As the Interior Master taught by shedding his own light, the human teacher taught by his personal influence. Both teachers, human and divine, taught by sharing with their students what they were. Teaching—any genuine teaching—was a holy and highly personal activity. It was never a job like another").

40. See, e.g., Brian D. Robinette, "Surprised by Conversation: A Reflection on Core Renewal at Boston College," *Conversations in Jesuit Higher Education* 55 (2019): 39 ("The impact of these [new Enduring Question and Complex Problem] courses on faculty and students has been overwhelmingly positive").

41. Claude Pavur, S.J., "The Curriculum Carries the Mission," *Conversations in Jesuit Higher Education* 34 (2008): 32.

42. O'Malley, "Jesuit Schools and the Humanities," 32. See also Robinette, "Surprised by Conversation," 39 ("Drawn into sustained conversation *with* their professors, students are not left to their own devices for integrating their core curriculum studies, as is often the case, but shown *how* by faculty who themselves are engaged in rigorous and sustained conversation. I can think of few learning outcomes as important as this").

Reflection and Core Renewal

Jack Butler, S.J.

Essential to this theory of formative education is the concept of reflection. All people reflect but Jesuit education uses Ignatian reflection as a deliberate template. This concept of reflection grew out of Ignatian spirituality and its understanding of prayer. Its educational form can be expressed in the language of psychology: lived personal experience is processed with the intellectual learning of the classroom and the experiential learning of student life. The reflection is facilitated by one or more of the "educators" in a student's life. The process elicits emotions and unmasks desires. The feelings arising from the reflective process are either congruent with the person and lead to a sense of harmony and contentment or incongruent and lead to a disruptive dysphoria. For a Jesuit this interplay begins the quest for God and is the raw material for the communicative relationship with God in prayer. For the psychologist and educator, this interplay feeds the quest for authenticity and homeostasis of the human organism. This also leads to the barometer known as "discernment" within Ignatian formative education.

— JESUIT CATHOLIC FORMATIVE EDUCATION AT BOSTON COLLEGE

Boston College is a Jesuit Catholic university. Over the last twenty years it's begun to understand itself as a formative community and culture that tries to optimize the learning experience. This was not always the case. The very word "formation" produced anxiety for those who understood the term as a prescription for a predetermined way of life. Education is about the unencumbered search and quest for knowledge and any resistance to such a pursuit of knowledge was considered contrary to the notion of the university's purpose. Over the last two decades at BC, this particular understanding of the concept has softened as a deeper understanding of formation has developed. Life itself ubiquitously and naturally forms all human beings. Unless an individual partners with natural "formational development," the end result is a haphazard life and maybe even a limited one. If intellectual and affective life develops in a random indiscriminate manner, purpose and meaning could be unexplored and not discovered if given to chance. At Boston College, formative education means connecting with the inevitability of growth in a purposeful and intentional way. The "end result" for human flourishment is freedom. An individual's life is not predicted or ascribed by this type of formation. Rather, at BC, "our" formation ensures that a person is consciously and deliberately involved in what they are becoming; formation is to enhance the lived experience. In this sense, "Formative Education" grew out of Jesuit pedagogy which was used in the training of Jesuits from the very beginning: Formative education has a history. The hope of this type of education is to involve the entire person within the educational process.

In a breakfast shop not far from Boston College, an impactful discussion began about formative education between the dean of the business school, the provost, and myself. Formative education had become a part of our culture; that early morning conversation over coffee underscored the reality and fact that care for the student was the driving factor behind our style of education. Faculty, administrators, and staff share a deep desire for Boston College students to have a greater and more fulfilling experience of education itself. Our educators wanted Boston College students to be involved in their education in a more significant way. From these initial conversations grew a larger-scale project that eventually led to the Core Renewal process. Student engagement and meeting scale were the focal points of these initial discussions. We were already doing something distinctive (we thought) in education; how could more students and faculty be involved in this endeavor? How could our formative education be enhanced? The heart of formative education, at a Jesuit Catholic school, is the liberal arts tradition. BC's motto is "Ever to Excel"; how to enhance our type or brand of education (formative) led to the refreshing of the liberal arts experience, which in its most concentrated state is the Core. We thought our Core courses needed to have an intentional "formative educational" element added to their curriculum. Formative education is about integration. The conversation that started over breakfast led to a quest for what an integrative system of education could look like within the first two years of college.

At Boston College we want cognitive development to intersect with emotional intelligence, producing overall intellectual growth. This learning dynamic is intended to stimulate grand ideas while eliciting an emotional response within the learner. The affect and the intellect are thus encountered simultaneously, touching on an individual's psychodynamic impulses and volitional drives. The hope for this kind of education is that the learner, as well as the community, taps into a system that is robust and rigorous. Learning is not passive but active! Our hope at Boston College is that as the intellect develops, the spirit soars, the heart is engaged, and imagination is the synthesizer of what is being learned. Throughout this process, the person achieves greater self-understanding and becomes more aware of what the world needs. Self-appropriation and thus the empowerment of one's gifts and talents are the goal of a formative education. It is more than simply finding a job.

The classroom and faculty have always been the sacred space and agent at the center of the academic enterprise and the formative process. However, at Jesuit Catholic universities, particularly Boston College, programs offered by Student Affairs and Mission and Ministry have tried to help and support students as they integrate what they are learning in the classroom with their lives. A well-developed human being who functions at the highest levels intellectually, socially, emotionally, and spiritually is the goal of a liberal arts–formative education. Those initial conversations, which grew into that larger process of renewal, morphed into a different kind of wondering. If integration is the goal, could a scaffolding for integration be externally replicated to aid the integrative process desired for the individual? Could the divisions of Student Affairs and Mission and Ministry aid Academic Affairs in a collaborative fashion to enhance learning? Might the three divisions develop an integrative conversation among themselves, paralleling the process each student was having internally as personal integration was sought? Getting the educators within Student Affairs and Mission and Ministry involved in the larger conversation with those in Academic Affairs on how to do whole-person education was new and innovative for Boston College. Professors were still at the center of the process, but now new colleagues were invited into the discussion to be collaborators shaping the learning environment within the classroom and course design even more than they had already been doing before. The three divisions were seriously and deliberately working together to help the educational process and overall learning experience. The hope was that this new discussion and possibly new style of learning, which was influenced by the Jesuit pedagogical method, would produce a better system of incorporating all aspects of a human being within the structured quest for knowledge found in an academic course.

There were many debates and maybe even arguments about whether it could be done or should be done. If it was done, what would it look like and what would be that "thing" that made it unique? These were the emerging questions.

External consultants were brought in. What began to slowly develop through a university-wide discussion was a notion and concept of reflection that many thought distinctive to our brand of education. The consultants mirrored back to the BC community that this recurring theme of reflection was the essential element of how to understand the formative process at Boston College; it was the key concept the consultants kept hearing from faculty, staff, and administrators. Although reflection is not the only element found within formative education, it was becoming a core element and a unifying aspect of education for our faculty and institution. Reflection had always been a significant part of Mission and Ministry and Student Affairs. It was now being given consideration for space within the classroom itself. As a result, how to incorporate reflection into an individual course became the challenge and desire for renewing the Core.

Before actually figuring out how to incorporate reflection into the Core Renewal courses, we had to reach a common understanding of reflection. Personally, I believe reflection is often misunderstood as a religious concept and/or a form of prayer/meditation. As such, this notion could have been an impediment to our using it within academic courses. That definition could be understood as sectarian and limiting in an institution that values academic freedom. Those in the conversation were trying to articulate and wrestle with a better understanding for this concept of reflection. Reflection as a concept is an active process of intellectual engagement. It's the integration of the cognitive and the imaginative, eliciting the affect. In many ways it's a progression of integrative learning. Reflection parallels or stimulates a form of emotional intelligence; it is an act, however, of the mind. Reflection is primarily cognitive. Reflection itself is not unique to Boston College. All people reflect; reflecting is part of human life and is a function all have. Reflection is in fact used in all of learning. Historically, reflection has held a privileged place in philosophical, theological, and psychological disciplines; yet it's found in all spheres of study. Analysis is the primary purpose to reflection. If all people reflect, it must be used and found in all places of learning and life. Why would BC single it out as distinctive? Simply put, not all people utilize reflection as deeply or intentionally as they can; it is an underdeveloped integrated skill. At Boston College we want students to be very intentional in their reflecting and to pay attention to details internally in a systematic, structured way. This is what our university wanted to develop and promote as an essential element to Core Renewal.

The literal meaning of reflection is to bend back, to take stock or assess. In this context it uses the imagination at various levels, creatively seeking options and a broader perspective. Reflection is a process of becoming aware of and attentive to different views and possibilities. These views and possibilities cause internal reactions that stimulate a plethora of emotions. These emotions help discern the validity of a thought and its congruency, which rests at a person's core. Reflection gets to the center of an individual's world view, their hermeneutic. A hermeneutic or world view can only be modified or changed through a reflective process.

The BC manner of reflection within a course, or the curriculum in general, is a particular technique of seeing or discerning different possibilities, scenarios, or outcomes. The horizons that emerge from reflection help lead to intermediary conclusions, which in turn lead to definitive action. What is to be done is the desire and object of this type of reflection. This form of reflecting is achieved within the sphere of the mind and allows for the imagination to see a course of action without trial-and-error or cost of time. For reflection, a person needs data: in this context, any experience or stimuli. Data within the human context is both external and internal. A dialectical process begins when data is analyzed through a reflective procedure. Whatever is being learned (no matter the discipline) is an external practice and the consumption is the internalization of that which comes from the outside. A topic or theory is being revealed through the learning dynamic between teacher and learner. Of course, sociological or cultural structures themselves can also be teachers; it doesn't have to be an individual professor. Learning and the appropriation of information is external. This form of data is then re-experienced within the acts of apprehending and comprehending through the internal forum of one's own experience. Internal experience develops through one's upbringing; the personal and emotional stimuli get interpreted through cultural, familial, and personal schemas appropriated as the person grows and matures. These affective memories are then internalized within each and every individual, based on past experience. These internalized interpretations of past happenings are known as internal data. The external and internal stimuli/realities (data) of experience are mediated through the reflective process; understanding, purpose, and meaning are then developed through this type of Hegelian procedure both within the person and externally through the learning dynamic. Assessment happens as the external data is reviewed by means of the internal data, and decisions of authenticity are made as a result of that encounter. Formative learning is achieved and actualized by means of reflection because the person appropriates the internal and external data in such a way as to form "new understanding." Some might say wisdom. This type of understanding/wisdom leads to a course of action or "how to live."

Reflection understood this way has been used by Jesuits for centuries. What a Jesuit learns is then tested through "experiments." These experiments are experiences that occur either in everyday life or through particular tasks analogous to internships. What the Jesuit is learning externally is then reflected upon through the mediation of the internal realities of life. What the Jesuit has learned is then being continually tested for validity, appropriation, and re-finement. Decisions result from such a process. Reflecting on these decisions is meant to aid one in becoming who one is and in how one chooses to live. This kind of reflection enables freedom; autonomy is achieved. This ongoing process of assessment, if done habitually, becomes a continuous method of learning that helps develop the self. This is the Jesuit method of formation and the one that BC was trying to assimilate into its formative mission.

The Core Renewal discussion sought to incorporate this method, developed by the Jesuits for the training of Jesuits (particularly in their spirituality) into a broader system and a more general approach to life. Student Affairs profes-sionals and Mission and Ministry practitioners have been doing this type of work (knowingly or unknowingly) in their programming, service trips, and vol-unteering practices for years. The goal now was to bring it into the classroom. At Boston College, PULSE has invested in this type of learning for fifty years. The Core and this new idea of formative education needed to be expanded from merely a philosophical and theological course with a service component. The new courses were going to be for all the liberal arts. These new courses would provide a space for reflection.

Courses were developed and two prototype models were put forth: Com-plex Problems and Enduring Questions. In both sets of courses, a reflective component was to be built into the course. The courses themselves were to be multi-disciplined approaches that tackled present-day problems or enduring questions throughout the centuries. The different disciplines and their pro-fessors would approach a question or a problem from their own professional training and engage the students by means of a problem or a question while helping them acquire the core competency skills of a particular discipline within the liberal arts ethos. As students grappled with different problems or questions from a variety of different disciplines, they were being asked to re-flect on what they were learning in regard to their own everyday lives. Was what they were learning consistent or not with what they thought, had been taught, or felt based on their experience? Active models of reflection were to be put into the course to achieve this goal. The professors, by means of the course, were to get the students to engage on how what they were learning resonated with their personal experience. This is where the new leaning was to take place! The hope was to elicit passions in how people felt around topics and issues while equipping the students with new intellectual data. Emotional intelligence was employed, and a deeper appropriation was achieved. Hope-fully individual desires were revealed as a result of this new process. The goal for these courses was to inspire new interests, passions, pursuits of truth or knowledge, and possibly to change or reinforce behaviors that the individual was currently living by or had based their knowledge sets on.

No professor is given a mandate or an archetype of how to engage their students in formative learning and reflection. Certainly, none were given in the Core Renewal process. The professors themselves were challenged to figure out ways to engage the students within their multi-dimensional lives. They did this by engaging students and what they were learning with where they lived, what they believed, where they came from, and with their dreams for a better tomorrow. Professors discussed among themselves how to engage students around these topics. In the past some professors might have seen these types of questions as potentially value laden. The trick in formative reflection is not to impose an opinion and/or a value but to allow the values and the opinions of the students to interact with the new "data" and knowledge being shared. This active engagement would affect the learning paradigm positively. Mission and Ministry and Student Affairs professionals were brought in to have discussions with faculty around issues of student engagement and best practices for reflection. The desire was to empower the learning experience, allowing our students to participate in active learning and enhancing their engagement not only with the material itself, but also with their own lives and the world at large. To date, the feedback from faculty and students has been positive; they appreciate this style of learning and the concept of reflection within the classroom and course.

Now, the parallel process begins. Deans, associate deans, faculty, and administrators in Student Affairs and Mission and Ministry must now reflect themselves. New data is on the table. The educators need to engage in the same process that Boston College is asking of the students; reflecting on what it was like for faculty to put together the courses; reflecting on how the faculty felt while teaching; reflecting on the actual work produced by the students; reflecting on the overall participation and affective response of the students in the courses; reflecting on the time and effort that was put into trying to achieve such a course; and reflecting on the data being collected through the assessment process. All of this reflective process will lead to a refinement of how we understand the role of reflection within Core Renewal. The reflective process is an ongoing system; it never ends. It is a mindfulness practice that is continuously assessing in its quest to gain a more adequate appropriation and comprehension of the data. In turn, this depth of felt and processed experience leads to an action of either refinement, changing course, or the development of the very thing being studied within the Boston College Core and the person themselves.

Surprised by Conversation

A Reflection on Core Renewal at Boston College

Brian D. Robinette

Ten years ago I wrote an article for *Conversations* titled "Beyond the Core Wars: Intellectual Charity and Knowledge as Ecstasy." At the time I was a newly tenured professor at Saint Louis University and relatively fresh to the challenging conversations around the core curriculum at Jesuit institutions. The article was occasioned in part by Pope Benedict XVI's message to Catholic educators, which he delivered during his April 2008 visit to the United States. Calling all educators to resist a primarily calculative and utilitarian approach to learning—a tendency as strong now as ever—the pope sketched out a bracing vision of higher education animated by wonderment and awe, by a self-transcending eros that is responsive to beauty, affectivity, justice, and the aspiration for human wholeness. In a word, intellectual ecstasy. Such a call was not a merely rhetorical exercise, however elevated it may have seemed, and neither did it favor some disciplines over others, say, those in the humanities over the sciences. Rather, it was an all-inclusive, dynamic, and quietly urgent summons to interdisciplinary collaboration and conversation across all boundaries; for when fully awakened, argued the pope, the impulse for truth pushes us well outside of ourselves, outside of our disciplinary silos and intellectual habits, and toward one another in dialogical relation. As my beloved colleague Fr. Michael Himes likes to put it, a university is "a rigorous and sustained conversation about the great questions of human existence among the widest possible circle of the best possible conversation partners."

Much of what I wrote ten years ago strikes me as relevant as ever, but having participated in numerous conversations around the core since then, and at two different Jesuit institutions, I have come to identify one of the conditions that significantly impedes the possibility of meaningful conversation around the core, and thus the prospects of interdisciplinary collaboration in its renewal: the feeling of scarcity. By this I mean the impending (and often inarticulate) sense that something precious is about to be lost, with little hope for recovery or creative reinvention. Scarcity is not necessarily a bad thing, and many conditions of scarcity can generate remarkable creativity and collaboration with others. People are often at their most resourceful when pressed up against challenging constraints. For better or worse, some forms of scarcity are inevitable given the intense pressures many institutions of higher learning now face, including budget crunches, teetering enrollment numbers, demographic shifts, growing bureaucracy, and the constant push for academic productivity. Add to this the declining support for the humanities and the increasing curricular demands for students preparing for more technical professions. Little wonder that our fists clench and imaginations shrink when relentlessly subjected to pressures like these. Having internalized a sense of scarcity, and ever anxious to retain our precious piece of the core, the scope of our conversations grows narrower and narrower and our willingness to risk interdisciplinary collaboration diminishes.

It is understandable that under such circumstances some colleges and universities have opted for a learning outcomes approach to core renewal. Rather than defining core requirements primarily along disciplinary (and thus departmental) lines, a learning outcomes approach organizes the core around an array of skills- and content-related goals that can be met in a variety of ways. While granting that some skills- and content-related goals are directly tied to specific disciplines, and thus to specific academic departments, a learning outcomes approach shifts the overall emphasis to a profile of goals that together constitute the core curriculum experience. This shift potentially relieves some of the pressures of a discipline-based distribution of requirements by giving departments a broader range of opportunities to contribute to these goals. Depending upon how it is fostered, this approach may encourage greater interdisciplinary cooperation and innovation among academic departments. Well-crafted learning goals can establish zones of contact for diverse disciplines to fill out together. On the other hand, a skills- and content-related approach may only intensify the sense of scarcity among faculty who contend that it undermines the expertise, rigor, and specificity that constitute each discipline. Rather than freeing up space for interdisciplinary engagement, the integrity of disciplines are potentially undermined, and academic departments threatened, as they must vie against one another in order to justify their share of the core.

It is not my aim here to offer an overarching judgment about the merits of a learning outcomes approach—I leave that to others in this issue—but I would like to highlight some of the distinctive features of the Core Renewal process underway at my current institution, Boston College, in light of the above pressures. One way to characterize this approach is in terms of a "third way" that fully embraces the distinction of disciplines while placing interdisciplinary collaboration directly in the hands of faculty. Without modifying the overall footprint of the core, or redistributing the departmental allotment of required courses, this approach proceeds more organically, and at an initially smaller scale, by inviting faculty to participate in Core Renewal by identifying another faculty member with whom they might like to collaborate.

Faculty can choose one of two formats for their collaboration. The first is a six-credit, team-taught "Complex Problem" course. Organized around a problem of significant complexity (e.g., climate change, war, racial violence, etc.), faculty bring their respective disciplines to bear upon a common set of challenges that demand innovative thinking and unprecedented cooperation. Some examples include "Science and Technology in American Society" taught by faculty in history and biology, or "From #BlackLivesMatter to #MeToo: Violence and Representation in the African Diaspora" taught by faculty in Romance languages and literatures and sociology, or "Global Implications of Climate Change" taught by faculty in sociology and environmental sciences. Consisting of a combination of lectures and labs, as well as several evening sessions dedicated to reflection and integration, these courses allow students to fulfill two core requirements in a highly interdisciplinary, goal-oriented manner.

The second format available to faculty is a pair of three-credit courses linked by a question of fundamental significance. Rather than team-taught, these "Enduring Question" courses retain greater independence while nevertheless establishing strong thematic connections across disciplinary lines. With a cap of nineteen students (compared to seventy-six for Complex Problem courses), Enduring Question courses move along more intimate lines that unpack such questions as "What does it mean to be human?" or "What is the good life?" or "How might we engender empathy?" or "How do we face illness, disability, and death?" Some recent examples include the following pairs: "Your Brain on Theatre: On Stage and Off" (biology) and "This Is Your Brain on Theatre: Neuroscience and the Actor" (theatre); "Being Human: The Philosophical Problem of Nature and Mathematical Knowledge" (philosophy) and "Understanding Mathematics: Its Philosophical Origins, Evolution, and Humanity" (mathematics); "Spiritual Exercises: Engagement, Empathy, Ethics" (theology) and "Aesthetic Exercises: Engagement, Empathy, Ethics" (music/fine arts).

The impact of these courses on faculty and students has been overwhelmingly positive. Based upon extensive assessment and ongoing consultation among faculty, students, and staff, the Core Renewal efforts have significantly enhanced the overall experience of the Core among those participating in it, leading more and more departments and programs to consider ways to contribute more fully. By starting with smaller-scale, faculty-led experimentations—all of which have been supported through teaching workshops, networking opportunities, modest faculty incentives, and promotion among students—the Core Renewal process has established deep roots in the university and is continuing to expand its scale. While there are still many challenges to work out as the Core Renewal process continues its second major phase of implementation—challenges such as staffing, expanding course selection, constraints of classroom and lab space, assessment of long-standing academic programs, and so on—the initial success of its first, more experimental phase has significantly modulated the sense of scarcity that typically aggravates these (and other) issues. They are felt more like the pressures of growth than of dearth.

As a faculty member who has taught in the new Core at Boston College and participated in numerous formal conversations around its assessment and expansion, I am surprised by how a sense of collaborative innovation has pervaded the entire effort. More than any other initiative I can think of, involvement in the Core Renewal has pushed me outside of my disciplinary-departmental framework and greatly expanded my circle of conversation partners. But more than this, because this form of core renewal is deeply rooted in faculty collaboration, and because such collaboration entails a host of creative risks and unanticipated outcomes among all those involved, students are far more likely to experience the excitement of interdisciplinary learning for themselves. Drawn into a sustained conversation *with* their professors, students are not left to their own devices for integrating their Core curriculum studies, as is often the case, but are shown *how* by faculty who themselves are engaged in rigorous and sustained conversation. I can think of few learning outcomes as important as this.

Note

This essay was previously published in *Conversations*, no. 55 (Spring 2019): 37–39.

PART II
Teaching the Renewed Core

Complex Problem Courses

Complex Problem courses are team-taught interdisciplinary courses that address a contemporary problem from two different disciplinary perspectives. Each of these courses enrolls seventy-six students and is worth 6 credits. A CP course makes up two courses of the teaching load for each of the two faculty members and also employs a Core fellow or teaching fellow to run the weekly labs. Students attend 150 minutes of lecture, a 75-minute lab, and a 110-minute evening reflection session each week.

Complex Problem courses have proven to be more difficult to develop and teach than Enduring Question courses. These are truly co-taught courses so faculty members must work together to develop a single course and are in the classroom together. In addition to 150 minutes of lecture, faculty (working with a Core fellow) must develop a weekly lab session that will use hands-on problem- or project-based exercises to reinforce course material. Faculty members must also come up with programming for (and in many cases, lead) a weekly evening reflection session that helps students learn to reflect on their lives and connect course material to life beyond the classroom. This is a lot!

These three faculty essays address three different aspects of the Complex Problem courses. Juliet Schor and Prasannan Parthasarathi reflect on teaching "Planet in Peril," discussing how they flipped their classroom, developed strategies for active learning, integrated the different parts of the course, and managed students' distress at learning more about how much peril our planet is in. Core Fellow Jenna Tonn writes about the ambitious lab that she helped develop and run for "Science and Technology in American Society" in which students built Arduino-based devices and then designed and carried out experiments using them. While most Complex Problem courses feature reflection sessions that are led by the course instructors, Tara Pisani Gareau and Brian Gareau developed a model of peer mentorship in which juniors and seniors were trained and supervised to lead evening reflection PODS (sessions for Purposeful Ongoing Discussion) in their course on "The Global Implications of Climate Change." Other faculty have adopted the POD model with as many as seven CP courses employing it in the 2021 academic year.

Teaching about a Planet in Peril

Prasannan Parthasarathi and Juliet B. Schor

In the fall of 2017, we taught our first Complex Problem course, Planet in Peril: The History and Future of Human Impacts on the Planet. We are a historian and a sociologist (although we both received our doctorates in economics, so the interdisciplinary part of the Complex Problem course comes almost naturally), and we are married. This class was by far the best teaching experience either of us has ever had, in our combined sixty years in the classroom. We decided to write this piece to encourage others to try something like a Complex Problem class, and to offer a bit of what we've learned along the way.

Preparing for Pedagogical Innovation

The first time through a six-credit Complex Problem course can be daunting. There are so many moving parts—the regular fifty-minute sessions three times a week, the labs, and the evening reflection sessions. We were managing eight lab sections (each with its own TA) that first semester. We were fortunate for two reasons. First, Juliet was on the committee that designed the Renewed Core, so she was familiar with the purpose of each part of the class. And second, we had been teaching a version of this class already, together. It was called Humans and Nature (same subtitle). The semester before the class ran as a Complex Problem course, we were able to do a kind of "dry run" by turning some of our class meetings into labs, and beginning to morph the course into what it would become. We would advise doing something like this if at all possible. It made the first time through much smoother.

With the dry run we were also able to introduce the major pedagogical innovation that we used for the Complex Problem course—a flipped classroom. Over time, we had grown increasingly dissatisfied with the conventional lecture format. We knew that some students were multitasking during lectures, as they clicked back and forth between social media and notes, or watched videos or texted. While there was always a group in the front rows who paid full attention, we learned that the farther back one went in the lecture hall, the less engaged the students were. When we were offered the chance to tape our lectures, we jumped at it. We produced just under one hundred short videos, because shorter lectures are easier for students to digest. They ranged in length from five to six minutes to fifteen to twenty, with most in the eight- to ten-minute range. We varied the format a bit. Most were the conventional type with a PowerPoint and a small picture of one of us talking. But we also did some in front of a screen, standing up, jointly or alone. And about fifteen were interview segments with guest speakers. Variety keeps students more engaged. Watching the lectures allows students to go at their own pace, which is ideal for difficult material. Short lectures also result in better retention of the content.

The other virtue of flipping is that it allows us to spend most of the fifty minutes of class time in interactive ways. We do a combination of small group discussions, design tasks, role-playing exercises, debates, unstructured back-and-forth with the class, and guest speakers. We are not rushed in the classroom. We have the students do all the reading and lecture viewing before Monday's class, and we start the week with a short quiz so that they will be rewarded for preparing. In the same way that it is important to provide incentives to students to do the reading, we feel we should also give them "credit" for watching the lectures. For us an additional benefit of the flipped model is that so much of the preparation for the class is done before the semester begins. This allows us to concentrate on pedagogical innovation, and to have a less pressured teaching experience. One caveat we would give about a flipped classroom is that it is easier to start with first-year students who aren't already socialized into the more passive learning mode of lectures. The first time we used the flipped model, on a group which included many juniors and seniors, the response was mixed. Subsequently we've had only first-year students, and they all like it.

A key aspect of flipping a classroom is developing "lesson" plans for the class time that force students to use the material they've learned from lectures and readings. We've found it's important to vary these plans over the semester, which requires imagination and a willingness to try new things. Once we find something that really works (a role play, an exercise where we ask the students to design a "common pool resource," one of the things we study) we work on refining it to make it work more smoothly. Since we do so many of these, we feel free to experiment. We strongly endorse the flipped classroom model. And if you have an opportunity to do it first with a small class, we advise doing that first.

It's hard to pinpoint exactly why teaching this class has been so rewarding. One reason is that the students are highly motivated and engaged. A second is that because we all spend so much time together, we become like a family. For first-year students, the class is an important site of social bonding. We suspect the "familial" aspect is heightened because we are married, and therefore more "parental," but this may happen to some extent in all team-taught classes. We also ask them to write a one-page personal bio-sketch in the first week, in which they tell us about their families and lives. We do the same for them. This helps avoid an impersonal classroom. It also sets the stage for the fact that the Complex Problem classes are designed not just for "academic" learning but also for personal engagement with the material. We turn now to that issue.

Teaching about Difficult Problems

The intention of a Complex Problem class is to explore a global issue that is important, interdisciplinary in nature, and difficult to solve. Many of these are also considered "wicked problems." Examples are global poverty, the rise of authoritarianism, slavery, terrorism, and gender violence. These are heavy issues that evoke challenging emotions in students. Because our topic is environmental destruction and the climate crisis, we are dealing with material that is terrifying and disempowering to whoever encounters it. But it is particularly so for young people. These kinds of classes do not work if they leave students depressed and demoralized, because then it's too likely that they convert their anxiety into denial and disengage. Even if they test well on the material, that's still a failure, because the courses are designed for engagement.

We learned this lesson the first time we taught the course. We assigned a new book by a prize-winning journalist who agreed to come as a guest lecturer. We hadn't realized how deeply pessimistic she and her book were. Her visit came early and it proved emotionally devastating for the students. Although the class also had more hopeful material, it was at the end of the semester, too late to counter the effect of this book.

This experience led us to revamp the way we organize things. We no longer put solutions at the end, but include them within each unit of the course, and not just at the end of the unit. We also present examples of both ecological degradation and sustainable arrangements throughout the historical material. It's important that students see that whole societies have had sustainable economies for long periods of time, given that there are almost no contemporary examples of sustainable countries. So we pair the smaller-scale successes of the present with more substantial historical cases. This helps us avoid fatalism, which we also counter with the more theoretical material, such as a unit that counterposes the conventional (fatalistic) Tragedy of the Commons model with Elinor Ostrom's commons management approach. We also talk openly about the emotional reactions that students may be having to the content of the course, and find that the "familial" aspects of the classroom atmosphere make it a safe space for students to express their feelings.

Finally, we pay a good deal of explicit attention to the tension between individual and collective solutions. For our topics of ecocide and climate crisis, there's no question that we must develop collective responses. We believe that is also true for many other complex problems. For this reason, we read about and lecture on collective responses. We also bring in guest speakers who are organizing for solutions, such as representatives of NGOs who work to save rain forests, alternative energy experts, and climate activists. But during the course of a semester most students won't have an opportunity to join a collective effort. If they are feeling an urgent need to do something, as many are, we also offer opportunities for individual behavior change. One of the things we've done is a (voluntary) Eating Challenge in which students form teams and try to reduce the carbon footprint of their diets. This consists of reducing or cutting out meat and dairy, the two largest dietary contributors to greenhouse gas emissions. The Challenge goes on for about a month, and is a fun but also demanding activity for students. We end it with a vegan ice cream party and for the two winning teams—a catered vegan meal at our home. Personal behavior change opportunities are easy to design, or you can use off-the-shelf options such as the student-oriented version of No Impact Week.

The other place we are able to address the need to take action is in the lab section of the course. The first few times we taught the class we partnered with the office in the City of Boston Environment Department that was focused on small-scale neighborhood activity to reduce carbon emissions. We had representatives from the office visit the class, and they assigned neighborhoods to the lab sections. Students met with residents and came up with a plan for an inexpensive mini-project that would reduce emissions and improve quality of life. The plans were posted on the city's website. The project was modest enough in scope to be feasible for the class, but the fact that it was a collaboration with the City of Boston enhanced its value for students. We have now run out of neighborhoods and projects so we will be designing a new approach for the lab. It will also be scale-appropriate and will likely have a real-life partner organization.

Conclusion

As we reflected on our experiences in the course of writing this essay, we came to better understand why teaching Planet in Peril was not only the most fun teaching experience we've had, but also the most rewarding. We think it's because the engagement in the issue we hoped to create for students also happened for us. That's not because we weren't already heavily involved in the topic—we teach about, research, write, and are politically active on issues of climate and environment, and have been for decades. But somehow with this new group of students, new pedagogy, and new format, we developed another way to engage. Partly this was because we developed stronger and more substantive bonds with students than is typical, especially in large classes. Part of it was because the course stretched us and forced us to confront how much more we (and others who study these areas) need to learn to confront this "wicked problem." So in the end, the deep and satisfying immersion that we hoped to develop for our students also occurred for us.

Experimenting with Science and Technology in American Society

Jenna Tonn

The Complex Problem class "Science and Technology in American Society" (STAS) offers first-year students the opportunity to take an interdisciplinary course that fulfills Core requirements in natural science and history. In STAS, students learn about big ideas and controversies in science and technology since 1945 through lectures, laboratory practicums, and weekly reflection sessions. Co-taught by three faculty from the departments of biology and history, STAS integrates content, such as the religious consequences of the Darwinian revolution or major developments in particle physics, with practice, or the hands-on experience of doing research.[1]

In STEM Lab, the laboratory practicum embedded in STAS, students get the feel for science and technology in action. During a typical mid-semester STEM Lab session, students in groups of three or four can be found working outside of the classroom. Some teams will be using CO_2 sensors to measure gas emissions at the nearest MBTA stop. Other groups might be carrying around a small GPS receiver to track their locations on campus within several meters. Still others might be sitting by the Chestnut Hill Reservoir waiting for birds or squirrels to trigger their infrared camera devices. Within STAS, STEM Lab is an iterative, process-based academic experience that turns first-year students into experimental researchers and the college campus into a living laboratory.

Lab Organization

STEM Lab's primary learning objective is creating a robust pedagogical space for students to engage with science and technology as a practice of trial and error. Students jump into this process quickly, figuring out how to program an

82

Arduino-based device to gather data about the local environment, the animals we live among, and/or the people we interact with on a daily basis.[2] Lab extends discussions from lecture and weekly reflection sessions by emphasizing that these Arduino-based devices must be deployed within a specific social, cultural, and technical context. For instance, students using a Pulse Sensor to record changes in pulse rate before and after meditating might connect their observations to both the latest neurobiological research and the current American cultural obsession with mindfulness.[3]

STAS enrolls 76–80 students a year. We hold four 75-minute STEM Lab sections, each with 16–20 students working in groups of 3 or 4. Currently, we offer five different types of Arduino-based devices for experimental use, which come with predetermined "problem streams": a CO_2 sensor to be used in the context of climate change; a GPS receiver for surveillance; a pulse sensor and an accelerometer for biomedical applications; and a remote camera associated with biodiversity. These problem streams guide students in the development of research projects that are in conversation with pressing issues in science and technology.

STAS demonstrates that innovations in science and technology rarely progress in simple linear directions from one major discovery to the next. Instead, scientific and technological advances might emerge due to a lucky break, or suddenly after years of failure, or through a tedious, resource-intensive cycle of trial and error. We have designed STEM Lab to model this experience. This framework is often a challenge to our students because it makes research-related tasks unpredictable. In addition, when we offer this course in the fall, we work with students who are navigating the college environment for the first time while also participating in a course that requires mastering new academic and interpersonal skills. Students balance troubleshooting sensor malfunctions, figuring out how to allocate research responsibilities to willing and at times unwilling peers, and learning how to do college-level research and writing. We designed STEM Lab's curriculum to anticipate these obstacles and to ensure that students can progress in their research with them in mind.

Curriculum Structure

Design Thinking and Thinking in Groups

Design thinking frames the first week of STEM Lab. To model the tone and pace of lab sections, we invite students to jump into a design thinking exercise based on methods from the Stanford University d.school.[4] Design thinking emphasizes human-centered design, leverages teamwork, celebrates brain-storming, and encourages an iterative process of active research and development. Using a basic supply of Post-it notes and markers, we ask students to redesign either an everyday technology, like an iPhone, or an everyday practice, like breakfast, for their partners. While at times silly, this exercise breaks the ice and delivers the message that STEM Lab is student-centered and action-oriented.

We have found that the best way for students to succeed in STEM Lab is to work in groups of three or four people (preferably four). This allows students to manage a semester-long project as part of a team and to share what is a significant workload. The best way to sort students into groups remains unclear, however, especially given how quickly STEM Lab moves forward after week one. We try to take into account educational research on group dynamics and how small-group work can promote interest in STEM fields for underrepresented students.[5] Each group spends significant time writing up a group contract that addresses minor concerns (e.g., how group members will contact each other about class assignments) as well as major expectations (e.g., how groups will approach conflict).[6] We are continually revising how we approach group work and the role of the instructor in mediating group dynamics as the semester unfolds. STEM Lab advances as a series of iterative modules. (See Appendix A at the end of this chapter.)

Module 1: Getting Sensor Data (3 Weeks)

The first three-week challenge for newly formed STEM Lab groups is to rapidly get up to speed with the basics of using an Arduino-based device and to design a quick experiment that takes their device through its paces. We provide all of the technical supplies as well as protocols that familiarize students with the Arduino microcontroller and IDE and each of their sensors. It is up to the students to manage their time wisely and allocate group responsibilities so that they are both learning Arduino basics and designing and executing their first experiment.

Students present their preliminary findings at the end of this module in the form of a PechaKucha presentation.[7] PechaKucha presentations follow a strict format (in our case, fifteen slides at 20 seconds each). We require students to briefly explain how their sensor works, the results from their first experiment, and outline what, given this experience, the next iteration of their experiment will be. We invite students to give their pitches to the entire course over two reflection sessions as a way of gaining expertise in public speaking and communicating scientific ideas to an interested audience. Students report that the PechaKucha presentation exercise is one of their favorite parts of STEM Lab.

Module 2: Experiment 1.0 (4 Weeks)

In Experiment 1.0, students think through the strengths and limitations of their sensor based on their PechaKucha presentation and design a four-week experiment that will use their sensor to gather data about a specific problem. A team with a GPS device might decide to track where students from different classes spend the most time during the day. A Pulse Sensor group might wonder what happens to pulse rates when students are taking simple math tests under intense time pressure. Students do not invent an experiment out of thin air. During these four weeks, they follow guidelines in our Experiment 1.0 guidelines (see Appendix B at the end of the chapter), which break down the components for a manageable experiment, point students in the direction of how to do responsible research using Boston College's library resources, and provide a series of assessment checkpoints to ensure that students are not stuck.[8] By the end of Experiment 1.0, we have found that students are just beginning to realize that their initial experimental design could be modified to produce better data, or that their sensor data could be collected in a different way, or that their expected hypotheses are totally off base and need to be revised. This awareness is a critical part of the research process.

Module 3: Experiment 2.0 (4 Weeks)

Experiment 2.0 builds off of the results and experiences from Experiment 1.0. It asks students to take a step back and redesign or iterate their initial experiment. (See Appendix C at the end of the chapter.) This might include rethinking independent or dependent variables; introducing clearer controls; expanding on preliminary data sets; collecting new, more convincing sets of data; cleaning up data in preparation for analysis; figuring out how to best visualize results; and/or sharpening the contextual stakes of the project. For many groups, Experiment 2.0 is a point in the semester when they finally know how their sensor works and suddenly have new insights into how to make their experiments more interesting. The limiting factor during this period is time. Experiment 2.0, as a result, turns into an occasionally frantic exercise in data collection and time management. The final product for this module is an extensive Experiment 2.0 lab report that details their experimental aims and results and includes the first draft of the group talk or poster for the STEM Lab Annual Conference.

STEM Lab Annual Conference

One of the major aims of STAS is for students to become aware of how scientific breakthroughs and technological innovations are communicated. We hope that students will come away from the course with an understanding of how the American public engages with science in the news and an ability to critique science communication and outreach. In both iterations of STEM Lab, we decided to organize a conference for students to communicate the results of their experiments to their peers, instructors, and a panel of guest judges. In 2017, we experimented with a daylong conference. Each group gave a short science talk and fielded questions from the class and guest judges. In 2018, we shifted gears and held a poster session, with each group interacting more informally with their audiences. In both formats, students gained experience honing their public speaking skills and presenting their research to an educated audience and concluded STEM Lab with a feeling of accomplishment. Each STEM Lab Conference ends with a competition, with the guest judges (a panel of four to six graduate student scientists and postdoctoral fellows) selecting the winners and runners-up of the presentations.

Student Research, or, What Is a Living Laboratory?

Locations and Emotions

In 2017, a four-person team called SCIEnce Squad used an Arduino-based GPS device to ask a simple question: "What is the relationship between a student's emotions and his or her location on Boston College's campus?" During the semester, they tracked five BC students going about their daily routines. They pinged them with short online qualitative surveys at random intervals, asking where they were (e.g., academic building, outside, dorm) and how they were feeling (e.g., joy, contentment, anger, frustration). SCIEnce Squad hypothesized that BC students would feel happiest when in their dorms not working and the most frustrated in the classroom. Instead, they found that students reported a mix of emotions at different locations—for instance, feeling both frustrated (negative) and motivated (positive) in a classroom and relaxed (positive) and frustrated (negative) in their dorms. They concluded that understanding this mix of emotions could help BC students as well as BC's University Health Services to think more strategically about the emotional lives of students on campus.

Campus Landscapes

In 2017, a team of students used an Arduino-based ArduCAM to document plant biodiversity on three local college campuses, including BC. Their research asked whether "the biodiversity of different plant species differ[s] between Boston College, Emmanuel College, and Boston University." They situated this question in two contexts: first, how green spaces can promote wellness; and second, how plant biodiversity contributes to a college's landscaping program and public relations strategy. Taking their sensor on the road, this group programmed their device to take photos along three predetermined transects at each institution—one by the main sign, a second by a major residence hall, and a third by the library. From these images, they calculated the percentage of plant coverage and number of plant species for each transect. They found that BC had the highest amount of plant coverage and the highest number of plant species. To put this into context, the group took the initiative to speak with Regina Bellavia, BC's director of Landscape Planning and Services, to better understand BC's landscaping goals and how they change during the seasons. The group concluded that attending to plant biodiversity is an important part of how an institution of higher education brands its campus.

Perilous Walking

In 2018, a group of students used an Arduino-based accelerometer to compare how BC students' movements are impaired while walking and wearing drunk goggles (alcohol impairment simulation goggles) versus walking and texting. Placing this experiment into context, they noted that while there has been a significant amount of research on how alcohol impairs gait, it is less clear how texting influences a student's passage through campus. They attached an accelerometer to each participant and recorded each participant's baseline movement, how this movement changed while wearing drunk goggles (which they used under the supervision of the BC Police Department), and how it changed again while walking (without goggles) and texting. After this first round of experiments, the team tested the same movements but added the element of a crowd of students the participants had to walk through. They concluded that students had different baseline reactions to walking while impaired or texting but overall it seemed like walking through a crowd in both cases resulted in a more variable gait. To address this issue at BC, this group proposed additional signage and education about texting on campus, especially by popular pedestrian crossings.

The Air Up There

In 2018, a four-person group used an Arduino-based CO_2 sensor to test how different organic materials emit different levels of CO_2 when burned. The group worked with the director of introductory chemistry laboratories and biology faculty to figure how best to burn their selection of organic materials (e.g., bark, grass, leaves, and paper) and capture the emissions in their sensor. They found that these organic materials emitted more than 400ppm of CO_2, the highest level of atmospheric carbon dioxide considered to be safe. They situated their results within the context of increasing numbers and intensities of wildfires in the U.S. West, which suggests that wildfires are both an indicator of climate change and a public health threat.

Biorhythms

One of the most successful sensors in both course iterations (2017 and 2018) has been the Pulse Sensor.[9] Groups have used the Pulse Sensor to track how the pulse rate changes for self-described gamers playing more or less violent video games, for students taking elementary math tests under intense time pressure, for individuals participating in a polygraph test, and for individuals responding to different tempos and genres of music. In one of the most striking experiments, the Pulse Sensor revealed how anxiety—as seen in a rapid increase in pulse in response to a suboptimum test-taking environment—manifests in the body, leading several groups to conclude that testing conditions for BC students might be altered to take into account physiological responses to quizzes and exams.

Revision, or, Lessons Learned

STEM Lab is an ambitious undertaking, and we have learned a number of lessons along the way.

Technical Frustration

Every group runs into problems with their Arduino-based sensors. Devices don't work or aren't calibrated correctly. Data isn't recorded or saved. Experimental designs change mid-semester requiring an overhaul of the whole process. The available devices are limited in their capabilities. We currently do all of our STEM Lab work in a regular classroom without access to makerspace or laboratory facilities. While STEM Lab offers students the experience of doing science—and part of that experience is based on the process of trial and error—we don't want to set students up for endless frustration. With this in mind, we are mindful to reevaluate the available sensors each semester; to develop assessment checkpoints to make sure that students are progressing in their work over the semester; to create a grading scheme for the lab that values process over results; and to reserve time in class every week for one-on-one assistance.

Teamwork Is Hard

STEM Lab is an active, student-centered learning environment organized around group work. We have frank conversations with our students that group work has its pros and cons. Group work allows for divisions of labor and the specialization of expertise. Ideally, it makes the workload for a major semester-long research project more manageable. In practice, however, group dynamics can be difficult to manage from the perspective of both the instructor and the students. Issues related to shirking work, busy midterm schedules, and personality clashes make it challenging for everyone involved. We are still revising how we approach group work—from assigning students to groups to creating mechanisms that allow for the continual assessment of group dynamics as the semester continues.

What Is a "Good" Project?

How do you define a rigorous and original experiment before you know what you are doing? In many ways, STEM Lab is all about building a bicycle as you are riding it, which can be an uncomfortable feeling for some students. We don't offer pre-scripted experimental projects. Instead, we individually advise each group in the development of their research. This means that although multiple groups might be using the same sensor, they are often drawing on different literature, have created very different experimental designs, and are coming up with divergent conclusions about next steps. For the instructors, this means advising nineteen or twenty separate research projects. When students are offering feedback on their peers' conference presentations by the end of the semester, they are able to articulate the stakes of a good project and whether or not the data is convincing. This ability to recognize the outlines of a solid project only develops over time. We are still working on figuring out how best to balance structuring the learning experience in a way that encourages all teams to succeed (e.g., through evaluation rubrics, lab reports, and other assessments) and allowing the STEM Lab environment to remain unstructured enough to encourage individual research interests to flourish.

Conclusion

STEM Lab is a unique liberal arts experience. Succeeding in lab requires leveraging skills from STEM fields, such as programming and quantitative data analysis, as well as from the humanities, such as conducting research to contextualize experiments and arguing for the stakes of experimental results. In our experience, some of the most interesting research projects have come from groups with cross-disciplinary expertise who are able to put the ideals of interdisciplinary education into practice.

Appendix A: STEM Lab Semester at a Glance, Fall 2018

Week	Lab Dates (TTh)	Activity	Assignment due
Week 1	Aug. 28 & 30	Introduction to STEM Lab	
Week 2	Sept. 4 & 6	Introduction to Group work	Group contract
Week 3	Sept. 11 & 13	Arduino 101	*DPD #1 & Lab #1
Week 4	Sept. 18 & 20	Getting Sensor Data	DPD #2
Week 5	Sept. 25 & 27	Getting Sensor Data	DPD #3 & Lab #2
	Sept. 25 Reflection	PechaKucha Round 1	5-minute pitch
Week 6	Oct. 2 & 4	Experiment 1.0:	DPD #4
		Experimental design	
	Oct. 2 Reflection	PechaKucha Round 2	5-minute pitch
Week 7	Oct. 9 & 11	Experiment 1.0:	DPD #5 due 5 P.M.
		Data collection	Oct 12
Week 8	Oct. 16 & 18	Experiment 1.0:	DPD #6 & Lab #3
		Data collection & analysis	
Week 9	Oct. 23 & 25	Experiment 1.0:	DPD #7 & Lab #4
		Data analysis & project synthesis	
Week 10	Oct. 30 & Nov 1	Experiment 2.0:	DPD #8
		Experimental redesign	
Week 11	Nov. 6 & 8	Experiment 2.0:	DPD #9
		Data collection	
Week 12	Nov. 13 & 15	Experiment 2.0:	DPD #10 & Lab #5
		Data analysis & project synthesis	
Week 13	Nov. 20 & 22	No STEM Lab— Thanksgiving break	
Week 14	Nov. 27 & 29	Poster design & research talk workshop	Posters due 5 P.M. Nov 30
Week 15	Dec. 4 & 6	STEM Lab Wrap-up	
	Dec. 4 (6–9 P.M.)	Mandatory STEM Lab Conference	

*DPD Guidelines

Weekly DPDs must be posted on the course blog within 24 hours from the beginning of lab.

DPDs must seek to answer four questions:

Content. What happened this week in the design process?
Attribution. Who contributed what to the team's work?
Contextual thinking. How does the project at hand connect to bigger questions or themes in the course?
Forward motion. Where will you begin next week?

DPDs also must include:

A group name and an appropriate subject line
At minimum 250 words in readable prose
At least two images reflecting the team's progress

Appendix B: Experiment 1.0, Fall 2018

Duration: 4 weeks (4 STEM Lab meetings + 4 DPDs + 2 Lab Reports); Timeline follows

Date	Task	Assignments due
Week 6: Oct. 1–5	Data logger integration and experimental design	DPD #4
Week 7: Oct. 8–12	Data collection (Note: TTh STEM Labs cancelled due to fall break. Data collection & DPD writing should continue.)	DPD #5 (*due 5 P.M. Oct. 12)
Week 8: Oct. 15–19	Data collection and analysis	DPD #6 & Lab #3
Week 9: Oct. 22–26	Data analysis and experiment 1.0 synthesis	DPD #7 & Lab #4

*Assignments due on Canvas 24 hrs after beginning of STEM Lab w/exception of DPD #5

Data Logger Integration
New materials for all sensors (except biodiversity camera)
SD card module x1
8GB SD card x1
SD card adapter x1
9V battery connector x1
9V batteries (as needed)
Breadboard + additional jumper wires (as needed)
Biodiversity camera
9V batteries (as needed)

Basic protocol to add SD Card Module

1. Figure out how to integrate a SD card module into your sensor setup
   a. Wire up your SD card module and add it to your sensor setup (see above for wiring diagram)
      i. Reference for wiring SD card module: https://electrosome.com/temperature-humidity-data-logger-arduino/
      ii. You may need to use a breadboard to daisy chain the power between your SD card module, the Arduino board, and your sensor
2. Modify the sensor code in your Arduino IDE to write data to SD card
   a. Copy/paste the existing sensor code into a new Arduino sketch
   b. Hack together your existing sensor code with SD card code
      i. Copy/paste the SD card code into a new Arduino Sketch and then integrate it into your existing code.
      ii. Pay attention to what gets added to the preamble/messages vs. the void setup vs. the void loop.
      iii. Useful references:
         1. SD Library basics: https://www.arduino.cc/en/Reference/SD
         2. See how someone else used a similar approach for their temp and humidity data logger: https://electrosome.com/temperature-humidity-data-logger-arduino/
3. Exception: Biodiversity camera
   a. Just add a 9V battery to your setup and you should be ready to go

Experiment Version 1.0: Labs #3 and #4

In this first experimental iteration, you will pursue a line of inquiry that produces data that can be used to intervene in the area of your stream—in other words, to encourage change in some field of social or cultural practice. What do we mean by this? Perhaps you want to use your pulse sensor data to design music tailored to the heartbeat or your CO_2 sensor data as the basis of a local public health campaign to raise awareness about pollutants on campus. Although your intervention needs to have quantifiable data behind it—data produced by your experiments—it can be made in the natural sciences, humanities, social sciences, or popular culture.

Formatting: Lab #3 and Lab #4 should be written in polished prose and turned into Canvas > Modules. They should be double-spaced, in 12-pt font with 1"-margins, and uploaded as a Word doc, a PDF, or a Google doc link that instructors can comment on by the deadline.

Lab #3: Experimental framework and design

Due on Canvas during Week 8 (Oct. 17 or 19)
For Lab #3, please consider the following questions and answer them in prose. The resulting lab report should be well organized, clearly written, double-spaced, and in 12-pt font with 1"-margins. Total length: 4–6 pages.

1. Experimental question: Define your group's research question for this four-week experiment. *(1–3 sentences)*

   A successful experiment begins with a solid research question.
   The best research questions are specific, narrow, and answerable,
      e.g., How does the biodiversity of local plant species vary between
      campus, the Hammond Reservation, and the suburbs of Newton?

2. Potential hypothesis: Develop one or two clear, straightforward hypotheses based on your research question. *(1–3 sentences)*

   It's hard to come up with a research question without also thinking
      about the anticipated results of the experiment (i.e., whether or not
      any of a few hypotheses will be rejected or supported).
   Hypotheses, however rough they might be, help to narrow the focus of
      a research question, e.g., We hypothesize that there will be fewer
      plant species on campus than at the Hammond Reservation, due to
      human design. Depending on the location in the Newton suburbs,
      the number of plant species could be higher or lower.

3. Sensor studies: Describe how the sensor will be used in the context of this experiment. Be sure to note the sensor's strengths and weaknesses and how the experiment will leverage or navigate around them. *(1 paragraph)*

4. Research: Ground your experiment in rigorous, well-sourced research. You must include (and cite) at least 5–7 sources from accredited publications. *(2–3 paragraphs)*

   What should this research do? It should use well-sourced informa-
      tion to provide background for the experiment at hand. Think
      about this as important context for your project.
   This research should be much more specific and more constrained by
      your experimental question than the research for your Pecha Kucha
      presentation.
   The subject of your research will vary in accordance with your
      research question. If you're using human subjects and using the

pulse sense or accelerometer to track some form of movement, it would be useful to understand standards around exercise physiology in humans or acceptable BPMs or sleep-related movement data. If you are doing a project about local biodiversity or environmental justice, it might be important to learn more about the neighborhoods you are visiting or the types of animals/plants that are native/invasive in the local area.

This research should be well organized, well written, and interesting.

Possible sources (refer back to the Reflection Session about research):

Science-related publications (e.g., Science, Nature, Scientific American, Wired, etc.)

Peer-reviewed databases (e.g., Oxford Bibliographies)

Newspapers (Boston Globe, New York Times, Washington Post, Wall Street Journal, Guardian, etc.) → Access via BC Library Nexis Uni

Historical newspapers from BC

Policy papers, think tanks, and .edu sources (e.g., RAND, Cornell Climate Change)

State and federal scientific organizations' websites (e.g., EPA, NOAA, etc.)

Databases of animals or plants (or field guides from the BC Libraries, see also eBird and the Global Biodiversity Information Facility)

Political coverage in newspapers, online, on Twitter, and on TV

5. Experimental Design: Detail the experiment that will be taking place. The experiment need not be focused on a "natural science" context. It can focus on questions from the sciences, social sciences, or humanities. It must, however, produce quantifiable data and include a control and multiple variables (or treatments). (1 page)

   Baseline/control: You will need to collect data to establish a baseline/control with which to compare future data. What will be the baseline for the experiment? What will you do to establish this baseline? Think about running the experiment in which everything is the same except the one variable of interest that will later be changed. For a gas sensor, this might mean taking measurements in a place where you don't anticipate a change in CO_2. For a pulse sensor, this might mean before/after testing anxiety during a math exam recording the heart rate during a pleasant/benign activity for the same amount of time.

   Variables: What is your rationale behind the different variables or treatments that will be involved? Why did you select them? How does their manipulation contribute to answering your question/ evaluating your hypothesis?

Participants/trials: Who will be participating? For human subjects, you will need to have them sign a consent form that addresses risks and privacy (format for consent forms). Aim for at least 5 participants/ trials (each with and without a control).

Strengths/Limitations: What are the strengths and weaknesses of this experimental design? How could you imagine changing it with a different sensor or different research question? What will be tough to control as confounding factors that could alter the outcome of your experiment (e.g., for the GPS, going inside buildings)?

Data collection: How will you be collecting your data? What are the units to be analyzed? What will be quantified? If you are using surveys to collect social/cultural data from your peers, how will these surveys be drafted? How will they avoid bias?

Lab #4: Experimental results and next steps

Due on Canvas during Week 9 (Oct. 24 or 26)
For Lab #4, please consider the following questions and answer them in prose. The resulting lab report should be well organized, clearly written, double-spaced, and in 12-pt font with 1″-margins. Total length: 2–4 pages.

1. Experimental summary

    Summarize the state of the experiment to date, including the experimental question, hypotheses, and experimental design. If any components of the experiment have changed, please describe them in detail. (*1 paragraph*)

2. Results: Present the results of the experiment in a clear, logical manner. (*1+ figure + 1 paragraph*)

    The results of your experiment should illustrate some kind of change. If you didn't find a change, then the results should explain why no change has occurred.

    Rather than mere lists of data, convert your results into an easily interpretable, visually comprehensible form. Ideally, these graphs, images, and/or maps should be accurate, interesting, and visually striking. They should also have clear labels.

    Interpret these results in straightforward prose. Evaluate what the data mean for your hypothesis.

3. Intervention & next steps: Think creatively about how you could imagine using the results of your experiment to intervene in the world. How might you need to redesign your experiment to do so? *(2–3 paragraphs)*

Do your results support a negative or positive intervention in the world?

How might you scale up your findings to change a behavior, a point of view, a policy debate?

Where could this intervention raise issues related to risk, ethics, and morality?

How might you amplify the reach of your intervention? (e.g., commercialization, deployment of device in different populations in different parts of the world)

What form would your intervention ideally take?

Continued scientific research
Science/tech policy suggestion
Public health awareness & prevention
Outreach, education &/or learning
Arts, culture, & design
Local history & politics
Social or environmental justice
Commercial products or services
Pop culture & entertainment
Public relations campaign
Editorial in the local, regional, national paper
Come up with your own!

Appendix C: Experiment 2.0, Fall 2018

Duration: 3 weeks (3 STEM Lab meetings + 3 DPDs + 1 Lab Report); Timeline follows

Date	Task	Assignments due
Week 10: Oct. 29–Nov. 2	Iteration: Redesign experiment and collect new data	DPD #8 (DPD must include plan for 2.0)
Week 11: Nov. 5–9	Implementation: Data collection (continued)	DPD #9
Week 12: Nov. 12–16	Synthesis: Data analysis and project synthesis	DPD #10 & Lab #5
Week 13: Nov. 19–23	*No STEM Lab—Thanksgiving Break*	

*Assignments due on Canvas 24 hours after beginning of STEM Lab

Iterating on Experiment 1.0

The goal of Experiment v 1.0 was to provide you with the opportunity to pilot an experimental design, work out the kinks of your technology, and start to collect data and analyze results. Redesigning your experiment allows you to learn from the lessons of your first series of trials and observations. Now that your technology is (mostly) working and you know the kind of data that your sensors produce, it's time to iterate—to execute an improved version of Experiment 1.0 to generate better results.

Things to Think About for Experiment v 2.0

We encourage you to iterate your project at every level from experimental question to intervention. Below are some suggestions for areas of improvement.

6. Experimental question: Refine your group's research question for this experiment.

   Add rigor: Learn from the results of Experiment 1.0 to ask a more rigorous experimental question.

   Refine language: Ask your experimental question in a way that is specific, tangible, and direct.

   Modify query: Experimental questions should not have simple yes or no answers. (e.g., Go for "How" questions over "Does X → Y" questions)

7. Potential hypothesis: Develop one or two clear, straightforward hypotheses based on your research question.

   Add rigor: Learn from the results of Experiment 1.0 to posit a better-informed and more specific hypothesis.

   Revise content: Perhaps your experiment has changed directions or your research has shifted focus. Rewrite your hypothesis to reflect that change. Your experimental question and hypothesis should fit together in scope and specificity.

8. Research: Ground your experiment in rigorous, well-sourced research. You must include (and cite) at least 5–7 sources from accredited publications.

   Refine focus: If your experimental design has changed, then your basis of research needs to shift as well.

Add rigor: If your group does not already cite 2–3 recent scientific sources, then it should return to the research process to determine what scientists or medical practitioners have shown about the subject in question.

Consult the BC Libraries Research Guides & Databases to find up-to-date scientific articles

General science research guide from BC Libraries

Biology databases: See esp. PubMed, Medline, News@Nature, PLoS, and Science Direct

Revise context: Connect the base of research directly to the experiment at hand while also gesturing at wider course themes.

Amp up style: This research should be well organized, well written, and interesting.

9. Experimental Design: Detail the experiment that will be taking place. The experiment need not be focused on a "natural science" context. It can focus on questions from the sciences, social sciences, or humanities. It must, however, produce quantifiable data and include a control and multiple variables (or treatments).

Clarify participants: Finalize participants and collect all consent forms (which might need to be modified given changes in the experimental design).

Add rigor: Experiment 1.0 provided a small sample for the experiment at hand. Determine as a group how you will add rigor to the experimental design. Some ideas:

If you only tested your experiment with 1 participant, enroll additional participants to test your experiment with more participants (5 is ideal).

If you visited multiple locations once, go back a predetermined number of times to collect additional data. This might take the form of simple repetition (e.g., go back multiple times to collect more data), a time course (e.g., return over a long period of time to see how that data changes), explorations of different environmental conditions (e.g., go back to the location at different times of day or during different weather to see how data changes), or changes in location (e.g., find a better set of locations).

If you used multiple variables, work to tease out their effects. For example, if you fed birds at different times of day, you could vary the kind of food used or test to see if over time the birds learn that there will be free food at a particular location. If you tested the relationship between stress and music genres, see how stress changes within musical genres (e.g., separate BPM from genre).

Rethink the baseline/control. Randomize treatments, clarify the control, think about placebo effects.

Add to data collection: Continue collecting data on a more substantial set of experimental components.

10. Results: Present the results of the experiment in a clear, logical manner. *(2+ figures)*

Synthesize results: Weed through the vast amount of data that you have collected to identify striking patterns (or changes). This might be tedious! Make an appointment with Prof. K to clarify your use of R.

Visualize results: Produce 2+ figures that capture your results effectively.

Clarify results: Ideally, these graphs, images, and/or maps should be accurate, interesting, and visually pleasing. They should also have clearly written labels.

Notes on figures:

Always label the axes (what's being show **AND** the units)!

There needs to be a figure caption explaining the figure in enough detail so that it stands alone (i.e., "Data from neighborhood" is insufficient).

Figures should be numbered (in the captions) so that they can be referred to in text. So that, "We found elevated cadmium at Site 1 (Figure 1)" is possible.

11. Intervention & next steps: Think creatively about how you could imagine using the results of your experiment to intervene in the world. How might you need to redesign your experiment to do so?

Crystalize intervention: Decide on 1–2 concrete interventions that your research supports.

Further research: Gesture toward next steps.

Lab #5: Experiment 2.0 poster draft

Due on Canvas during Week 12 (Nov. 14 or 16)

The goal of this assignment is to encourage you to think about your final presentation for STEM Lab well in advance. Final presentations will take the form of a traditional conference poster and a short research-based poster talk. Each team must also develop a short research talk that briefly highlights the research question, results, and implications/interventions of the project at hand. Both the poster and the research-based poster talk will be assessed by the instructors, the class, and a group of expert judges.

For Lab #5, upload your poster draft (as a PDF) to Canvas > Experiment 2.0 > Assignments > Lab #5.

Posters should be clear, visually pleasing, and present experimental data in a compelling manner. Most of all, posters should demonstrate to the audience that your group has asked and answered an important question related to science and technology and addressed any ethical, moral, or social concerns raised by the development of your experiments.

How to create a scientific poster

1. Familiarize yourself with what a scientific poster looks like
   a. NYU has a great set of "How to Create a Research Poster" guidelines. This includes examples of well designed and poorly designed posters.
   b. Look at these examples to get additional ideas about design and organization.

2. Familiarize yourself with the final presentation rubric, which includes information about poster content, visual clarity, and visual creativity

3. Design your poster using PowerPoint (or Illustrator if you know how to use it)
   a. Use our template as the basis of your poster (see: Canvas > Week 14)
   b. Or follow these guidelines to create your own template
   c. *Note:* If you use our template, you are expected to modify it to make it more visually interesting/compelling
   d. Regarding poster size: Limit poster size to 40″ × 32″.

4. Upload your poster draft to Canvas as a PDF file.

STEM LAB: Final Conference Poster Presentation Rubric

Criteria	Excellent	Proficient	Needs improvement	Deficient
Presentation of Research:	Prominently positions title/ authors of project.	Positions title/ authors of project adequately.	Positions title/authors of project.	Title/authors of project absent.
Poster content	Thoroughly but concisely presents main points of introduction, research question(s), hypotheses, research methods, results, and conclusions or interventions in a well-organized manner.	Presents main points of introduction, research question(s), hypotheses, research methods, results, and conclusions or interventions in a fairly well organized manner. Some points might be better presented than others.	Presents main points of introduction, research question(s), hypotheses, research methods, results, and conclusions or interventions but not as sufficiently and not as well organized. Some points might be lacking.	Does not sufficiently present main points of introduction, research question(s), hypotheses, research methods, results, and conclusions or interventions and is not well-organized. Points might be missing or incorrect.
Presentation of Research:	Pitch narration and answers to questions are engaging, thorough, and add greatly to the poster presentation.	Pitch narration and answers to questions are adequate and add to the presentation.	Pitch narration and answers to questions lack clarity and organization.	Pitch narration and answers to questions unclear, disorganized, and/or reference incorrect information.
Pitch content	Group members contribute equally.	Group members contribute mostly equally.	Unequal contribution to pitch narration by group members.	Unequal contributions by group members.
Visual Presentation:	Overall visually appealing.	Overall visually appealing.	Visual appeal is adequate.	Not very visually appealing.
Poster clarity	Not cluttered; colors and patterns enhance readability.	Not cluttered; colors and patterns support readability.	Somewhat cluttered; colors and patterns detract from readability.	Cluttered; colors and patterns hinder readability.
	Uses font sizes/ variations which facilitate the organization, presentation, and communication of the research.	Adequate use of font sizes/ variations to facilitate the organization, presentation, and communication of the research.	Use of font sizes/ variations to facilitate the organization, presentation, and communication of the research is inconsistent or not uniform, or distracting.	Use of font sizes/ variations to facilitate the organization, presentation, and communication of the research is inconsistent, not uniform, or distracting.
	Graphics (e.g., tables, figures, maps etc.) are engaging and enhance the text.	Graphics (e.g., tables, figures, maps, etc.) enhance the text.	Graphics (e.g., tables, figures, maps, etc.) adequately enhance the text.	Graphics (e.g., tables, figures, maps, etc.) do not enhance the text

(continued)

STEM LAB: Final Conference Poster Presentation Rubric (*continued*)

Criteria	Excellent	Proficient	Needs improvement	Deficient
Poster clarity (continued)	Content is clearly arranged so that the viewer can understand order even without the pitch.	Content is arranged so that the viewer can understand order without the pitch.	Content arrangement is confusing and does not adequately assist the viewer in understanding order without the pitch.	Content arrangement is confusing and does not adequately assist the viewer in understanding order without the pitch.
Visual Presentation: Poster creativity	Overall design is an expansion and improvement upon the template.	Overall design is a modest deviation from the template.	Overall design is a simple reproduction of the template.	Overall design is clearly not guided by any template.
Research and documentation	Research is well sourced, up to date, and substantial. Cites all data obtained from other sources. APA citation style is accurate.	Research is adequately sourced, up to date, and substantial. Cites most data obtained from other sources. APA citation style is accurate.	Research is poorly sourced, not up to date, and does not support project. Cites some data obtained from other sources. Citation style is inconsistent or incorrect.	Research is nonexistent. Does not cite sources.
Spelling and grammar	No spelling and grammar mistakes.	Minimal spelling and grammar mistakes.	Noticeable spelling and grammar mistakes.	Excessive spelling and/or grammar mistakes.

Notes

1. STEM Lab applied for and received Institutional Review Board exemption from the Boston College Office of Research Protection for this in-class research, which is not intended to create generalizable knowledge.

2. Arduino, https://www.arduino.cc/.

3. Pulse Sensor, https://pulsesensor.com/.

4. Stanford d.school, the Hasso Plattner Institute of Design, "A Virtual Crash Course in Design Thinking," 2017, https://dschool.stanford.edu/resources-collections/a-virtual-crash-course-in-design-thinking. See also the chapters by Andy Boynton and Toby Bottorf in this volume.

5. Marina Micari and Denise Drane, "Promoting Success: Possible Factors Behind Achievement of Underrepresented Students in a Peer-Led Small-Group STEM Workshop Program," *Journal of Women and Minorities in Science and Engineering* 13, no. 3 (2007), https://doi.org/10.1615/JWomenMinorScienEng.v13.i3.60.

6. STEM Lab's Group Contract template is adapted from "Making Group Contracts," Centre for Teaching Excellence, University of Waterloo, https://uwaterloo.ca/centre-for-teaching-excellence/teaching-resources/teaching-tips/developing-assignments/group-work/making-group-contracts.

7. PechaKucha, https://www.pechakucha.org/faq.

8. We have been very grateful to BC's librarians, who have come to class to introduce students to the resources available at the BC Library as well as to discuss what counts as responsible research.

9. Pulse Sensor, https://pulsesensor.com/.

Global Implications of Climate Change

Importance of Mentorship in a Core Education

Tara Pisani Gareau and Brian J. Gareau

The first year of college is a formative period in one's life. For many it is the first time of living away from home and making day-to-day decisions independently. Strangers, perhaps from a different religious, ethnic, racial, or cultural background, take the place of family members as roommates. Freshmen students are exposed to new ideas and experiences within the campus community, which can be exhilarating and eye-opening, as well as overwhelming and disorienting. At the minimum, students must get their bearings and figure out how they are going to make their way through the next several years of college—which major to choose, with whom to spend their time and to confide in, and in what parts of campus life to participate. All of these decisions will ultimately affect who they will become and their life's work. Boston College's Core Curriculum, rooted in the Jesuit education ideals of intellectual, self, and spiritual formation, is an opportunity to help students during this journey into adulthood.

During the three-year pilot of Boston College's Core Renewal effort, we taught two iterations of an interdisciplinary Complex Problem course, "Global Implications of Climate Change," for first-year students. Certainly global climate change qualifies as one of society's most urgent and complex challenges, requiring interdisciplinary problem solving. Students in our course learn about the science of climate change, the impacts of climate change on ecosystems and human communities, the sociopolitical juggernaut that has hampered society from changing course, and the technological and political solutions needed to move toward sustainability.

To help students consider the ethical dimensions of climate change and their personal connection to this complex problem, we recruited upperclass students with academic training in environmental and social justice issues (as well as experience with Boston College's various formative programs offered through its Center for Student Formation) to facilitate reflection sections. We called these reflection sections "PODs," an acronym for "purposeful ongoing discussion," but also a term that embodied our goal for developing a supportive community of peers (as in a pod of whales that communicate and cooperate with one another to protect their young and to hunt for food) rooted in Jesuit pedagogy. We found that POD leaders provided critical mentorship to first-year students that extended beyond the time frame of the course. In addition to helping first-year students understand and reflect on the significance of climate change, students looked to their POD leaders for advice on engaging in the campus community and navigating student life.

Value of Mentorship to Formative Education

Mentorship is the guidance and nurturing provided by an experienced person (mentor) to a less experienced person (mentee). A good mentor provides sage advice, encouragement, and acts as an attentive sounding board to test one's ideas. Mentorship is not so common in the undergraduate classroom, where the student-to-teacher ratio and lack of administrative support can be obstacles to the development of mentoring relationships.[1] Yet, when mentorship is incorporated into the classroom, students and faculty find the relationship highly valuable.[2]

How Can Mentorship Be Integrated into Undergraduate Education?

If mentorship plays a role in student formation, how can we integrate it into undergraduate education? We discovered support and space for mentorship and reflection within the structure of Boston College's Renewed Core Curriculum. Since 2015, all faculty teaching courses that contribute to the Core Curriculum are asked to engage with the Core Renewal Learning Goals. While established courses will undoubtedly require time in order to achieve this contribution in a central way, newly proposed Core courses must explain at the outset how they contribute to Core Renewal. The goals are written on the Core Curriculum website and feature in the guiding document, "The Vision Animating the Boston College Core Curriculum" (see Appendix A at the end of the book). While not all Core courses can (or perhaps even should) engage with all these learning goals in a single course, as students complete all of the fifteen Core requirements they will engage with all of them in some fashion. We have found that being attentive to the goal of forming whole persons has allowed us to incorporate more of these learning goals into our Complex Problem course than we might otherwise have been able to. Indeed, we have discovered that our course topic of climate change, combined with mentorship through the POD program, has helped make our course a place in which intellectual, moral, and spiritual formation are encouraged. Focusing on mentorship has made it possible for us to link the intellectually rigorous content of our two disciplines to the affective components that drive our passion for studying and resolving complex problems.

Climate Change as a Complex Problem

Humanity depends on planet Earth and its diversity of resources, yet human activity has destabilized our climate via the increasing production of greenhouse gases that accumulate in the atmosphere and trap heat. Climate change is a complex problem because it is a planetary response to the way humans live and consume resources. Greenhouse gases are released to the atmosphere through transportation, industrial activities, production of goods, urban development, agriculture, land use changes, heating and cooling of buildings, and electricity generation. We are already seeing the devastating effects of climate change with increasing frequency and intensity of hurricanes, sea level rise and flooding in coastal cities and island nations, droughts, and destructive wildfires. But the predictions for what lies ahead are even more dire.[3] Furthermore, the Intergovernmental Panel on Climate Change (IPCC) 2014 forecasted with very high confidence, "that climate change and climate variability worsen existing poverty and exacerbate inequalities, especially for those disadvantaged by gender, age, race, class, caste, indigeneity and (dis)ability."[4]

Combating climate change requires ambitious policies and cooperation at every level of government, an investment in clean and renewable fuel sources, and a fundamental shift in human culture and behavior. Despite overwhelming scientific consensus and high confidence of dangerous global warming, policy makers have dragged their feet to pass the type of legislation that would bring carbon emissions down to levels that will ensure the future of the planet's habitability, and U.S. consumers have not changed behavior in any substantive way. For example, from 1980 to 2016 registered highway vehicles in the United States rose from 161,490,159 to 268,799,083.[5] Plug-in electric vehicles make up less than 1 percent of these—in 2018 there were 1,000,000 plug-in electric vehicles on the road.[6] Global annual carbon emissions have risen sharply since 2000 from 24.6 billion tons to over 35 billion tons of CO_2 in 2013.[7]

In the 2015 papal encyclical *Laudato Si'*, Pope Francis, the leader of the worldwide Catholic Church, made an urgent appeal to the people of the world

> for a new dialogue about how we are shaping the future of our planet. We need a conversation which includes everyone, since the environmental challenge we are undergoing, and its human roots, concern and affect us all. . . . All of us can cooperate as instruments of God for the care of creation, each according to his or her own culture, experience, involvements and talents.[8]

In our course, students are not only exposed to the social and natural sciences, but also to the wisdom of Pope Francis: "The climate is a common good, belonging to all and meant for all. At the global level, it is a complex system linked to many of the essential conditions for human life."

Structure of Global Implications of Climate Change

We designed a Core Complex Problem course, EESC1501 and SOCY1501 "Global Implications of Climate Change." The six-credit course, which satisfies both the Natural Science and Social Science Core requirements, as well as Cultural Diversity through Engaging Difference & Justice, is composed of three 50-minute lectures, one 110-minute laboratory and one 75-minute evening reflection session each week. The format for our class is to have students gather in one group for the lecture and into smaller groups for both the labs and reflection sections. We use the lectures to teach the principles and key concepts of climate change science and the social complexities of the problem. The labs, which are taught by a Core Fellow,[9] contain hands-on activities designed to meet the first and fifth learning objectives of the Core. In labs, students make use of public climate data, interdisciplinary research methods, scholarly literature, and analytical tools to answer directed questions about climate change patterns, interactions, anthropogenic influences, and societal and ecological impacts. The reflection section known as POD is where we give students the space and time to dive into ethical questions and moral dilemmas of climate change and to reflect on their personal connection to the topics. In our syllabus for POD, we state that students will "critically engage with the content of the course, intelligently discern the evidence of climate change and its impact on society, and respectfully debate, deliberate, and decide on potential solutions."

Our starting point for integrating reflection into our course was the belief that students would feel most comfortable in expressing their ideas and feelings in a small group setting with people they trust. Since our class enrollment would be a maximum of seventy-six students, we organized POD into five groups with no more than fifteen students to a POD. (Labs were organized into four different groups with no more than nineteen students per group.) Next we needed discussion facilitators. The obvious first choice was for each of us and the lab instructors to take one or two POD sections to lead, but because all the reflection sections were scheduled at the same time of the week, we would have had to hire another instructor to cover all the POD sections. Additionally we were cognizant about not wanting to assign more work to the lab instructors beyond their normal responsibilities, and we wanted POD leaders to be able to focus on their tasks of facilitating conversation about the course material and its importance to their own lives. Thus, we opted for utilizing experienced upperclass students as POD leaders, who enrolled in a pass/fail three-credit course, which we called the POD Leadership Program. We paired two POD leaders per section and defined their role as the following:

1. Provide students with a comfortable environment where they can express their ideas and questions
2. Serve as role models as scholars and moral citizens of the Boston College community
3. Mentor students by way of advice on accomplishing their personal goals while at Boston College

Incorporating upperclass students into our first-year level course to facilitate POD sections turned out to be one of the best decisions we made about our course. First, in the two pilot years of the course, we found that first-year students bonded quickly and gained trust with their POD leaders and their fellow students in the section. Even before course evaluations were in, we heard from students about how POD was their favorite part of their week and how much they looked forward to those sessions. The comfortable and safe environment that POD leaders create allows for meaningful reflection and dialogue. Second, as upperclass students, POD leaders are able to provide expert advice about campus life and academics, which students greatly appreciate. Third, POD leaders took their role as mentors and role models seriously, often expressing their fulfillment at being able to give back to Boston College and to be a positive influence on students' experience. There is a strong culture of service at Boston College, where many students participate in volunteer and service learning programs. POD leaders often exceeded our expectations of their time commitment to their POD section. For example, one pair of POD leaders would meet individually with students in their section over coffee to check in with them about the class and college life. Several PODs formed group chats, where they continued class conversations. Most striking to us is how the students expected these relationships to continue long after the course concluded. One student wrote in the course evaluation, "I feel like our POD group has become really close and moving forward into the next semester and year, I feel like I would still be able to reach out to them about help picking classes and just discussing life at BC."

Finally, the POD leadership program added another dimension of student formation to the class. The formation of the POD leaders themselves was something that we had not anticipated in the first iteration of the course but have come to embrace and prepare for in the subsequent iterations. We play an important role as mentors to the POD leaders. Before the classes begin, we hold a full-day retreat with POD leaders to discuss roles, expectations, and small group facilitation skills. The retreat helps POD leaders bond as a group and sets the stage for the semester. We then meet weekly with POD leaders to reflect on their personal paths, to review how POD sections went that week, to go over the plan for the following week, and to provide leadership training. Our weekly meetings typically buzz with students' eagerness to share and learn from one another.

Overcoming the Challenges of Integrating Mentorship and Reflexivity in Undergraduate Education

There is one main challenge of integrating mentorship in the classroom—investing the time to do it right. Mentoring undergraduates takes more time than just lecturing, no matter how you slice it. We invest our time in mentoring the POD leaders so they in turn can mentor the first-year students, some of whom then want to become future POD leaders. Adding ten POD leaders to a course means more people to direct and manage through meetings, conversations, and emails. However, we feel it is well worth the time investment. The value to students is reflected in our student evaluations, which often contain comments about how POD was important for making their first-year experience a positive one, providing a space in which they could connect with fellow students in a safe, constructive way. It is not just about learning content, but also a way of being. As a Core course, we aim to create a truly formative experience. The benefit of co-teaching cannot be overstated. While preparation is more time-intensive for a Complex Problem course, we share this responsibility and benefit from bringing different ideas, skills, disciplines, and passion for the subject matter to the course.

Building reflection into course content can also be challenging because most of us are less trained in this area of introspection. How do we get students to personally connect to and care about the subject matter? What questions do we ask? How much time do we spend on discussing matters of the heart versus matters of the mind? How do we respond to the diversity of emotions and perspectives and when the discussion goes in an unexpected direction? We are still answering these questions for ourselves but have developed a general framework that we find useful for the POD section.

We break each POD class into four parts: (1) Student formation activity, (2) discussion on a homework assignment, (3) introduction of a new topic with an activity, and (4) introduction of the next week's assignment. We worked with Boston College's Center for Student Formation, which runs several successful programs on campus, to come up with specific student formation activities. An example of a formation activity is "Three Pillars," where students reflect on three formative experiences in their life during childhood and adolescence. Formation activities may involve background music, complete silence, art or other creative expression to help students tap into and communicate their ideas. We aim to have topics discussed in POD tie in with curriculum learned in lecture. For example, in the "one-minute elevator speech" activity, students are asked to draft a scientifically accurate and convincing response to a relative or close friend who challenges them on the validity of anthropogenic climate change. Students pair up and take turns role-playing the climate skeptic and practicing their elevator speech. This activity ties into lecture topics on climate science, climate change skepticism, and communication of science. The POD activity is rehearsal for their assignment for the following week, which is to have a conversation about climate change with a relative or friend and then to write about how the conversation went in their reflection journal (what did they learn and how might they approach the conversation differently next time?). All of the assignments involve a journal entry in which students respond to specific questions. Journal writing allows students to come to the next class prepared to discuss their experiences, perspectives, and ideas related to the assignment. The purpose of each POD meeting is for members to consider a variety of viewpoints backed by the evidence they bring to the discussion and to work as a group to come to a conclusion that moves the conversation forward. The conclusion is not predetermined, which means POD leaders must be prepared to facilitate the dialogue. Thus we spend time with the POD leaders on this important skill.

While the structure of POD is fairly consistent, the content and format is diverse and dynamic. We encourage POD leaders to use a different approach each class to facilitate an open and inclusive discussion. This usually involves a combination of small-group and whole-group discussions with guidelines. For example a whole-group discussion might make use of a talking stick (or ball or bean bag for that matter), where the stick gets passed to participants who can respond to a question without interruption for a given amount of time.

Another example is the fishbowl, where an inner circle of participants discuss a topic while the outer circle listens, observes, and reports back what they learned and then the group roles switch to discuss a related topic. Key to achieving an interactive and productive discussion are the prompts and questions. For prompts we use short videos, current events, readings, and simulations. During our weekly meeting with the POD leaders, we discuss and determine the discussion questions that go with the prompts. In particular we are striving for open-ended questions that connect to and challenge students to find ways to integrate the material into their lives.

Now that some of our POD leaders have graduated, we have been able to have conversations with them about what the experience meant to them at Boston College, and how the experience is influencing them in the workforce. These personal reflections on the POD experience have helped us prepare the next generation of POD leaders for what is to come and help promote the program at the university. Reflecting on her time as a freshman in POD, one of our POD leader alumni commented, "I was consistently challenged to go beyond the usual memorization and critical thinking techniques that I used as a student. . . . I was able to utilize systems thinking techniques that I use today in my current job at a sustainability nonprofit." Another POD alumna, now a law student, commented, "I've been able to . . . develop a more interdisciplinary perspective . . . as a second-year law student specializing in environmental and international law . . . and ask deep questions about the way our society functions." Another former POD leader, commenting on the process of renewing the Core Curriculum in general, noted, "Core Renewal provides important skills in applying topics to multiple disciplines of study and helps students learn to translate the knowledge they gain in one course to a socially significant level." Another was able to connect the experience of being a POD leader to the core values of a Boston College education: "Providing concrete mentorship opportunities that can help students discern their vocations is a core value of Boston College." Another, currently a PhD student, commented on connections between intellectual and moral formation: "I have used these techniques [learned as a POD leader] to help my undergraduates working in the lab, and my fellow graduate students to better understand the importance of science and how to make connections between the mind and the heart, between knowledge and action."

Conclusion

The POD model supports the Jesuit tradition of educating the whole person. While we certainly believe the content of our course is deeply important, it is what our students go on to do after our course experience that is the true measure of what we have passed on to them. If our students leave our course with some tools to engage deeply with difficult problems that are worth our effort to try to resolve, and they do so with the intent of being active, moral citizens, then we have accomplished something useful. If we have encouraged our students to take seriously their own spiritual growth and to see all forms of life as truly valuable and worthy of our respect and attention, then we've helped Boston College in its Jesuit Catholic mission to educate the whole person. Since 2015, the POD Leadership Program and POD have been adopted by faculty in seven more Complex Problem courses, and a foundational Core course in International Studies, meaning that hundreds of students have experienced this form of intellectual reflection in a Core course, and hundreds more will in years to come.

Recently, one of our senior POD leaders from 2017 told us that she was going out to eat with her former POD leader, who still lived and now worked in the Boston area. Like many of our former POD leaders and students, the two had been in contact since their POD four years ago. The BC alumnus was excited to get together because he wanted to catch up on how things were going at Boston College in the area of tackling climate change and to celebrate the news that he was getting married. The current student was excited to share with her mentor her own rewarding experiences as a POD leader and to thank him for being the inspiration that made it possible. It is through meaningful dialogue that connects both the intellectual and the personal that solutions will be found to society's difficult issues. These connections are beyond any explicit learning objective in our course syllabus, but they point to the formative potential of Core Renewal that integrates mentorship and reflection in the class experience.

Notes

1. D. Morales, S. E. Grineski, and T. Collins, "Faculty Motivation to Mentor Students through Undergraduate Research Programs: A Study of Enabling and Constraining Factors," *Research in Higher Education* 58 (2017): 520–544.

2. Nicola Livingstone and Nicola Naismith. "Faculty and Undergraduate Student Perceptions of an Integrated Mentoring Approach," *Active Learning in Higher Education* 19, no. 1 (2018): 77–91. A. M. Navarra, A. Witkoski Stempfel, K. Rodriguez, F. Lim, N. Nelson, and L. Slater, "Beliefs and Perceptions of Mentorship among Nursing Faculty and Traditional and Accelerated Undergraduate Nursing Students," *Nurse Education Today* 61 (2018): 20–24.

3. O. Hoegh-Guldberg, D. Jacob, M. Taylor, M. Bindi, S. Brown, I. Camilloni, A. Diedhiou, R. Djalante, K. Ebi, F. Engelbrecht, J. Guiot, Y. Hijioka, S. Mehrotra, A. Payne, S. I. Seneviratne, A. Thomas, R. Warren, G. Zhou, "Impacts of 1.5°C

Global Warming on Natural and Human Systems," in *Global Warming of 1.5°C*, an IPCC Special Report on the Impacts of Global warming of 1.5°C above Pre-Industrial Levels and Related Global Greenhouse Gas Emission Pathways, in the Context of Strengthening the Gobal Response to the Threat of Climate Change, Sustainable Development, and Efforts to Eradicate Poverty, ed. V. Masson-Delmotte, P. Zhai, H. O. Pörtner, D. Roberts, J. Skea, P.R. Shukla, A. Pirani, W. Moufouma-Okia, C. Péan, R. Pidcock, S. Connors, J. B. R. Matthews, Y. Chen, X. Zhou, M. I. Gomis, E. Lonnoy, T. Maycock, M. Tignor, and T. Waterfield (Cambridge: Cambridge University Press, 2018).

4. L. Olsson et al., "Livelihoods and Poverty," in *Climate Change 2014: Impacts, Adaptation, and Vulnerability. Part A: Global and Sectoral Aspects. Contribution of working Group II to the Fifth Assessment*, Report of the Intergovernmental Panel on Climate Change, ed. C. B. Field, V. R. Barros, D. J. Dokken, K. J. Mach, M. D. Mastrandrea, T. E. Bilir, M. Chatterjee, K. L. Ebi, Y. O. Estrada, R. C. Genova, B. Girma, E. S. Kissel, A. N. Levy, S. MacCracken, P. R. Mastrandrea, and L. L. White (Cambridge: Cambridge University Press, 2014), 793–832.

5. U.S. Bureau of Transportation Statistics, "Number of U.S. Aircraft, Vehicles, Vessels, and Other Conveyances," https://www.bts.gov/content/number-us-aircraft -vehicles-vessels-and-other-conveyances.

6. "Plug-In Electric Cars Sales In U.S. Surpass 1 Million," https://insideevs.com/1 -million-electric-cars-sold-us/.

7. Our World in Data, https://ourworldindata.org/co2-and-other-greenhouse-gas -emissions.

8. *Laudato Si'*: http://w2.vatican.va/content/dam/francesco/pdf/encyclicals /documents/papa-francesco_20150524_enciclica-laudato-si_en.pdf.

9. For more about Core Fellows, see https://www.bc.edu/bc-web/schools/mcas/ undergraduate/core-curriculum/core-fellows.html.

Enduring Question Courses: Bringing Together Divergent Disciplines

Enduring Question courses have proven to be, in many ways, easier to develop and teach than Complex Problem courses. These consist of two separate nineteen-student seminars that address large human questions across time and are connected by common topics, readings, and assignments. Each class is worth 3 credits and each meets for the standard 150 minutes each week. Common scheduling patterns are to offer one class on Monday, Wednesday, and Friday and the other on Tuesday and Thursday, or else to offer them on the same days back-to-back. Both faculty members meet with the students for four 110-minute evening reflection sessions in the course of the semester. It turned out to be important to leave the nature of the connection between the two courses as open and flexible as possible. It would have been much harder to match faculty for these courses if the nature of the connection were predetermined and rigid. Although students occasionally felt that a given pair of courses was not clearly connected, most faculty found ways to make the connections clear and to highlight the different disciplinary approaches to common readings, questions, and topics. Common reflection sessions also helped establish thematic connections between the two courses.

The following faculty essays demonstrate some of the different ways that faculty found to connect two different courses, to integrate and differentiate two different disciplinary perspectives, and to connect their courses with life outside the classroom.

Some faculty who had never met before and who worked in very different disciplines were brought together by the Core office and decided to work together to develop Enduring Question courses. Elizabeth Kowaleski Wallace of the English Department, and Dunwei Wang of the Chemistry Department met at a social event organized by the Core office to help faculty find teaching partners. Beth works on eighteenth-century English literature, and Dunwei Wang is a chemist working on finding combinations of material components that could replicate the process of photosynthesis. Their essay describes how they brought together their very different approaches, educations, backgrounds and expertise to create courses titled "Living in the Material World." Daniel Callahan of the Music Department had never met Brian Robinette of Theology. Both were corresponding with Mary Crane in an attempt to find teaching partners and at the last minute, only a few days before course proposals were due, met for a beer and found common ground in their interest in human attention and how it might be exercised and focused. Their essay explains how "Spiritual Exercises: Engagement, Empathy, Ethics," and "Aesthetic Exercises: Engagement, Empathy, Ethics" lead students to develop different forms of attentiveness.

How to Live in the Material World

Two Perspectives

Elizabeth Kowaleski Wallace and Dunwei Wang

Our pairing could not have been more counterintuitive: an English professor with a disciplinary focus on eighteenth-century British literature and culture who was trained in the late twentieth century at Columbia, and a chemistry professor with a focus on energy conversion and storage who was trained in the twenty-first century, first at a Chinese technological university and then at Stanford. Yet the first time we met to discuss the possibility of team-teaching, the chemistry (pun intended!) was palpable. After a brief conversation, we could see that we shared a series of clear goals: to help our students be humble in the face of the material world; to encourage an awareness of responsible citizenship in an age of extraordinary climate change; and to foster the kind of critical and creative thinking necessary to meet the climate challenges ahead. We quickly settled on the title "Living in the Material World" and began our discussion, plans, and negotiations. How would we each fashion a course that modeled a disciplinary approach and that taught students the basic intellectual moves necessary for further work in that academic field?

For Beth, the opportunity to work with someone in the sciences was welcome. For several years, she had been supplementing her traditional training in literature and literary theory with readings in an emerging field called New Materialism. In the words of Diana Coole and Samantha Frost, New Materialism returns us to "the most fundamental questions about the nature of matter and the place of embodied humans within a material world."[1] New Materialism (also sometimes referred to in the plural, "Materialisms") functions as an umbrella term for a series of related academic endeavors. On the one hand, it covers a range of literary, philosophical, and cultural theories exploring materiality itself. Jane Bennett's 2010 study *Vibrant Matter* provides one much-cited example.[2] On the other hand, the term extends to recent work in science studies and the history of science. Here the work of physicist Karen Barad is often cited.[3] All New Materialists recognize that, in order to combat the extraordinary challenges now presented by our rapidly changing environment, humanists and scientists must speak to one another and find common ground: Rather than isolating ourselves within our disciplines, rather than promoting one kind of knowledge at the expense of another, those in the academy must identify shared vocabulary, shared concepts, and shared commitments. So, for Beth the opportunity to listen to and learn from a physical chemist and to hear what matters both in another discipline and in a classroom rooted in that discipline was a most exciting prospect.

For Dunwei, the desire to reach out of his comfortable zone in chemistry had a lot to do with his personal experience. Growing up in the rural China that preceded the recent industrial boom, he was fortunate to see what pristine nature had to offer; being trained as a scientist at the heart of Silicon Valley, he was given an opportunity to peek into what modern civilization could enable. This experience prompted him to ask questions concerning the role played by *Homo sapiens* in modern times. It was obvious to him that answers to questions like these could not be found in the sciences alone. A bridge was needed. Then there was the first meeting with Beth, which was like a lightning strike. It became clear to Dunwei that a partnership with an English professor would be a great place to start. After all, Dunwei's internal struggles rooted in his personal and professional experiences were not new; being able to tap into the great minds crystallized in literature, with the help of Beth, would simply make sense. Dunwei's contribution, as it later proved, would be to help present the insights in a new light made possible by the latest developments in the scientific community. Together, we were presented with power neither of us alone could possess.

Neither one of us could reasonably aspire to become proficient in the other's field of expertise. Yet our conversations and our dialogues, especially as we began the process of shaping two interconnected syllabi to be taught to the group of students we would share, continued to focus on shared pedagogical commitments. In particular, we would come at the topic of materiality from two perspectives—one literary, philosophical, and historical (Literature Core) the other empirical and experiential (Science Core). Beth's class would introduce some ethical and moral concerns about the human relationship to the natural world, beginning with comments by Pope Francis in *Laudato Si'*. Then, her class would consider the history of how humans have thought about materiality, beginning with selections from Lucretius's *On The Nature of Things*, through seventeenth-century science as glimpsed in *The Blazing World* by Margaret Cavendish, through the eighteenth century and forward to various twentieth- and twenty-first-century writings on materiality, including Jane Bennett's vitalist materialism. Beth's class would also briefly survey the history of science and would create opportunities for both critical and creative thinking about materiality.

Dunwei's class would focus on an empirical approach to real-life questions about human materiality and energy use. Students would review basic information such as the energy/matter conversion principles. They would study the mechanisms by which energy is released from chemical bonds and discover how it is transferred to human bodies. In addition, Dunwei's class would study the rate of metabolism in a healthy body. Later units would focus on the carbon, nitrogen, and oxygen cycles and atmospheric composition, as well as the reactivity of hydrocarbons, inorganic products in smog, and effects of smog. Dunwei's class would culminate with a discussion about renewable energy.

We designed our joint reflection sessions as a place where we would bring our different disciplinary perspectives to a common experience, for example, a movie viewing, a visit to the science museum, or a visit to a rare books library. In the second year, a trip to Dunwei's laboratory allowed the students (and Beth) to see Dunwei's cutting-edge energy research. As they commented in their evaluations, students reflected on the eye-opening experience of seeing the settings within which science is done. The class visit helped to demystify science, removing a critical barrier that discourages our youth from even taking a science course, let alone choosing STEM (science, technology, engineering, and math) as a career.

One especially successful reflection session involved viewing the 2015 film *The Martian* in conjunction with *Robinson Crusoe*, which students had read in their Literature Core class. Students prepared for the reflection session by doing small-group research projects on one feat that Crusoe claimed to have single-handedly accomplished on his island, whose topography is said to resemble that of Trinidad. In such a place, what would it actually take for Crusoe to grow wheat; tame, kill, and skin goats; make a basket or a pot, and so on? From this assignment, students learn how fiction engages with the real, but they also discover how a text structures reality in order to privilege some ideas over others. Crusoe's fortuitous discovery that he can easily grow wheat (with no insects, for instance, to trouble his crop) may distort agricultural verisimilitude, but it also allows the novelist to develop the idea of divine providence. Elsewhere in the book, how does the novel engage with facts about the material world, distorting some facts while putting others forward, in order to create its mythic and isolated creator? In the meantime, in their Science Core, in an additional lesson on how fiction engages with "the real," students learned the chemical processes involved in the making of clay products such as porcelain.

The evening reflection session allowed students to compare the novel and *The Martian* and to tease out similarities between Crusoe and Mark Watney: How is Watney's situation on Mars another version of Crusoe's archetypal experience? How is Mars like and unlike Crusoe's Caribbean island? Students quickly observed how Watney mastered his environment with the same bravado as Crusoe. In response to the often-cited scene where Watney (a self-identified botanist) grows life-sustaining potatoes using human excrement, Dunwei brought a scientific observation to bear. While the scene humorously celebrates human acumen and ingenuity, it fails to acknowledge the presence of the microbes within the excrement. These, we could say, are the invisible and silent chemical partners of Watney's ingenuity. What we can learn, then, is not only something about biological process, but also about human agency in connection to the material world. The full cycle of energy and nutrients, from the Sun to human and back to the environment, would not have been possible without the invisible partners. At the heart of this cycle is human agency.

A later reflection session also did the work of knitting together scientific perspective and humanistic concern. In this session, we considered the ongoing problem of plastic pollution. Or to take an example from another one of our reflection sessions, how does a physical chemist think about the problem of non-biodegradable plastic? At the same time, how does a humanist approach the issue of public awareness of plastic use, exploring, perhaps, creative and even potentially eye-opening approaches? A humorous video of an errant plastic bag, sung to a lively ballad, can focus audience attention on a simple chemical fact: The bonds that hold the elements together to make plastics useful and durable are exceedingly difficult to break, at least by nature's force alone.

Beth believes strongly that working with Dunwei Wang helped her rethink which literary works to teach and to reconsider how she teaches them. In addition, it inspired her to see that truly innovative pedagogy must encourage students to discover how complex problems require multiple, supple intellectual solutions. For example, as an eighteenth-century scholar, Beth had long taught the it-narrative, or a narrative told from the point of view of a thing. This genre is often taught in relation to certain themes: for instance, the rise of commodity culture, new interpretations of what it is to be human, or pre-novelistic explorations of the possibilities of narrative. In one remarkable example, readers follow the path of a silk petticoat. The narrative culminates when the petticoat, now ragged and dirty, is purified and turned into a spotless sheet of paper. In this class, we ask about the material processes of transformation that created the silk petticoat and then, ultimately, the blank sheet of paper. Then students write their own it-narratives, tracing the path of everyday items from their origins, to their manufacture, to their transport, their use, and finally their destruction. If the story of the silk petticoat is also a story of the humans who come across its path, how do the objects of our everyday lives also tell a story about us and our relationship to the planet?

The partnership with Beth was a positive double blast for Dunwei. The unlikely combination of a chemistry course and an English course brought to Dunwei not only Beth's rich literary knowledge but also students Dunwei would not teach in a normal chemistry course. In one memorable reflection session during the first year of teaching the course, students' deep, reflective discussions on the connection of pencil and paper with human beings offered Dunwei a profound pride and hope for our next generation. The thoughts went far beyond the chemical makeup of the pencil "lead" and its interaction with the cellulose molecules in paper, which would be Dunwei's primary teaching point in a normal chemistry course. Such deep thoughts could only be evoked by the matching course. In addition, the overwhelming power of the literary really astounded Dunwei, who had read only Asian philosophy prior to graduate school. The remarkable similarities between Eastern and Western philosophy regarding materialism, and the relationship between human beings and the world, are profoundly reassuring to Dunwei, in both his teaching and research in chemical sciences.

Toward the end of the semester, Beth's class turns to a set of philosophic concerns taught via a graphic novel titled "Here" by Richard McGuire. In his work, McGuire depicts one suburban location (in fact the place where he grew up in New Jersey) in "deep time"—that is, from the very origins of the universe to some point in a very distant future. The effect can be unsettling, as students start to process the diminution of the human footprint against the vast sweep of time. The idea of human agency—and indeed of a human imprint on the planet—can appear to be insignificant from a perspective that affords the human being so little importance relative to cosmic time. How does such a perspective avoid a fatal pessimism, a sense that humans really don't matter that much? How does one deal with the impression that, at any rate, we have done too little and that it is "too late" to make changes?

At this point, the two classes work together to ask, in an honest and straightforward manner, about the potential gap between a philosophic trend away from humanistic (or human-centered) solutions (which is sometimes called post-humanist) and a scientific optimism that focuses on solutions. In both our classes we argue that it is extremely important to invest in human intellect and in the human capacity to generate ideas and strategies for survival.

On conclusion, here is what we have both come to think: Though we must continue to be humble in light of how unremarkable *Homo sapiens* are in terms of our biochemical nature, it is critical to recognize the unique place we hold in the cycles of energy and materials. Our disproportionally large energy and material footprints demand conscientiousness in our responsibilities, which is hard to instill in young students by literacy or science alone. And though we must realistically acknowledge the daunting challenges we face as a result of overconsumption, it is equally important to realize that scientific understanding of the world is accelerating at an unprecedented pace, offering us new power and tools to combat the daunting challenges. In many ways, this joint course represents a great step forward. We firmly believe that in the future, socially responsible scientists and scientifically savvy humanists will find more common platforms to foster the healthy growth of our next generation.

Notes

1. Diana Coole and Samantha Frost, eds., *New Materialisms: Ontology, Agency, and Politics* (Durham, N.C.: Duke University Press, 2010).

2. Jane Bennett, *Vibrant Matter: A Political Ecology of Things* (Durham, N.C.: Duke University Press, 2010).

3. Karen Barad, "Agential Realism: Feminist Interventions in Understanding Scientific Practice," in *The Science Studies Reader*, ed. Mario Biagioli (New York: Routledge, 1999), 1–11.

Aesthetic and Spiritual Exercises, in and beyond the Classroom

Daniel M. Callahan and Brian D. Robinette

Exercising Education

What does it mean to be engaged? To be mindful? To be rapt? What is empathy and how does it relate to sympathy, imitation, and compassion? Do experiences of the beautiful just "happen," or are they learned? Are spiritual encounters spontaneous and fleeting, or can we prepare for them and work to integrate them into our lives? If aesthetic and spiritual experiences are not just passively received but also cultivated, are there certain forms of life or a reliable set of exercises we might draw upon as resources? What dispositions, embodied skills, and habits of mind are conducive for living a more authentic and beautiful life? Are aesthetic or spiritual practices universally good and just, or must we always ask "for what" and "for whom"? Are they best undertaken individually, or is community essential to their fuller realization? To what extent might aesthetic and spiritual exercises help us engage the world, transform ourselves, and ultimately better the lives of others?

These are the enduring questions that animate our linked courses, "Aesthetic Exercises and Spiritual Exercises." Framed as a joint exploration into the role of "exercise" (or *askesis*) as key to human flourishing, these courses introduce students to various modes and theories of aesthetic and spiritual practice in the West, from antiquity to the present, and invite critical inquiry into the forms of life they foster. As course offerings that satisfy the fine arts core requirement and one theology core requirement, "Aesthetic Exercises and Spiritual Exercises" are designed to bring academic rigor together with personal appropriation. With a scholarly focus on the form, content, and history of these practices, which includes careful reading of texts and analysis of diverse modes of creative endeavor, these courses also highlight the phenomenological and experiential dimensions of such practices, with the hope that students might discover them from "the inside." The shared pedagogical principle at work here is that students will not really understand, or be able to critically evaluate, the significance of aesthetic and spiritual exercises if they are studied only from afar; they must also be inhabited, experimented with, and to some extent "undergone." In this way, the learning environment promoted by our linked courses is highly participatory. The classroom experience itself, along with assignments and several excursions beyond campus, function as living laboratories. They allow for, and even strongly encourage, the reflective distance necessary for critical analysis, but by first inviting students to try things out for themselves, to gain the inside knowledge that is possible when fully immersed.

One of the foundational texts that inspires both of us as teachers and scholars is Pierre Hadot's *Philosophy as a Way of Life: Spiritual Exercises from Socrates to Foucault.* Committed to the view that ancient philosophy is best understood in terms of *praxis*—as a "way of life," as a process of perceptual, affective, and cognitive transformation through the cultivation of embodied skills and mental habits—Hadot surveys various schools of ancient philosophy, as well as the life-practices supporting them, and traces their influence on subsequent eras of philosophy and theology, noting along the way how later traditions both received and adapted them. Perhaps more than any other scholar in recent memory, Hadot has rehabilitated our understanding of ancient philosophy as a process of *training*, not only concept-formation. Reading selections of Hadot early on in the semester allows our students to readily apprehend the organizing theme of the two courses. Just as the athlete trains long and hard for competition, or the musician devotes countless hours to rehearsal, so too must the philosopher undergo a process of formation and incorporate a distinctive set of disciplines that unfold over time. One doesn't just "do" philosophy. One must "become" a philosopher. Likewise, one doesn't just "do" theology. One must "become" a theologian. Theology requires the right preparation and mind-set. It calls for the development of certain faculties. It requires the right type of exercise and familiarity with traditions in spiritual formation. So too with traditions of aesthetic formation. One doesn't haphazardly appreciate the presence of beauty in art, or in nature, but one must refine capacities for beholding it, for being available and responsive to its diverse manifestations. It requires attunement: a discerning eye, a sensitive ear, a developed taste, an ability to judge. Aesthetic formation helps us more readily recognize, prepare for, and further explore encounters with beauty in everyday life.

In addition to Hadot, each of our courses includes some engagement with the *Autobiography* and *Spiritual Exercises* of Ignatius of Loyola. Very much an inheritor of ancient philosophical exercises, Ignatius is also an innovator and especially inspired by the life of Christ and the tradition of the saints. In Ignatius we find a fascinating and complex integration of Greco-Roman, Christian, and humanistic sensibilities. With a strong emphasis on the use of imagination, the discernment of desire, and a commitment to serving others, Ignatius develops a detailed regimen of personal formation that has undergirded Jesuit education (and the broader tradition of Ignatian humanism) for over four centuries. Connecting our courses with the heart of Jesuit education allows our students to better appreciate the relationship between the liberal arts and the distinctive ethos of the university they attend. The diverse elements of the core curriculum at Boston College are meant to be integrated, both intellectually and personally, and the university community itself should help foster a way of life for students, a sense of vocation, and not only advancement toward an occupation. By working to integrate our courses around the theme of training, it is hoped that the classical sense of education as *paideia* can be realized, that the cultivation of aesthetic and spiritual exercises can be seen as integral to the overall aims of a liberal arts education.

A Closer Look at Aesthetic Exercises

Unlike its co-requisite, "Spiritual Exercises," "Aesthetic Exercises" is not named after a classic text. Google "aesthetic exercises" and you will get links to pages outlining exercise routines and photos of chiseled v-shaped torsos first; links to pages referring to the eighteenth-century philosopher Alexander Baumgarten and our recent Boston College courses farther down the hit list. This proximity of athletes and aesthetes provides a serendipitous introduction to the course. Arts and physical education—both demoted to extracurricular "play" and most likely to be cut in United States schools today—formed the backbone of *paideia* in Ancient Greece, where philosophy was taught in the *gymnasion*, including that at the Academy of Plato. In the second week of "Aesthetic Exercises" students read Plato's *Republic*, which espoused that *gymnastikē* (physical training) and *mousikē* (training in not only music but also literary and performing arts) were necessary for a good and just citizenry. The engagement of players and, key to "Aesthetic Exercises," audiences of sports versus those of the arts look different—football fans screaming and rising off the couch in anticipation as a player runs toward the end zone, sitting still and silent while an orchestra plays a symphony—however, in both arenas audiences have learned what and how to pay attention to what is present before them, and in doing so their lives seem more worth living. In "Aesthetic Exercises" students focus on their own attention, habit formation, and experiences of beauty, whether the object of aesthetic experience is a beautiful play in a hockey game, a moving monologue in a tragedy of Sophocles, the live performance of a Mozart symphony, or the combination of images, lyrics, and music in a Beyoncé music video.

After reading Plato on training and mimesis, Aristotle on catharsis and sympathy, Kant on beauty and autonomy, Hans Ulrich Gumbrecht on presence and epiphanies, and David Foster Wallace on beautiful "plays," students in the first third of "Aesthetic Exercises" are challenged to see how, for audiences, the form and function of sports and the performing arts are more similar than different. Their first of three longer essays for the course is based on their own unique experiences of viewing *Oedipus Rex* and attending a Boston College game (either football or hockey, depending on the semester). Beyond exploring similarities both superficial (people in masks playing in front of an audience) and more conceptual (the presence of beauty and, following Kant, its attendant autonomy or "purposiveness without purpose," ineffability, and subjective universality), students are charged with detailing, reflecting on, and analyzing their own experiences of these events, specifically with how they were (not) engaged and to what extent they did (not) experience empathy (feeling as if one is another) or sympathy (feeling for another) with the players on the stage and field/rink. Taking notes throughout each event, students highlight the contours of their attention and focus, when they experience what Gumbrecht has called "moments of intensity," and to what extent they feel catharsis or somehow changed by the event. The purpose of the student's synchronous note-taking, their low-stakes 1,600-word draft-y writing exercises due twenty-four hours after the event, and their considered and polished essay due a week later is *not* that the student arrive at a thesis (e.g., "Catharsis cannot occur in agon-focused stadia"). Rather, the goal is that they convey their experiences of attending to these events, reflect on their own subjective embodied engagement, and analyze this practical experience of highly charged events (a seemingly impossible pass and touchdown during a Boston College football game; the peripeteia and anagnorisis in *Oedipus Rex*) by drawing on, and challenging, classics of aesthetic theory.

The second third of "Aesthetic Exercises" focuses on a very specific type of attention that is daunting for the majority of students: following a longer piece of purely instrumental music, a four-movement classical symphony, in live performance and appreciating (and writing about) what is unique about that performance. Our first co-course evening reflection session usually occurs at the beginning of this module on music. In that reflection session we ask students to attend to the sound of silence served two ways: spiritually (during a silent meditation, done first in stillness and then while walking) and aesthetically (we witness a live performance by student musicians of John Cage's silent piece, 4'33", followed by music more traditionally understood). Back in the classroom, the second third of "Aesthetic Exercises" progresses from an introduction to the fundamentals of Western music to homing in on the specific four-movement symphony that they will hear performed live at Boston's Symphony Hall. Having learned the basics of sonata form, students are tasked with listening to several different recordings of the first movement of the symphony we will hear, and creating their own listening charts that note both where the main elements of sonata form occur in each recorded performance and what sounds unique about each performance of the same score. This exercise, although challenging, increases familiarity with the music while also cultivating more attentive listening habits. This intense preparation allows students to feel their way through the form of symphony in live performance, and to better appreciate the difference between a musical score and its interpretation, between text and act. As after the football game, students complete low-stakes, 1,600-word writing exercises in reply to five prompts, which progress from a description of the concert hall and its audiences to describing specific moments in the music that stood out to them and how they compared to the recordings with which they were familiar. The goal is that students leave Symphony Hall not just with newfound appreciation of Beethoven—whose name is emblazoned in gold above the stage—but of the creative and physical labor of the living musicians before them. Many students in their final essays are even able to describe how they toggled between identifying with the music (which is the original definition of "empathy," a translation of *Einfühlung*, whereby one projects oneself into an artwork), appreciating the techniques and movements of the musicians, and following the overall sound and form of the music.

Following our focus on music and its performance, the final third of the course turns toward visual art, film, and digital multimedia. We consider the many relationships that exist between an artwork's medium and an artist's message from romanticism through modernism and postmodernism, and in popular culture today. Although the larger history and stylistic traits of these periods are presented in broad strokes, our focus remains the students' engagement with these artworks and what they understand the ethical stakes of the art and their engagement with it to be. Students complete a series of viewing exercises individually at Boston's Museum of Fine Arts. These always start with Turner's *Slave Ship*, in which students are asked to spend time in front of the canvas both from afar, appreciating Turner's use of color and overall form, and up close, where the horrifying images of drowning black bodies is visible. Their self-guided tour and exercises wind a familiar art-historical path toward medium specificity and non-representation: from Monet's Impressionist haystacks to more "difficult" modernist canvases (most recently, Mark Rothko's all-black final canvases on loan to the MFA). Students contrast their experiences with viewing these paintings in person versus as hi-definition digital reproductions online. This provides a segue to considering photography and film, and the special power accorded them by Walter Benjamin, whose "Work of Art in the Age of Its Technological Reproducibility" essay students put into dialogue with their experiences in the museum and when devouring multimedia every day. In our final weeks students consider Laurie Anderson's "O Superman" and *Heart of a Dog*, Beyoncé's *Lemonade*, and a music video of their own choice as we explore postmodernism and/as the popular: its embrace of pastiche; its mixing of media, genres, and histories; and its undercutting of binaries like high-low, art-pop, playful-serious, flippant-earnest.

While the whiplash tour of art and media history in the final third of the course exposes students to a lot of artwork very quickly, the ultimate goal is that students use their own aesthetic experiences to confront questions about the specifically ethical dimension of art and entertainment. How have artists and their artworks made people's lives better? Does students' engagement with these works make their lives better? How? After a century of being increasingly confronted with the aestheticizing of politics, should art and audiences respond by a "politicizing of aesthetics," as Benjamin advocated? Or, as Gumbrecht suggested, do we engage these works only because "we long for such moments of intensity although they have no edifying contents or effects to offer" and are separate and apart from our everyday world? These are the enduring questions that students tackle in their final essays and course exit interviews—and that they hopefully continue to reflect upon throughout a lifetime of encountering beauty in the world.

A Closer Look at Spiritual Exercises

As a companion to "Aesthetic Exercises," "Spiritual Exercises" introduces students to a variety of spiritual exercises that have helped shape the philosophical and theological traditions of the West, and which allow students better to appreciate how philosophical and theological practice is not just a conceptual enterprise but a way of life. As important as theory is and remains in these disciplines, the course explores the ascetical and contemplative roots of theory (*theoria*) by exploring those practices of perceptual, emotional, and cognitive transformation that contribute to "the good life." Examples include concentrating on the present moment, meditation upon death, becoming indifferent to indifferent things, practicing gratitude, meditative reading, the art of dia-logue, systematizing the passions, curtailing possessive desires, observing moods and states of mind, discerning desires, examining conscience, and in some traditions, cultivating non-conceptual awareness through prayer or med-itation. Beginning with Platonic and Stoic philosophy, the course highlights these exercises while tracing their adaption and transformation in ancient, me-dieval, and modern contexts, particularly in light of the biblical traditions and their diverse appropriation within the history of Christianity. In addition to Socrates, Plato, and Seneca, figures such as Saint Augustine, Saint Ignatius of Loyola, Saint Teresa of Avila, Henry David Thoreau, Simone Weil, Thomas Merton, and Etty Hillesum are featured.

Tracing these exercises and traditions, while noting their convergences and mutations, demands serious academic work. But the subject matter naturally invites personal investment. I refer to this as the "lab" portion of the class, mak-ing explicit from the outset that students should expect to experiment with these exercises throughout the semester. To facilitate this, I assign an "Observational-Experiential Journal" (OEJ) in which students reflect on their engagement with these exercises. While reading Plato's *Phaedo*, for example, students are provided adaptable instructions for meditating on death—a cen-tral feature of Socrates' summons to the philosophical life. Or while reading Seneca, students are asked to "become a Stoic for three days" by implement-ing a handful of disciplines outlined in his letters. Or as we read Henry David Thoreau, we visit Walden Pond and learn how to ruminate while walking—or what Thoreau called "sauntering." Students readily embrace these experimen-tations. It's as though they only needed the slightest permission to take inter-est in observing their moods, their sensory perceptions, their thoughts, their patterns of desires, that is, to pay attention to themselves.

By first introducing spiritual exercises within a philosophical context, vir-tually all students become quite open to them in a theological context. When students encounter Augustine's spirituality of interiority, or Teresa of Avila's "prayer of quiet," or Ignatius of Loyola's rules for discernment, or the practice of *lectio divina* in monastic traditions, they can readily see how much they share with the spirit of ancient philosophy. Incorporating insights from other disciplines and contemporary voices also makes a difference in fostering open-ness in the classroom. When introducing meditation and contemplative prayer to students, we read classic texts from the tradition while comparing them to contemporary "mindfulness" practices. Because many students are at least generally aware of secular approaches to mindfulness, and perhaps have some experience with them, they may find that the psychological and cogni-tive neuroscientific framing of mindfulness provides perspectives on ancient

wisdom they might not otherwise have. This turns out to be especially important when entering into silence together in the classroom. When instructing
students on the basics of meditation practice in class—body posture, breath,
noticing sensations, feelings, and thoughts, opening the heart, etc.—students
are encouraged to adopt the framework that is most conducive to participation. For some this will involve a theological intention, while for others it may
be more broadly philosophical or psychological in orientation. Some students
may not even know where they stand on these issues, or what their intentions
really are, and yet here too they will find spiritual exercises amenable to them.
Should they keep up with the practice beyond the course, they will discover
more about what their intentions really are and what role such practices might
assume in their lives. As they do, they are encouraged to ask, What is a spiritual
practice really *for*? How do we discern a fruitful from an unfruitful practice?
What difference does a community make, or a tradition? What role is there
for spiritual teachers, for spiritual benefactors or saints, for the wisdom of
others as we undertake a philosophical or theological way of life? What are
some of the dangers or pitfalls to serious spiritual practice, and how might we
navigate the inevitable ups and downs that attend it: for example, ecstasy and
aridity, conviction and confusion, integration and brokenness? Above all, how
does one's spiritual practice benefit *others*? Is it primarily about "my" inner life,
or does it contribute to love, justice, and peace in the world?

Exercising beyond Discipline

Having taught our paired courses three times over the first three years of the
Core Renewal Pilot Program, we have increasingly realized that our work as
pedagogues here is less a matter of "discipline," with its implications of control and mastery, and better thought of as "exercise": open-ended, though no
less rigorous, and focused more on process and becoming, on the movements
and actions through which a body learns. "Exercise" derives from roots that
literally mean "remove restraint," in the sense of driving cattle out to fields to
graze or plow. Beyond the substantial amount of reading and writing both our
courses demand of students and ourselves, we place an even greater stress on
a non-discursive element, on putting our students out there, on leading them
through embodied practices that aim to cultivate habits of mindfulness, openness, and readiness for attending to and reflecting on the spiritual and the
aesthetic for the rest of their lives. Practically, this means that—although Daniel's lectures on Benjamin's "Work of Art" essay have become more streamlined
and Brian's discussion questions about Etty Hillesum more targeted—we spend
a substantial amount of time and effort planning and leading in-class exercises,

extra-class evening reflection sessions (contracting a yoga instructor, finding available student musicians), and multiple off-campus trips (to Walden, Symphony Hall, and elsewhere). Beyond leading students out of the classroom and their comfort zones, we have also found ourselves taken beyond our normal disciplinary bounds and cultivating new techniques and habits that we have translated to the many more courses we teach outside of the Core Renewal Pilot Program. For example, Daniel has increased the number of pre-report writing exercises he requires of both music majors and non-majors. Meanwhile, Brian has introduced various spiritual exercises in his upper-level undergraduate theology courses, as well as graduate level courses, with the aim of further integrating the academic and personally formative dimensions of theological education. Though undeniably challenging at first, teaching our linked courses has become ever more rewarding over the years, a habit that we now cannot imagine quitting.

What have these exercises been like for our freshmen? On their anonymous course evaluations, students consistently state that our courses demand more time and "attention," both in class and outside of it, than they had expected, but that they actually enjoyed the challenge. Attention can seem like a contemporary buzzword: the increased interest in mindfulness and meditation over the past few decades, the increased number of diagnoses of attention deficit/-hyperactivity disorder. The desire to cultivate attention is, of course, nothing new, as classic texts like Marcus Aurelius's *Meditations*, the Buddhist sutras, and Ignatius's *Spiritual Exercises* attest. "Although people seem to be unaware of it today, the development of the faculty of attention forms the real object and almost the sole interest of studies." Simone Weil wrote that in 1942, but her words seem even more applicable in an age when we all mindlessly scroll through apps on our phones. Just as an athlete cannot afford to lose her attention while exercising with a heavily loaded barbell, engaging transformative practices like meditation or appreciating an artwork demands attention. Cultivating such attention and the application of the senses through exercises, and then reflecting on those exercises with others can seem odd and embarrassing to our freshmen at first. By the end of the semester, it has become a habit, and one that they discuss and write about with considerable joy and without shame.

Enduring Question Courses:
Differentiating Similar Disciplines

In some cases, faculty paired by the Core office taught in similar disciplines and faced different challenges: finding ways to highlight different disciplinary approaches for students and also finding ways to connect classes that covered quite different material, albeit with a similar approach. Hanne Eisenberg and Thomas Epstein both teach courses on literature and culture, Hanne studying ancient Greek religion and literature in the Classics Department, and Tom, originally a professor of the practice in the BC Honors Program, focused on the Russian novel. Hanne's course "Death in Ancient Greece" could fulfill the history (1) requirement while Tom's course "Death in Modern Russia" fulfilled the literature core requirement. Their essay describes how they used the reflection sessions to both connect and differentiate their courses. Robert Bartlett and Aspen Brinton, coming from the Political Science and Philosophy Departments, both study political theory. Bob's essay describes how in their paired courses on "Justice and War," he spent a semester reading Thucydides and studying ancient war, while Aspen had students focusing on modern philosophical approaches to war and justice. Min Hyoung Song is a professor in the English Department and Holly VandeWall is a professor of the practice in the Philosophy Department. Min and Holly had similar interests in the history of how human beings have thought about their connection to the natural world. Their courses moved in parallel chronologically from classical antiquity to the present, studying imaginative and philosophical texts grappling with the human relation to nature.

Death in Ancient Greece and Modern Russia

Reflecting on Our Reflection Sessions

Hanne Eisenfeld and Thomas Epstein

Death: the subject pushes right past the brief of an "enduring" question and into the territory that resists all inquiry. Nevertheless, our paired courses, "Death in Ancient Greece" (Hanne Eisenfeld) and "Life and Death in Russian Literature" (Thomas Epstein), set out with the modest goal of equipping our fifteen freshmen to interrogate the nature of death, emphasizing especially its paradoxical status as both a universal reality and a social construct, an object of academic study and an urgent human concern. The specific subjects of our courses invited our students to grapple with difficult—even distressing—material at a geographical and temporal remove (modern Russia and Ancient Greece respectively), a move that we hoped would allow them to approach death as a subject of rigorous academic inquiry subject to our respective methodological approaches of cultural history and literary analysis. At the same time, we wanted to empower them to think about the place of death in their own lives and in our contemporary world. This, it seemed to us, was perfect work for the reflection sessions, the four extracurricular meetings that are a required component of each Enduring Question course, but whose nature and content is left entirely up to each teaching partnership.

When we set out to design our reflection sessions, a centerpiece of our collaborative work on the two classes, we asked ourselves how we could invite students to come to grips with three shared questions at the heart of our courses by inviting them out of the classroom and into the laboratories of experience. The first of these questions, "What is death?," was meant to open up questions of a biological, cultural, and religio-philosophical nature. The second, "How should we think about death?," encouraged our students to ask themselves how death "stands" in their lives—near, far, nowhere? Finally: "How do the ways that different cultures represent death inform the values of that culture and what do these representations tell us about the human condition?" It was this third question, which in some sense sought to synthesize the first two, transforming them into an answerable inquiry, that served as the guiding question-concept for our collaboration.

In planning our reflection sessions, we decided that the best way forward was gradually to "abandon" the Ancient Greece-modern Russia parallel lines and instead to converge in contemporary treatments of death, "close to home." In so doing, we would seek to triangulate among foreign experience, ancient experience, and familiar experience: all with the aim of defamiliarizing-refamiliarizing ourselves with the idea (and construction) of "death." We sought to craft a structure that would allow our students to be not only receivers of knowledge but also its creators. This meant transforming the concept of the reflection session from an inward-directed discussion of course materials to the construction of a series of ever more complex encounters with the world in which we are living and the ideas that shape it.

We developed a schedule of reflection sessions that moved from the familiar to the unfamiliar while gradually shifting responsibility for framing questions and modes of understanding from us to our students. We began with a visit to the Museum of Fine Arts in Boston in late September where we preselected works around which to focus our discussion; the second reflection took us to Mount Auburn Cemetery in Cambridge, Massachusetts (mid-October), where a guided tour and discussion introduced students to the funerary practices of Boston elites in the nineteenth century; for the third, our so-called "death panel" (November), we invited a panel of experts in the fields of bereavement, counseling, and funerals, and guided our students in preparing the questions for the panel; finally, as our capstone session (December), we asked our students to become experts on a particular issue tied up with death in the modern world and to use the skills and approaches of the course to teach that issue to us and their peers. Taken together, then, the four reflections charted a semester-long itinerary for introducing, practicing, and developing mastery of skills from our courses applied to phenomena alive and at work in the world.

For our first and most traditional activity, our visit to the Museum of Fine Arts (MFA) in Boston, we established formal guidelines for our students, including, for each of our separate courses, a list of five objects in the museum's collection, with guiding questions to focus their viewing and to foster discussion. For both of us, this first reflection session was tied more or less directly to our course syllabi and to the skills and approaches to materials we were then working on. For the Ancient Greek course, Hanne Eisenfeld identified two sets of objects: those directly derived from funerary contexts such as a Cretan *larnax* (coffin) or a funerary *stele* (gravestone), and artistic and household objects depicting death scenes, including a vase with a scene familiar from the *Iliad* (Achilles dragging Hektor's body). The former objects embodied the physical realities of death and funerary practice that students had already begun to encounter in an early unit of the course on death in the Mycenaean world, the latter asked students to consider, in conversation with the epic texts that they were encountering as sites of both ancient education and entertainment, how death infiltrated and even decorated daily experience. As the Boston Museum of Fine Arts is without a Russian collection, Thomas Epstein chose five paintings focused on modern representations of death, ranging from the late eighteenth century (John Singleton Copley's *Watson and the Shark*) to the mid-twentieth (Hyman Bloom's 1947 *Female Corpse* and Pablo Picasso's 1963 *Rape of the Sabine Women*). These selections were chosen to resonate with conceptions and descriptions of death in Tolstoy's "The Death of Ivan Ilych," "Three Deaths," and "Sevastopol" and encouraged students to apply the practices of close reading to each painting. Our first goals of re- and de-familiarization were achieved. Our students marveled at the physical immediacy of the holes in the bottom of the Cretan *larnax* that allowed for decomposition and drainage and were individually and personally moved by the sculptures of a husband and wife who lie together in relief on an Etruscan sarcophagus. They brought those experiences to the modern collection, debating the depiction of the body in Bloom's painting and the way the colors of the corpse expressed to them both beauty and disgust. We could see them, throughout the visit, trying out new ways of knowing and perceiving and bringing those approaches into conversation with their preexisting expectations of museums, death, and art.

Several weeks later, on a classic New England fall day, we set out together for Mount Auburn, America's first "garden" cemetery. A celebrated site, the cemetery not only continues to function as a "home" for the dead but has become a tourist destination that provides guided tours for interested visitors. As opposed to the MFA visit, this one had no *direct* bearing either on representations of death in Ancient Greece or on the "Russian way of death" in modernity: Rather, we stood at an epicenter of mid-nineteenth century (and forward) American New England funerary culture (while a given for several of our students, we also had an international student and several first-generation Americans for whom "Yankee" burial rituals were not native or even familiar). In terms of architecture, the first "layers" of Mount Auburn reflects New England nineteenth-century Neoclassicism, so many of the graves were decorated with Classical sculpture and other Greek and Roman motifs, which Hanne Eisenfeld pointed out to the students. While it would have been quite possible for the two of us to have led a tour narrowly oriented to the concerns of our courses and the sociology and anthropology of the site, we decided it was better to experience directly the cemetery authority's own self-presentation (an emphasis on Boston-Brahmin values, famous people, and the ecology of the natural site). Stops included a monument to William Frederick Harden, one of the originators of express package delivery, which the Express Companies of the United States erected for him after his untimely death; the monument includes images of package delivery and functions as both monument and advertisement. Hanne Eisenfeld's class had just finished a unit on Athenian grave monuments and the students were well-positioned to recognize this maneuver, a distant echo of the way that Athenian families built large tombs along major roadways as a means of self-promotion. Our students were also struck by the idealized funerary landscape and its romanticizing effect, which in Thomas Epstein's class were later compared and contrasted with the desecration of cemeteries described in Isaac Babel's story-cycle "Red Cavalry," as well as to the denial of death and the project of its literal overcoming that pervaded Soviet culture. A subsequent assignment offered students the opportunity to design their own grave monument with both the Ancient Greek material and the Mount Auburn visit in mind. One such project adapted the mausolea from the Mount Auburn landscape while integrating statues of mourners, a nod to the Athenian concern with grave visitation and lament and a poignant demonstration of transience.

Immediately following the cemetery visit we adjourned to a Greek restaurant for lunch and an animated discussion of how and why "we," "they," and others bury (or not) and honor (or not) their dead.

By the ninth week of our fourteen-week semester both courses were in full flower. In both classes students had engaged in a variety of writing activities and class presentations. Moreover, as our group of fifteen students was made up of first-semester freshmen taking these two classes together, they developed strong bonds and trust in one another. This made it more natural and easier for us to introduce the concept of our third session, the Panel of Experts (colloquially, the "death panel"), where we expected more input from the students and anticipated discussions of difficult topics.

The composition of the panel was decided by the two instructors, and we shared the work required to bring off the event. In the end we had three extraordinarily willing and able "experts" in different aspects of confronting death: the university chaplain at Brown University, Janet Cooper Nelson; Sue E. Morris, director of bereavement services at Dana Farber Cancer Center; and Fred Dello Russo Jr., head of the Dello Russo Family Funeral Home headquartered in Medford, Massachusetts. For this third session we asked considerably more of the students than during the first two sessions by making them responsible for developing the questions they would pose to the experts. We scaffolded the project by first assigning them the task of individually generating questions they were interested in asking the panel. We encouraged them at this stage to think broadly and to feel comfortable including questions that struck at the heart of experiences too raw for usual conversation (course content to this point had included murder and suicide, disease, death in childbirth, infanticide, mass slaughter, and martyrdom both voluntary and involuntary). Class discussions had already helped our students develop the tools to think critically and emotionally about these issues, but they were unused to raising them outside the closed community of the course. Once the questions were generated, we gathered and collated them, then disseminated them in class, where we asked the students to first meet in small groups and talk together about recurring themes they saw in the questions and emphases they wanted to be sure to bring out during the panel. They then gathered in a single large group to talk about which questions were perceived as more sensitive or fraught and how the students' thinking about those questions was shaped by their experiences in our classes. These preparatory discussions revealed real development in students' ability to think critically and analytically about issues they had encountered through the distancing mechanisms of our courses and also their eagerness to understand what place was given—or not—to those experiences in the contemporary world.

The event itself was a great success. The panelists were enthusiastic about being with us and pleased to meet and hear each other speak. Chaplain Nelson, with decades of university experience behind her, answered our students' questions frankly (most of them having to do with what a university chaplain actually does) and then herself focused on an issue, and led a mini-discussion, that she considers crucial for university communities to face up to: student suicide.

Thanks to the group's cohesiveness and Chaplain Nelson's sensitivity, the discussion was open, frank, and compassionate. Dr. Morris engaged the students in a long conversation on grief and the grieving process; Mr. Dello Russo, who turned out to have been a former divinity student at Boston College, a sitting member of the Medford, Massachusetts, city council, and a second-generation mortician, spoke about the funeral industry as could only someone who loved and believed in it (he described his work as the front line of grief counseling). For the students (and for us), the encounter was eye-opening and brought the contemporary American way of death completely out of the closet and into common, but not banal, discourse. Students posed questions that revealed both their careful thought and the expertise they had gained through their academic study as well as their eager trepidation to approach and understand these issues as seen from the front line. Our panelists were impressed by our students' preparation, openness, and engagement, and we ended the session with the sense that meaningful connections had been drawn between the carefully framed units of our courses and the much messier and unbounded work around death that is ongoing, but often unseen, in the community.

The capstone assignment, culminating in the final reflection session, was designed to synthesize in miniature the knowledge, theoretical approaches, and skills attained over the course of the semester. We actively echoed the format of the panel of experts in our framing of the assignment, encouraging our students to step into the role of knowledgeable speakers while promoting the concept of open inter- and intragroup dialogue about death. We chose four topics that invited students, once again, into contexts beyond the scope of either course while also inviting them to analyze those phenomena within the frameworks of knowledge developed in our classes. Two of these topics, the movies *Amour* and *Grizzly Man*, offered our students an opportunity to analyze texts as aesthetic and artistic interventions into the understanding of death and mortality; the other two, Canada's legalization of physician-assisted suicide in 2015 and the memorialization of the 9/11 attacks at Ground Zero, invited them to analyze legal and cultural responses to mortality. Rather than summarizing the assignment further, we think it best in this case to reproduce the document that structured the Capstone event:

CAPSTONE EVENT: December 14, 7–9 P.M.

The big picture: analyze a modern phenomenon in light of frameworks, questions, value systems, and disciplinary models that you have worked with in both courses. As a panel, you will present your phenomenon to your peers, **then respond to their questions as well as pose to them at least one of your own.**

More specifically:

Step 1: Develop a set of questions that you think are worth raising about your topic. Be ready to articulate how the material of one or both courses helped you to develop these questions. (Due: 12/9)

Step 2: Dig into your material to propose answers to those questions. The frameworks that you used to develop the questions should also inform your approach to seeking answers.

Step 3: Develop and disseminate a short orientation for your peers to read/watch before your presentation. If you are doing one of the movie prompts, this should include a short paragraph or collection of bullet points and a c. three-minute clip from your movie that you'd like your peers to watch in advance. If you are doing one of the other prompts, this should include a short paragraph or collection of bullet points as well as a link to a piece of relevant primary material that you'd like your peers to think about before you present. (Due: 12/12, 5 P.M.)

Step 4: Present your take on your phenomenon to your peers at our Capstone event in a presentation of c. 20 minutes followed by c. 10 minutes of discussion. The active part of your presentation should conclude with a question framed to elicit discussion from your audience. (Due: 12/14, event 7–9 P.M.)

Step 5: Individually write up your own take on your phenomenon in an essay of c. 500 words. (Due: 12/19, noon)

The composition of the panels was based on student wishes (that is, after reading the prompt each student supplied us with her or his "ratings" of the topics, a process that ended with everyone working on either their first- or second-choice topic, though it meant that we gave up our ability to choreograph group composition with the goal of balancing varying strengths and enthusiasms). As a result—and as a result of our timeline, which we would strongly suggest expanding to anyone working with this assignment as a model—the resulting presentations lacked something in finesse and complexity, but they were rich in enthusiasm and showcased our students' ability to talk about wide-ranging and difficult topics with knowledge and confidence.

The group working with the 9/11 Memorial drew on their encounters with commemoration in both classes, highlighting especially the shared tombs of the war dead that Athens built at public expense and the monument erected at Chernobyl after the disaster. Using the digital access to the 9/11 Memorial and Museum, they asked their peers to consider the assertion of social values and reestablishment of social order through the organization of the museum. They highlighted, especially, the issues inherent in memorializing the first responders as a distinct group from the others who died that day and how those labels constituted identity and the way individual memories were valued. They also interrogated the nature and purpose of the gift shop and the unavoidable tensions between commercialism and tragedy. In regard to Chernobyl, having read Svetlana Alexievich's searing oral history of the disaster, the panel questioned the relationship between extreme human suffering and its subsequent monumental glorification by the state. By thinking about how past tragedies have been framed, defined, or ignored, they were able to leverage an examination of the site into a broader consideration of the way that a record of violence and tragedy has become an assertion of—not unproblematic—national values and to read those constructions against the distant yet recognizable landscapes of our courses.

The film assignments asked students to apply their cumulatively acquired knowledge and skills to artistic representations of contemporary encounters with death. With Michael Haneke's *Amour* our student panel described aspects of the film's artistry while focusing on its sensitive and intimate but nonetheless objectified depiction of an aged, long-married French couple's struggle to maintain the bonds of love in the face of the shattering experience of one of the spouse's deaths. With Werner Herzog's artistic documentary *Grizzly Man* the panel was faced with more familiar, if ultimately darker, terrain in the depiction of a decidedly contemporary American story of a young man (Timothy Treadwell) who seems to *charge* toward death in a tragically misguided rebellion against the American way of life.

Each of our four capstone panels, drawing on material from both courses, initiated critical and meaningful discussions that bound the subject at hand into the overarching questions of the course: What is death? How should we think about death? How do particular cultural reactions to death help us understand that culture as well as the shared human condition? Conversation in response to the capstone presentations developed within the framework of these overarching questions, inviting contemplation of how the way we construct our lives tells us a great deal about how we think about death in general and our own death in particular; how heroic narratives have been transformed and sometimes turned grotesque in modernity; on how a "good life" and a "good death" are or are not connected.

As we look back at our classes a year later, we are struck by the outsized influence that those four reflection sessions had on the coherence and efficacy of our courses. They proved to be the glue that brought Ancient Greece and modern Russia into conversation with each other and connected the two courses both for the instructors and the students. Our decision not to make the sessions into formal attempts at linking the curricula of the two separate courses (such as a discussion of a shared text would have effected) proved to be crucial. By framing them, instead, as a dedicated context for thinking about the implication of our course material beyond the boundaries of either class, we were able to use the reflection sessions as a lens that broadened our inquiry from our special topics outward to the universal question of the representation of death, while narrowing it to the personal and existential.

By inviting our students into the landscapes of Boston (MFA, Mount Auburn) and by inviting community members into the classroom (panel of experts) we encouraged our students to take the whole city—and the world beyond—as their laboratory during their remaining time at Boston College and thereafter. Beyond any concern with death in particular, we aspired to engender in our students the intellectual habit of thinking critically and creatively, of never taking anything for granted but always remaining open to the wonders of experience. We were able to introduce and model these habits in our classes, but our reflection sessions ultimately broke down the barriers between academic and lived experience and invited our students to take on the role of explorers and interpreters of our strange terrain.

Spending a Semester with "A Possession for All Time"

Justice and War in Thucydides

Robert C. Bartlett

As part of Boston College's Renewed Core Pilot Program in the spring semester of 2016, Robert Bartlett (political science) and Aspen Brinton (philosophy) each taught, to the same seventeen first-year students, one of two independent but coordinated seminars that shared a thematic focus and a title: "Power, Justice, and War." Among the questions we asked over the course of the semester were these: Why has war been a more or less constant presence in human life? In the face of that harsh fact, how have human beings organized political and social systems in search of justice or a just peace? Does the defense of justice necessitate that we wage war? How do relationships of power influence the outbreak and conduct of war? How does power sway our attempts to seek justice and maintain peace? What is the fate of justice in war, and under what circumstances, if any, can a war be said to be just?

This essay first sketches the link between the two seminars and some of the specific content of each. It then turns to relate some of my experiences leading a semester-long study of a single foundational text, Thucydides' *War of the Peloponnesians and Athenians*.

Some Preliminaries

Given our shared interests in political theory, political philosophy, and the moral questions that arise from war and conflict, Aspen Brinton and I conceived of pairing two courses, one of which would approach the question of justice and war from an ancient perspective, the other from a modern one. In this way we arrived at the decision to have one seminar focus on Thucydides' *War of the Peloponnesians and Athenians*, the other on a variety of modern texts, beginning with Thomas Hobbes's *Leviathan* and continuing through Reinhold Niebuhr's *Moral Man and Immoral Society*, with a good many other stops along the way (and beyond). Thus we would approach a shared set of questions from differing historical epochs, ancient and modern. In addition, our students would have the simultaneous experience of undertaking a sustained and concentrated study of a single text—Thucydides'—while also reading a good many shorter texts: a certain constancy combined with variety. We were also concerned to present students with a variety of *kinds* of texts, too, that went beyond chronology: not only Thucydides' hard-to-classify philosophical-historical treatise but also contemporary scholarship (Michael Walzer on just and unjust wars), modern philosophical treatises (Hobbes's *Leviathan*, Immanuel Kant's "Perpetual Peace," John Stuart Mill's "A Few Words on Non-Intervention," Hannah Arendt's "On Violence"), novels or short stories (Tim O'Brien's *The Things They Carried*), a film (*Death and the Maiden*), as well as writings from practicing politicians, diplomats, and other close observers (Vaclav Havel's "Power of the Powerless," Gandhi's *Political Writings*, Samantha Power's *A Problem from Hell: America and the Age of Genocide*).

Our pedagogical goals in teaching the two seminars were as follows:

To develop the ability to use philosophical ideas to better understand how power, justice, and war affect one's own life as well as the lives of others, both locally and globally

To learn how to undertake a close interpretative reading of different types of texts, including texts from philosophy, literature, and political theory

To begin developing analytical writing skills applicable to various humanistic disciplines

To learn how to ask good questions about the political and cultural forces that we live within today

To begin developing skills to engage in debate and discussion with those who think differently than oneself, as well as learning how to reflect critically about one's own thinking

To appreciate the value of the differences between the "ancient" perspective and the "modern" perspective by learning how to integrate those perspectives in light of perennial problems, as well as how to think critically about the relevance of the ancient/modern distinction

The "modern" course explored

the enduring questions of power, justice, and war by examining a series of modern political thinkers who have contributed to the perennial discussion about how to use power justly, how to balance

concerns about justice in the midst of war, and how to govern the
world through different modalities of power. Each of the texts will in
some way provoke students to think about the difference and interplay
between normative thinking (how should we do things justly?) and
empirical thinking (how do we actually do things?).

Aspen Brinton's syllabus

Brinton also split up the class into teams, each team being responsible for following and reporting regularly to the class on developments in "hot spots" around
the globe: Syria; North and South Korea; Ukraine; Yemen; Boko Haram/Nige-
ria and Northern Africa; Iraq; Afghanistan; Israel/Palestine; and Mexico.

As for the "ancients" component of the course, it was (to repeat) devoted to
a close reading of a single text, *The War of the Peloponnesians and Athenians*,
written by the Athenian general and philosopher, Thucydides. In this work
Thucydides not only details the course of the disastrous, twenty-seven-year-
long war (431–404 BCE) between the two superpowers of the day, Athens and
Sparta; he also elucidates the theoretical or philosophical questions that arise
out of political life at its gravest or most challenging. Above all, Thucydides
considers the argument, made powerfully by a number of leading spokesmen
in the war, that nations are compelled by nature to seek their advantage as they
understand it and that necessity must be seen to excuse what cannot be helped:
The very categories of "just" and "unjust" do not properly apply to international
politics—an early forerunner of what has come to be called "realism." This
momentous argument is of course also opposed by many speakers in the war.
Who is right? It was one of our chief tasks over the semester to master the
details of Thucydides' narrative and also to grapple as best we could with the
arguments that are put forward, especially arguments pertaining to justice and
injustice. Taking Thucydides as our guide and teacher, then, we tried to learn
what he has to teach us about power, justice, and war.

One peculiar feature of our seminars were the four reflection sessions we held
with our students over the course of the semester. These were the chief opportunity the two of us had to get together with our students as a single group
outside of regular class time. These sessions permitted us to take a different,
sometimes broader, view of the tough questions we had been grappling with in
the class. Our first reflection session took the form of a field trip in the greater
Boston area to a privately run, 10,000-square-foot museum documenting World
War II. The International Museum of World War II houses an extraordinary
collection of artifacts, ranging from actual tanks to clothing to weapons to war
propaganda and much else besides, all of it organized chronologically. Seeing
examples of the weapons used, the uniforms worn, some of the implements of

daily life in wartime, and so on brought home in a visceral way something of the conduct of war and its toll, especially effective since most students are familiar with the principal events at least of World War II. Our second reflection session was a lecture by and conversation with a former student of mine, Capt. John Warren, retired from the United States Marine Corps, who did two tours of duty in the course of the Iraq War. He gave a riveting account, complete with photographs and video, of his time in combat in Iraq, and set out in clear and frank terms the challenges, frustrations, and satisfactions of military service. Students were much taken with the experience, and a serious, thoughtful conversation ensued between the students and Capt. Warren. For our third reflection session, we took advantage of the presence on Boston College's campus of Fr. Paul McNellis who, in addition to teaching in the Philosophy Department and being a Jesuit priest, is also a Vietnam veteran. His remarks to our students were centered on the question of whether it is possible to be a Christian and a soldier—Fr. McNellis answered the question in the affirmative—but his reflections proved to be wide-ranging, from his day-to-day activities in the war, to his return to Vietnam as a journalist after he had left active duty, to his decision to enter the priesthood. Students found his comments to be of great interest, delivered as they were with a certain understated gravitas that powerfully conveyed to students the truly life-and-death questions that surround the conduct of war. In the final meeting, near the end of the semester, we simply met as a group ourselves and had a fine, extended, and truly thoughtful conversation about the course, its theme, and the specific texts that most moved or enlightened or frustrated or otherwise affected us.

On Thucydides

In the introduction to his history of the Peloponnesian War, that long and ruinous war between Athens and Sparta and their respective subjects or allies (the "Peloponnesians"), Thucydides admits that his account lacks the pleasures that stem from poetic or mythical tales, such as one reads of in Homer. Nonetheless, he contends, his book will supply the reader with a satisfaction all its own: He will set forth the truth, to the best of his abilities, with regard to both the deeds done and the speeches delivered in the course of the war. And evidently there is some satisfaction to be gained by understanding the truth, even of harsh things. Above all, Thucydides says, if his book "will be judged useful by any who wish to look at the plain truth about both past events and those that, at some future point will, in accord with human nature, recur in similar or comparable ways—that will suffice." And then Thucydides adds, in a justly famous sentence, that his book "has been composed as a possession for all time, not as a competition piece for the moment."

I suspect that it is rare for undergraduate students to spend much time with a single author or book—to say nothing of spending an entire semester with one. It is probably rarer still for freshmen, whose courses are mostly introductory and tend to follow the model of the ten-day tour through Europe: If it's Thursday, this must be Belgium. Today Descartes, tomorrow Hobbes. The risks of devoting a semester to a single book are fairly obvious, since students who fail to develop an interest in or taste for the book will find the semester to be a very long one indeed. And at first, Thucydides' book does appear formidable, in length and in its foreign character. The book more or less begins, for example, with a blur of foreign-sounding names, Dorians and Ionians, Corinthians and Corcyreans, Themistocles and Pausanias and a great many others. It also presupposes some familiarity with the great wars before Thucydides' time, the Trojan War (as detailed by Homer) and the Persian Wars (as chronicled by Herodotus). But these historical matters can be taught relatively quickly and painlessly, and with the aid of maps and a few charts and timelines, I was able to convey to students, as we made our way through the book, the most important information they needed to follow the narrative thread. In fact, I was much impressed by the students' mastery not only of the broad arc of the war, but also of many of its details—right down to recalling the name of this or that general in a battle waged a good many pages before. Some students responded most to the analysis the book makes possible of the conduct of warfare—matters of tactics and strategy—while others responded more to the broader theoretical arguments made by the principal actors in the war. It is probably an exaggeration to say that there is something for everyone in Thucydides' book, but in its impressive scope, and the gravity of its subject matter, it surely comes close. There is a quiet dignity to the book as "Thucydides an Athenian" details the eventual decline and defeat of the Athens that made possible the writing of such a book.

One of the most unusual features of Thucydides' text is its combination of narrative, in which Thucydides addresses us directly in his own name, with directly quoted speeches of the political actors themselves. (The book is therefore also a treasure trove for those interested in the practice of political rhetoric.) To take advantage of this feature of the book, I had each student select one speech and present it to the class: What precisely is the purpose of the speech, the concrete end it is meant to bring about? What obstacles—strategic, military, economic, moral—does the speaker face in trying to effect that goal? How—and how well—does the speaker overcome those obstacles in speech? This was one of the best features of the class, nudging each student to become an active participant in the discussion and giving each student a certain expertise as a foundation on which to build.

It was both a pleasure and an honor to teach this fine group of first-year students, many of whom I am still in contact with. There developed over the course of the semester a real esprit de corps among the students that I had not quite seen before (and haven't quite encountered since). Such are the bonds that can be struck in undertaking a shared endeavor that is elevated by a serious purpose. This is all the more true since the book in question is one that I regard, not only as a classic but as one of the very few books that reward painstaking study with a means to begin to understand the world and therefore also oneself. It seems to me appropriate that I end these remarks by sharing the reflections, written well after the class, of two students from our seminars, both of them (as I write these words) about to enter their senior year.

"One memorable episode from Thucydides' *History of the Peloponnesian War* was the Athenian defeat at Delium. This battle during the Boiotian Campaign highlighted how studying Thucydides can give the reader experience not only with military history, but also with political theory. From a strategic perspective, this event proved the dangers of Athens's growing ambition and expansionism that the city-state had adopted in its departure from Pericles' more defensive strategy for the war. This change in military approach, however, also brought up themes throughout Thucydides' writing, such as the natural human desire for conquest and prestige, or the justification of the strong ruling the weak. The human desire for glory, for example, was part of the reasoning behind both Athens's invasion at Delium and the Boiotians' pursuit of the fleeing Athenian army after winning the battle. Episodes such as this engagement provide plenty of context for the reader to assess and discuss the themes that Thucydides brings up throughout his account of the war." (Thomas Savage)

"Reading Thucydides was one of the greatest and most enjoyably challenging experiences of my college career. The book is long and often confusing, but the way in which he masterfully decides to present the events of the Peloponnesian War, the thoughts and the considerations of the men involved, and the future implications of individual momentary decisions is both impressive and important to modern political science students. The events mentioned include important lessons, political commentary, and a surprising amount of relevance to today's political climate. . . . If the book is not read in full, there are nonetheless definite events (e.g., the Melian Dialogue and Athens's decision to expand to Sicily) that should be read by every political science student at some point in his or her undergraduate experience." (Jeffrey Toomey)

Inquiring about Humans and Nature

Creativity, Planning, and Serendipity

Holly VandeWall and Min Hyoung Song

Together, we taught paired courses for all three years of the Renewed Core Curriculum pilot. The courses were designed to address questions of enduring importance from two different disciplinary perspectives. What is human? What is natural? What is the relationship between the two? These are the questions we explored from philosophical and literary traditions of thought. In planning our courses, we were interested in highlighting the differences between these traditions and, just as importantly, in facilitating dialogue between them. The goal was to model for students the ways in which different disciplines overlap in their interests, augmenting what can be known about a specific topic. Our feeling was that this is something students often realize later in their college careers. Somewhere in their junior or senior years, perhaps, they might realize while sitting in a class discussion that the professor was offering another way to talk about an issue they'd previously encountered in another course. Learning isn't siloed; there are exciting intellectual synergies happening all the time. What we wanted to do was to accelerate to the moment when our students realized this fact.

When we agreed to take part in these pilot courses, then, we thought the students would glean insights about disciplinary methods and about how to evaluate their own approaches to thinking through large questions. We also imagined ourselves discovering more about the methods of another discipline, and picking up some teaching and assignment strategies from another professor interested in student formation. These outcomes occurred as hoped, but it was the process of planning the courses together and discovering what the students taught us in return that made the experience so valuable. The students found ways to surprise and challenge us at least as much as we surprised and challenged each other. It wasn't the anticipated synergy we found most exciting, but the surprises that come with working with another instructor in leading discussions with a group of engaged first-year undergraduates.

Each year we tried not to change our syllabi too much. This allowed us to see how well our vision for the course worked with three different sets of students. At the same time, we did tweak the course in minor ways, learning from each year's experience, and we were struck by how in each year new serendipities happened. What follows looks more closely at the planning that went into our courses, the changes we implemented from year to year, and the ways in which spending so much time with the same small group of students affected our understanding of classroom dynamics. The experience of teaching these paired courses taught us many things, but perhaps what it most brought to the foreground is how important planning is for making serendipitous moments in the classroom possible.

Planning and Refinements

Designing a new syllabus is a time-consuming and usually solitary process for a professor. It is a luxury to be able to teach how and what you want. This is a luxury we have always appreciated. But course design usually happens in a bit of a vacuum chamber, and the results that enable us to assess what the students took away are only visible near the end of the experiment. Planning a paired course with another professor made us reconsider every step. We agreed that we wanted to have a historically structured course—to introduce students to how the relationship between the human and the non-human natural world has been imagined and negotiated in Western culture. This starting place led to a large number of questions. How much time to spend on each period? If we planned assignments to build skills, how would the skills of philosophical reading and writing contrast with those of literary analysis? How could our assignments interact and build on each other? What texts could both professors teach chapters from, to emphasize the ways that different disciplinary approaches gather meaning from texts? How could our final assignment link the course material together?

Addressing these questions took time. It was at least double the amount of time we would have spent in developing a new syllabus on our own, and it yielded some extraordinary benefits. One week we realized, only while discussing with the students, that they were considering Shakespeare's *The Tempest* and Bacon's *New Atlantis* on alternate days of the same week. The texts, whose authors are exact contemporaries, both feature mariners stranded on islands where the inhabitants exhibit extraordinary power over nature, but what a difference in style and goal they represent! We wish we could say we had planned that, but it really emerged as a result of a long-discussed commitment to asking some similar questions. More importantly, the interweaving of thematic questions and styles stimulated the students to raise issues that we could not have predicted in our planning. How separate were the ideas of science and magic in this period? Is control over nature a possible reality or an illusion? Is *The Tempest* part of the utopian novel genre? These were some of the questions students asked, teaching us in the process almost as much about the subject as we imparted to our students.

Much of the work of designing our respective syllabi occurred the summer before the first year. We were part of a semester-long seminar sponsored by Boston College that was meant to get us thinking about pedagogy in a deliberate, systematic way. While the seminar was interesting, its content tended to focus on abstract topics. For the most specific work of planning actual courses, we carved out two days in June to talk about the readings, goals, and assignments that would constitute the courses' primary content. It helped that we were organizing the courses chronologically, as this gave them a strong structure that compelled us to think through similar issues almost simultaneously with each other. We think that a more theme-based approach would have made it harder for us to facilitate such opportunities for unforeseen dialogue, while in our courses they happened because we were exploring similar time periods.

In deciding on which periods to emphasize, Min's own thinking about how to teach this material changed. He originally wanted to focus attention on the development of the pastoral from antiquity through the Renaissance, leading to the emergence of anti-pastoral tropes that question the classed basis of deeply conventional ways of imagining nature. It so happened, however, that in the second year Holly could not take the students to the Boston Museum of Fine Arts as she did in a previous year. At the museum, she asked them to choose a painting and then to later write about it at length. Min agreed to take this assignment on, and this forced him to teach the unit on the pastoral with a greater emphasis on the ways in which literary ideas of ideal landscapes developed in dialogue with a history of visual representation. It also led him to ask his students to choose a non-Western (maybe East Asian or pre-Columbian) piece of art to write about, so they could talk about how they diverge from the Western pastoral tradition.

In the first year of teaching the course, the film *The Martian* was released. Because Min wanted the students to reflect on the similarities between this film and *Robinson Crusoe*, one of the first texts he put on his syllabus, we took the students to see the movie for one of our night reflection sessions. Holly, who wasn't familiar with the narrative of the film, was happy to supplement

Min's class in this way. Only the day after viewing the film, in class, did she and the students find the many ways that this narrative illuminated, and was illuminated by, the selections from Francis Bacon, René Descartes, and Blaise Pascal that the students were reading in class that week. It was in reflecting on this unexpected synergy that we decided to show *The Martian* again in the following years.

As the semester progressed, we carefully planned for our courses to converge around a couple of shared texts: Thoreau's *Walden* and Rachel Carson's *Silent Spring*. As a result of the scheduling of specific classes, it worked out that Min went first with each book. So when it came time to teach *Walden*, he focused attention on the first half, trying in particular to get the students to appreciate the way it is written, the effect it has on the reader, and the ways in which Thoreau's ideas continue to resonate today, sometimes in unexpected ways. Holly turned more to Thoreau's biography, his vision for human transcendence, and helped the students trace the long and subtle argument he sustains throughout the book. Likewise, in discussion of *Silent Spring*, Min focused on the early short chapters to consider how they make use of genre, borrowing as they do from different kinds of fiction to connect with readers. Holly then turned her attention to the goals Carson sought to achieve through her use of rhetoric, and how they clashed with the almost religious faith in science that Carson's argument needed to confront.

Our final project was perhaps our most ambitious attempt to integrate the two classes, and getting the assignment right took some tweaking over the years. We asked the students to write extensively about a place or object that they might frequently encounter without much thought, to make that place or object deliberately unfamiliar so that they could think about it in ways they hadn't before. The goal was to provide the opportunity for students to question their underlying assumptions about their relationships to the natural world. Our students were required to write two essays, both in first person. The first, graded by Min, was a thick description about the space, object, or relation they selected for their final project, addressing such issues as: What are its boundaries and its chief characteristics? How does it relate to the environment that's around it? What about it catches your eye? What kind of dynamic is at play? The thick description also drew on quotations from the readings from Min's class. For example, students could consider—in a critical way, mindful of the way various readers have challenged this idea—the figure of the lone individual capable of reproducing civilization all on his own, exemplified by Robinson Crusoe, in thinking about oneself as a lone individual in a quiet field.

The students were then asked to analyze the same place or object through a philosophical lens for Holly's class. They chose two readings from her course that helped them to see their place through other lenses, restating the relevant arguments of their chosen authors, assessing what insight this argument offered in understanding the space, and discussing whether the authors and arguments they chose contrasted with each other, supported each other, or proposed two complementary ways of understanding the relationship between humans and nature.

We had carefully designed the short writing assignments in both classes to build the skills necessary to write these final essays, and found that many of the students produced technically accomplished essays. But too many seemed easily stumped by what we had thought was the easiest part of the assignment—choosing a space and learning to contemplate it with sufficient focus.

In the first year, we had grand visions of creating a visual map of the spaces, posting the students' images and descriptions on MediaKron (an online tool created at Boston College that is supposed to facilitate the creation of course-related websites), and having them respond to each other's essays for a third part of the assignment, which we planned to grade jointly. What we had not anticipated was the sheer time commitment this would require. Scheduling class time for all the students to learn to use the software, uploading essays right before finals week, requiring students to read and respond to each other's papers during their busiest time of the semester, and thus tying ourselves to a very delayed grading schedule all proved to be a bridge too far. In the next year, we scrapped the technology and commenting on each other's work parts of the assignment. Instead, we devoted time during the evening reflection classes to choosing and discussing their place of focus and learning how to look at it.

Our most successful use of the reflection time, however, was a trip to Walden Pond. Organizing the trip was one of the more time-intensive portions of planning the class, even with significant help from the Dean's Office. In the first year, we were unable to go because the parking lot could not accommodate even a small bus like the one we planned to use; the visitor center and gift shop—ironically, we thought—were being renovated and expanded. But, in the second and third years, the opportunity to visit Thoreau's pond in early winter, the day after reading his chapter on "The Pond in Winter," allowed us to use Thoreau as the paradigm example of thick description and philosophical analysis of place—a target for their final projects to aim toward as well as a chance to come together as a class and see what they had previously only read about. During our outing, the students walked together, engaging in casual conversation with us, and occasionally we pointed out something significant or relevant to our courses. We eventually ended up at the original site of Thoreau's house, where we talked a little about the site and how being there gave us new insights about some of the major and minor concerns in *Walden*. For instance, we pointed out how this area would have been farmland during Thoreau's time, so that there would have been significantly fewer trees around his clearing. We also noted the proximity of the train tracks, which almost abut the original location of his house. Seeing how close the train came gave all of us a better appreciation of the frustration Thoreau felt against the coming of the train to this area of Massachusetts.

If the first year lacked the trip to Walden Pond, it immensely benefited from the release of Pope Francis's encyclical on humans and the environment, *Laudato Si'*, the summer before the course began. Boston College organized a major international conference, "Our Common Home," in late September of that year to reflect on the encyclical and its call to sustainability and the need to address climate change. In light of the opportunity offered by the conference we agreed, during a last-minute course design meeting in August, to incorporate readings from *Laudato Si'* into both courses. We also required our students to attend at least two sessions of the conference and write about them for class. Chronologically, these readings should have come at the end of the semester— it doesn't get much more contemporary than published-this-summer. But the synchronicity of an international discussion of the relationship between the individual, the community, the divine, and the natural world being played out on our campus during the first month of class was too powerful to miss. The issues raised by *Laudato Si'* became central points of contact for a least a dozen other readings that semester. Even without the conference, Holly continued to assign several chapters from the encyclical in following years.

Looking back at our experiences, what seems to us one of the most salient benefits of teaching these paired courses is how they allowed a class to come together. Our shared students spent a lot of time with one another. They met in a seminar-sized classroom every day from Monday through Friday. While they alternated professors on these days, it's clear they were connecting the courses in their own persons in ways the syllabus could only hope for. We found, however, that dynamics changed from year to year, and focus became for both of us about how to manage these dynamics. The course chemistry varied a lot, and became an important component of pedagogy. Racial differences in particular came to the foreground in interesting ways, which also affected how we interacted with the material we were reading. Every class was majority white with one or two African American students and two or three Asian and Asian American students. Some of these students easily got along with their cohort while others, especially two who were international students, did not always seem to have a lot in common with their classmates. The intensity of the experience could make them stand out more than they otherwise would, since bonds became strong while those who felt left out were more left out. This was a dynamic we became more aware of—perhaps because it made something that's usually implicit more explicit for us as instructors—and we thought this gave us additional opportunity to reach out to these students and find ways for them to adjust to a campus that is majority white.

The outside-classroom experiences—museum trips, films, and visits to Walden—also gave us extra insight into how students interact with each other. It became clear that these experiences, especially the visit to the museum that came early in the semester and involved getting away from the classroom together, allowed students to get to know one another in a way that seemed to ease a lot of awkwardness. We noticed that after this first trip, students were more talkative in class and even seemed more playful. Perhaps the trip gave students a common bond, or a shared experience, that carried into the classroom. Or perhaps there was something familiarizing about being together in a less formal setting that lent classroom interactions more informality.

Who took these courses also changed from year to year. Many of the students in the first year were passionate about environmentalism—that was what had convinced them to try this new pilot course. This enthusiasm for the material led to intense conversations around a shared focus, which in turn allowed us to introduce the students to highly sophisticated ideas. The students in year three were less interested in the material and in engaging directly with their professors. Many in this class had enrolled on the recommendation of charismatic students from the first year. Nevertheless, they were also much more integrated and connected with each other, and in this way the course seemed to help them to adjust to college life faster and to find ways to do well in their studies. In all three years, it was for us a novel and unexpected luxury to have another professor with whom to discuss these class dynamics. We were each another lens for the other on the same view, a kind of reflectiveness we asked students to find for their final project. These courses not only gave our students exciting opportunities for discovering unexpected connections and new ways of looking at familiar objects, they also gave us, the instructors, opportunities to learn as well.

The Liberal Arts Core: Engaging with Current Events, 2016–2020

Our implementation of these new courses has happened during tumultuous times in our country and world. The fall of the second year of pilot courses coincided with the 2016 presidential election, which Enduring Question and Complex Problem faculty struggled in various ways to negotiate. When courses are intended to intersect with life outside the classroom, current events make themselves felt even more keenly. The Black Lives Matter movement, MeToo movement, changes in immigration policy, the epistemological crisis bound up with "fake news," and the pandemic all had significant impact on these courses.

Elizabeth Graver and Lynne Anderson are both faculty members in the English Department. Elizabeth is a full professor and novelist, while Lynne, also a writer, is an adjunct faculty member and director of our programming for English Language Learners. Elizabeth and Lynne developed paired courses that fulfill the Literature and Writing Core requirements. From the outset they wanted to teach courses on the topic of immigration that would be open to students who had been identified as needing extra support as English language learners as well as to students who were native speakers of English. Given the challenges of teaching students with such a wide range of English language skills, we reduced the size of their sections. In their essay they describe teaching about the American immigrant experience to this diverse group using a focus on food. Régine Jean-Charles co-taught a Complex Problem course with C. Shawn McGuffey called "When #BlackLivesMatter Meets #Metoo," and her essay reflects on the role of Black feminist pedagogy in integrating the parts of the course and creating a classroom experience that would be both disruptive and generative for students. Allison Adair, professor of the practice in English, and Sylvia Sellers-García, associate professor of history, initially designed their Enduring Question courses, "Truth-telling in History," and "Truth-telling in Literature," to unsettle students' assumptions about the kinds of truth to be found in the study of history and literature. In the Trump era, though, as consensus about a shared set of facts was lost from the public sphere, they grappled with the need to unsettle truth without destroying all belief in it. Finally, Assistant Dean of the Core Elizabeth Shlala describes how the Core office supported faculty in developing remote and hybrid teaching strategies during the pandemic.

Crossings

Teaching "Roots and Routes: Reading/Writing Identity, Migration, and Culture"

Lynne Anderson and Elizabeth Graver

What are the gifts and challenges of thinking and writing across languages and cultures? How do roots inform routes, and vice versa? What does "home" mean in our contemporary globalized but also increasingly balkanized world? What happens if you think of migration as a web rather than as a linear journey from Point A to Point B? How does language intersect with identity? Where are you *from?*

These are just a few of the questions behind "Roots and Routes," our paired first-year undergraduate writing and literature seminars. We designed the courses to be primarily targeted to Advanced English Language Learners, with a third of the seats reserved for native English speakers. The resulting group of seventeen students came from a diverse mix of linguistic, cultural, educational, and socioeconomic backgrounds. The course's first run, in Fall 2017, included international students (mostly with substantial financial resources, as Boston College does not offer financial aid to international undergraduates) from Mexico, South Korea, and Nicaragua as well as Generation 1.5 students (primarily low-income) who immigrated to the United States as children or teens from Ethiopia, Ghana, Nepal, Senegal, Guatemala, and Colombia. It also included U.S.-born students from a range of socioeconomic backgrounds and both rural and urban locales. A few students identified as "third culture kids" with transnational roots. While the course's diverse makeup was enriching for everyone, it seemed particularly important for our Generation 1.5 students. Many in this cohort arrive at Boston College needing some language support, but because they have attended high school in the United States and identify as Americans, they are not best served in our English Language Learning (ELL) writing and literature sections, which are predominantly populated by newly arrived international students. As one student noted in a course evaluation: "The benefits [were] that I didn't feel out of place."

The subject matter of "Roots and Routes" intersected with the students' own experiences and allowed for an invigorating interplay between text and world. Through a variety of assignments (narrative, reflective, analytic/close reading, profiles based on interviews), student writing became more fluid as the semester unfolded and contributed to a deepening conversation that built on the themes of both courses. As one student observed: "In [this class] you become a writer and create a sort of family of writers with your classmates."

Lynne Anderson, who directs English Language Learning at Boston College, taught the First Year Writing Seminar portion of the pairing. Elizabeth Graver, who teaches creative writing and contemporary literature, taught the Literature Core. Together, we designed evening reflection sessions and field trips, brought in speakers, and strove to put the two courses in meaningful dialogue with each other. Everywhere we looked for ways to encourage crossings—between the wide array of students, between texts and lives, reading and writing, history and our current moment, individual and collective identities. We worked to create a welcoming space that would then allow the students to ask rigorous and sometimes thorny questions of our texts, themselves, and the other people in the room. As instructors, we were energized beyond our expectations by the many connections enabled by this paired course.

Roots and Routes

Early in the semester, we introduced the students to Nigerian American writer Chimamanda Ngozi Adichie's TED Talk, "The Danger of the Single Story," in which she says that "the single story creates stereotypes, and the problem with stereotypes is not that they are untrue, but that they are incomplete. They make one story become the only story." Adichie's talk sets forth several themes that were central to the semester's journey, among them the importance of close reading and listening; the role of stories in unsettling preconceptions and enlarging understanding; the relationship between storytelling and power, and between storytelling and conceptions of the past.

In the Literature Core, Adichie's TED Talk was followed by a close reading of Zadie Smith's complex short story, "The Embassy of Cambodia," where students were invited to use Adichie's remarks to think about the story's peculiar collective narration, its exploration of insider/outsider status, its unsettling of stereotypes, and its persistent emphasis on literal or figurative crossings as it follows the path of Fatou, a domestic worker from the Ivory Coast working as an indentured servant for a Pakistani family in London. In a reading response to the story, one student wrote, "'She was a prisoner,' thought Fatou of the Sudanese slave she read about in the paper. . . . The story of the oppressed Sudanese girl made Fatou wonder if she, in fact, was also a prisoner. However, desperately trying to find any excuse to avoid that title, Fatou convinced herself she was far from being one. Unfortunately what Fatou failed to understand was that she, in fact, was a prisoner: a prisoner of the single story."

Other themes of the paired courses included the interconnections between language, power, and identity (texts included Yiyun Li's "To Speak Is to Blunder" and Costica Bradatan's "Born Again in a Second Language"). In the literature class, students did close readings and annotations of several essays to probe the difference between learning a new language as an externally imposed necessity and learning a language as a self-imposed free choice (see Gloria Anzaldúa's "How to Tame a Wild Tongue," Jhumpa Lahiri's "Teach Yourself Italian," and Lauren Collins's "Love in a Foreign Language"). In the writing class, students considered linguistic heritage and loss through the works of bicultural writers such as Sandra Cisneros, Eva Hoffman, Amy Tan, and Lev Golinkin (see "An Offering to the Power of Language," *Lost in Translation*, "Mother Tongue," *A Backpack, A Bear, and Eight Crates of Vodka*). While Cisneros notes the power of the past— "the language of our antepasados, those who come before us, connects us to our center, to who we are, and directs us to our life work"—Golinkin (a Boston College graduate) illustrates the losses that come when facing the language barrier: "You will never be seen as anything more than an immigrant, or a moron, or a child. . . . You no longer have opinions . . . or perspectives built over a lifetime."

These readings intersected with the multilingual students' experiences and allowed for a rich discussion about the complex dynamics between language and identity and language and power. A Generation 1.5 student from Colombia echoed Cisneros and Golinkin: "During my first year in America, every time I would hear a person speak Spanish, I would feel like a little kid in a candy store. . . . [Speaking English] I try hard to translate the words, but those words do not have the same meaning. . . . They lose the emotion behind them . . . so it makes it difficult to fully get the message across. After ten years of speaking two languages, I realize that languages are both bridges and walls." Since all the students, including the native English speakers, had studied a foreign language and inhabit an increasingly multilingual United States, the topic had widespread resonance. As one native speaker wrote in his reflection: "I've never known any other language other than English, so my privilege is often hidden and I personally have never been victimized because of my identity since I have been surrounded by a majority of English speakers . . . but I understand many people struggle and feel marginalized by the complexities and restraints it places on foreign speakers."

Texts and Lives

The varied backgrounds of our students and ourselves (we are both middle-aged, U.S.-born white women, though with different stories/heritages) proved to be tremendously enriching. A few examples: During a discussion of the Haitian call-and-response storytelling practice invoked by the title of Edwidge Danticat's collection *Krik? Krak!*, students born in Ethiopia, Ghana, and Senegal shared their own cultures' versions of call and response, which opened the door to a wider discussion of the African diaspora, the legacy of the slave trade in Haiti, questions of audience, and storytelling as an explicit or implicit invitation to dialogue and crossing. During the discussion of Chicana writer Gloria Anzaldúa's multilingual essay "How to Tame a Wild Tongue," the Spanish-speaking students in the room were invited to read a Spanish passage from the essay aloud. The other Spanish speakers then reported on what they could glean about each other's backgrounds through hearing different accents—a level of detail and "close reading" invisible to the non-native Spanish speakers in the room. This, in turn, led to a charged but vital discussion about social class, attitudes toward Indigenous peoples (one student, from Guatemala, had learned Spanish as a second language, having been raised speaking Q'eqchi'), colonialism, and the politics of language, returning us to the Anzaldúa essay in a fuller way.

In both these instances, the English Language Learners were able to offer nuanced, comparative perspectives that took the group beyond the expertise of the professors and other students and added to our shared experience of the texts. Differences of linguistic background and culture, which can sometimes feel like liabilities to ELL students, became strengths. Invariably, students were surprised by each other's depth of knowledge and experience, as by the wide range of backgrounds. One student observed, "I think [the class] made me a lot more aware of the different kinds of students we have at BC. Everyone in the class had a different story and a different path, yet we all ended up in the same classroom twice a week. It made the world feel smaller, in a way."

Elizabeth and Lynne

Elizabeth:

While I've taught creative writing and literature for many years, with a recent focus on literatures of migration, I am not a specialist in teaching English Language Learners and depended on Lynne to help me navigate the complexities of the students' varied language backgrounds and levels. Despite Lynne's having cautioned me, I started the course with an overstuffed syllabus and quickly learned that for this cohort (and probably for most first-year college students), less was definitely more. Devoting three class sessions to Edwidge Danticat's short story "Sunrise, Sunset" allowed us to move from basic questions of comprehension, narration, and point of view to a discussion of generational and cultural attitudes toward child-rearing, mental illness, and trauma in the story, and finally, to an exploration of how Danticat's treatment of literal and figurative memory loss in the context of migration resonated with several other texts.

Through conversations, readings, and the online resources she provides to the ELL instructors in the program she runs, Lynne helped me understand in more nuanced ways how a student's particular language and cultural background might impact not only her particular language transfer challenges but also her concepts of argument, essay shape, and even citation and attribution. The recent nonfiction work of writer Gish Jen, one of our class visitors, was also illuminating in this regard (see *Tiger Writing: Art, Culture and the Interdependent Self*, and *The Girl at the Baggage Claim: Explaining the East-West Culture Gap*). In response to our mutual feeling that the students needed better instruction and more practice in close reading, Lynne and I learned midstream how to use the online annotation program Perusall, a tool that is visual, interactive, and collaborative, and that proved highly effective. These various supports allowed me to maintain my high standards and explore subject matter I am passionate about, while also responding to the needs of our bright multilingual students, challenging all the students in the class and expanding my own range as a teacher.

Lynne also brought her experience as a chef and food writer with a focus on immigrant kitchens to the class, arranging a final project where students took over a BC dining hall kitchen and cooked food from their cultures side by side, making a shared feast. This ambitious project tied into the reading and writing students had done on food and culture, creating a through-line from the course content to the communal and joyful experience of creating and sharing a meal whose eclectic nature—mashed potatoes, tortillas, Senegalese soupe kandia, and tteokbokki from Korea—was as delicious as it was varied.

Lynne:

I witnessed the way Elizabeth shares her strategies as a fiction writer with students. For our first reflection session, she devised a group writing activity that I probably would not have undertaken so early in the semester because it required everyone to share something they'd just composed (with no time for revision or feedback). It was, however, a wonderful success (one student commented on it in his semester reflection for my class) and allowed us to hear the varied and idiosyncratic voices of the group. Students wrote a tactile description of an object we'd brought to the session (an old doorknob, a bone, sewing kit, traditional cooking implements, a woven cloth). We encouraged them to consider their objects within a context of movement and migration, recognizing that each possessed traces of the past. Elizabeth designed the activity so that she and I took part in it, something else that I would not have done, because I worried that students would compare their work to that of the teacher/expert and feel uncomfortable when it came time to share aloud. This was not the case. Our participation allowed students to witness the two of us crossing out words, reworking phrases, and starting again (just as they were), an important reminder that the composition process is hard work for all of us, whether we are newly arrived college students or published writers. The nineteen voices reading aloud at the end of the evening was a wonderful way to honor the individual members of our group and our collective creativity.

Elizabeth generously shared her own process as a fiction writer throughout the semester; on one occasion she spoke about the research that went into her novels and, when preparing students for the video interview assignment, discussed her own strategies when interviewing to uncover stories that gesture to the arc of a life's narrative in meaningful ways. I found this an interesting approach because so often in literature classes the focus lies solely on the texts themselves, without considering how the author brought the story or poem or essay to the page. An overarching theme in both of our courses was the danger of the single story (Adichie), and in sharing her own approach to writing, Elizabeth showed students how to recognize this in the texts they were reading and in their own quests to understand the world.

Inside and Out

Our field trips and evening reflection sessions involved creative writing exercises, guest speakers (in addition to writer Gish Jen, State Representative Adrian Madaro met with our class), a tour of Boston's Chinatown, and the final cooking session and celebratory meal. All of these activities were designed to foster community, to bring the world to BC and the students to the world, and to offer experiential ways of accessing the course's central themes of identity, migration, and culture. Institutional support in the form of a budget and help with logistics were key to our being able to offer this programming.

Each of us also worked to develop assignments that bridged inside and outside and invited students to connect lived life with texts in fresh and substantive ways. In the Literature Core, the students' final project was to make a video interview with an immigrant. The people our students chose to interview included fellow undergraduates, a food service worker, and a librarian. Some of the Generation 1.5 students interviewed their own parents, grandparents, or cousins. One American-born student interviewed his aunt's home healthcare worker from Haiti. Another student interviewed her mother, who'd been a refugee from Vietnam, and included a photo of her American-born father, who had met his wife in the refugee camp where he'd been volunteering. The students were also required to write a paper in which they compared and contrasted their interviewees' observations to key moments in the texts we had read together—another crossing. We screened the videos in class. Here, writ large, were seventeen examples of the importance of getting beyond the single story. Two of the students' videos were eventually selected for publication on *Global-Boston*, a professional website curated by our historian colleague Lynn Johnson— an opportunity that allowed students to contribute to a wider conversation and for their interviewees' voices to be heard in a public forum.

In the writing seminar, students went beyond the confines of the classroom to explore the way one's culture informs perceptions and expectations. Building from our reading of Gish Jen's *The Girl at the Baggage Claim* that posits an East/West divide where individualism is valued in the West and a more collectivist approach in the East, students conducted interviews to explore the way a particular cultural practice unfolds in different parts of the world. Topics included rituals related to mealtime, parent/child relationships, greetings, dating practices, perceptions of mental illness. Interviewees included members of the BC community and beyond. As one student noted, "This assignment gave me an opportunity to explore the cultural differences that I have noticed all of my life. I also enjoyed the interview process of this essay. I was able to talk to my parents and my cousin about topics we never would normally talk about. I was able to gain an insight on their childhood growing up, and could see how that shaped them into the person they are today."

A final writing assignment, a reflection on a food memory, was read aloud during the last day of class and followed the group cooking activity. With generous support from Boston College Dining Services, each student prepared a dish with resonance to his or her family. A student from Oklahoma made his family's biscuits and gravy while another cooked Thakali and wrote of his mother and aunts preparing this traditional stew in his village in Nepal. In a final reflection for the course, the Nepalese student wrote, "I will never forget the food and time we spent cooking together . . . because I felt like I was at home cooking with my family."

By the end of the semester, students seemed to recognize that coming to college was a mini-migration of sorts, a crossing into another world, which then allowed for a deeper understanding of the homes they had left behind. The paired courses were also a journey for us as instructors. The next time we teach "Roots and Routes," we will coordinate assignments better, spreading them out more, alternating due dates and teaching more shared texts. What we hope we *can* duplicate is this batch of students' mix of analytic rigor and emotional engagement, as well as their strong connections to us and each other—a gift, it seems, of these paired courses, which put students in the same classroom for twice as long as a typical class and offer additional opportunities for reflection and for experiential learning. One student wrote, "When writing the final journal about food, I started to tear up by the time I reached the last paragraph. . . . It wasn't until I had finished that essay that I realized the strong connection I had to my mother's cooking and how much I missed my family. Who would have thought that writing down my feelings would bring me closer to something I've had my entire life?"

The Architecture of a Black Feminist Classroom

Pedagogical Praxis in "Where #BlackLivesMatter Meets #MeToo"

Régine Michelle Jean-Charles

During the first week of our Complex Problem class, "Where #BlackLivesmatter Meets #MeToo: Violence and Representation in the African Diaspora," I have my students read June Jordan's "Poem About My Rights" aloud in front of their peers. The poem, written in 1978 by Black feminist poet, essayist, and playwright June Jordan connects the speaker's personal history of rape to a public narrative about violence that is global, informed by social justice, and born of multiple oppressions. The magnificent conclusion of "Poem About My Rights" in which the speaker narrates her private pain as a rape survivor reinforces the idea that histories of violence are raced and gendered, intertwined and embodied. It reads:

> I am the history of rape
> I am the history of the rejection of who I am
> I am the history of the terrorized incarceration of myself
> I am the history of battery assault and limitless
> armies against whatever I want to do with my mind
> and my body and my soul and
> whether it's about walking out at night
> or whether it's about the love that I feel or
> whether it's about the sanctity of my vagina or
> the sanctity of my national boundaries
> or the sanctity of my leaders or the sanctity
> of each and every desire
> that I know from my personal and idiosyncratic
> and indisputably single and singular heart

I have been raped
be-
cause I have been wrong the wrong sex the wrong age
the wrong skin the wrong nose the wrong hair the/ wrong need
the wrong dream the wrong geographic
the wrong sartorial I
I have been the meaning of rape
I have been the problem everyone seeks to
eliminate by forced
penetration with or without the evidence of slime and
but let this be unmistakable this poem
is not consent I do not consent
to my mother to my father to the teachers to
the F.B.I. to South Africa to Bedford-Stuy
to Park Avenue to American Airlines to the hardon
idlers on the corners to the sneaky creeps in
cars
I am not wrong: Wrong is not my name
My name is my own my own my own . . .[1]

Jordan's riveting conclusion establishes that the subject of the poem takes up and claims space. She occupies space as a survivor, as a commentator on social justice, as poet, and as a woman who understands how global networks of power such as capitalism and patriarchy calibrate her lived experience as a Black woman. On the page, she takes up space through the anaphoric use of "I" and "my own."[2] This gesture disrupts the idea of Black women subject to the ownership of others, whether they were forced into that position through the legacy of chattel slavery or the hetero-patriarchal structure of the family. The poet clears a space for Black women rape survivors to affirm their existence within the stanzas of the poem. By inter-imbricating her created space with global histories of violence and oppressive circuits of power she questions who gets to occupy which spaces even as she creates them. The poem thus emblematizes what Black feminist historian Barbara Ransby called the "dialectic of breaking boundaries and creating space."[3] Breaking a boundary is to refuse convention, creating a space is to imagine new possibilities beyond convention. The act of breaking and creating simultaneously is both disruptive (interrupting) and generative.

It is with that impulse in mind, a desire to be both *disruptive* and *generative*, that I invite my students to begin the journey of "transforming rape culture" at the heart of the class's mission. In this essay, I reflect on my experience teaching a class intended to disrupt and to generate. My thinking here is primarily animated by my belief that a Black feminist classroom can function as space of disruption, transformation, formation, and safety on predominantly white college campuses.[4] I argue that creating such a space requires a different relationship to the built environment as well as an intentional focus on reclaiming the space of the classroom, and moving beyond that physical space of both the classroom and the physical college campus. In my view, there are three ways in which our Black feminist pedagogy instructs students on how to break boundaries and create space: (1) by *setting* the classroom space, (2) by *claiming space* (taking up space) on campus outside of the classroom, and (3) *by moving beyond* the confines of the classroom to do work in the community off campus. Ultimately, and somewhat unexpectedly, the class emerged as a space for staging an encounter with Black feminism that only succeeded because of how it calls upon students to move beyond the built environment of the university campus and challenge the spatial configuration of the classroom.

My colleague, sociologist Dr. Shawn McGuffey and I taught "Where #BlackLivesmatter Meets #MeToo: Violence and Representation in the African Diaspora" for the first time in the fall of 2018. The class fulfilled the BC Core requirements in literature and one social science and was cross-listed with the African and African Diaspora Studies Program and the sociology department. Our course content was geographically diverse and intentionally global: We explore the problem of rape culture in multiple contexts based in the United States, the Caribbean, and on the African continent. As a part of the Renewed Core it was interdisciplinary in form and deployed methodologies from both the humanities and the social sciences. Our goal was to approach rape culture as not only a complex problem but also as an urgent problem that is global in scope. We came to the class with the explicit goal of equipping students to imagine solutions for intervening in and eradicating rape culture with constant attention to how intersectionality operates in gender-based violence. According to the editors of the collection *Transforming a Rape Culture*, from which our vision drew much inspiration:

> Transforming a rape culture involves imaginative leaps from our present state of institutionalized violence to a future that is safer and more just. *We must summon our imaginations for this task*, because history and society have so few precedents for us . . . transforming a rape culture is about changing fundamental attitudes and values.[5]

Taking this statement seriously, our students not only learned about the wide-ranging manifestations and ramifications of rape culture, and academic approaches to examining it, but they were also asked to summon their imaginations to envision a world without sexual violence and to consider how to challenge the norms that perpetuate rape culture. The imagination, the ability to dream or, as the theorist Ashon Crawley puts it, "to imagine otherwise," is an essential ingredient for the work of transformation. In other words, by imagining a world without sexual violence our students are encouraged to envision and work toward a more just world.[6]

To achieve these goals, we assigned critical readings from the fields of sociology, literary studies, and cultural studies. We read articles by Beth Richie, Andrea Ritchie, Barbara Christian, and Rhoda Reddock among others. We read fiction in different genres, including Toni Morrison's novel *The Bluest Eye*, Marie Chauvet's triptych novel *Anger*, Lynn Nottage's play *Ruined*, and Yvonne Vera's novella *Under the Tongue*. We watched films such as *NO! The Rape Documentary* about sexual violence in the Black community, *The Hunting Ground* about campus sexual assault, and *Spotlight* about the *Boston Globe* when it unearthed the sex abuse scandal in the Catholic Church. We asked questions like, "How do historical racialized, sexualized and gendered tropes help us understand current-day responses to sexual assault? How do definitions of what constitutes sexual violence shape how we respond to both perpetrators and survivors? Why is rape culture so pervasive around the world? How do writers represent sexual violence in their fiction? What is the relationship between rape and representation? How do representations of rape differ in various mediums? How are rape victim/survivors portrayed in literature and film? How do cultural workers reflect, challenge, or attempt to dismantle some of the basic premises of rape culture through their representations of sexual violence?" The development of these questions and the answers that students advanced to respond to them were central to our mission to interrogate and dismantle rape culture.

Per the Complex Problem structure, the class also included a weekly lab that involved students in collaborative work concerning historical and contemporary cases of sexual violence or working with local anti-violence projects in the Boston area. In these labs students made connections between the literary texts and critical readings from class and contemporary manifestations of rape culture, such as the crisis of campus sexual assault, sexual abuse in the Catholic Church, and the proliferation of sexual violence in refugee camps. By linking the study of rape culture to its modern-day incidence, our students were better equipped to create projects that intervene in the problem of sexual violence. The final element of the class structure was a weekly reflection session in which we considered specific cases of sexual violence—through films, speakers, and panel discussions. During these two-hour evening reflection sessions, we invited local community organizations like Black Lives Matter

Boston and The Boston Area Rape Crisis Center as well as nationally known leaders in the movement to end violence against women and girls such as A Long Walk Home co-founders Scheherazade Tillet and Salamishah Tillet and filmmaker Aishah Shahidah Simmons.[7]

It should be noted that the class structure that I just outlined was dictated to us by the university's Core Pilot Program. The structure was intentional; it was a deliberate effort to provide more contact hours for students to build in space for reflection and for the students to be able to apply their knowledge in the lab setting. Yet, although the structure of the class was created by the university, the architecture of the class was Black feminist. By architecture I mean the ways that we designed the class to suit our goals and our pedagogical praxis as Black feminist scholars, looking to have our students not only understand but also intervene in rape culture. Nowhere was this more clear than in the labs in which they developed their group projects as well as in the formative elements of the class. At the end of the semester, students in each lab presented group projects to the class about their own research and/or fieldwork undertaken in the labs. One group conducted a climate survey about campus sexual assault at Boston College; group 2 worked for the Boston Area Rape Crisis Center; group 3 created an arts-based project; and group 4 organized an event on campus. We were very purposeful in selecting our readings and created assignments determined to be attentive to intersectionality, consider contemporary problems in Black Studies, and include a rigorous community element that requires students to travel outside of the classroom.

One of my contributions to the class is to introduce students to rape cultural criticism, which is about how the images, narratives, and rhetoric surrounding rape are historically, politically, and socially informed. Because "the subject of rape and representation troubles the boundaries between literature, politics, law, popular culture, film studies and feminism," a cultural studies approach helps make connections between multiple forms and disciplines.[8] "Feminist modes of 'reading' rape and its cultural inscriptions help identify and demystify the multiple manifestations, displacements, and transformations of what amounts to an insidious cultural myth. In the process, they show how feminist critique can challenge the representations that continue to hurt women."[9] Using these tools, we ask questions like: What do representations of sexual violence tell us? We know that because of rape culture there are negative portrayals, but how might representation allow us, or empower us, to imagine differently. How might literature help us imagine a world without sexual violence?

Our pedagogy was motivated by a desire to bridge the gap between theory and praxis while emphasizing the idea of transformation. Again, we wanted our students to imagine a world without sexual violence and actively devise ways to intervene in, address, and ultimately end rape culture. Our assignments for students to move outside of these institutional spaces were informed by our understanding of the limits of the academy. Since the late 1970s and early 1980s Black feminists have regularly questioned the utility of the classroom specifically, and institutions of higher learning in general as spaces for engaging Black feminism. In a review essay of *All the Women Are White, All the Blacks Are Men, But Some of Us Are Brave* published in 1982, Cheryl Clarke describes how the anthology embraced a form of pedagogy designed to transcend the boundaries of a college classroom. As she writes:

> Pedagogy need not only exist in a college classroom. . . . I believe that the perpetuity of a radical Black women's studies is dependent upon its distance from traditional white and male institutions of high[er] learning and otherwise. In its philosophy and vision, *But Some of Us Are Brave* is adaptable to the struggle of naming ourselves to Black women who exist and survive outside the academic colony and who are in need of a "pro-feminist" and "anti-racist" perspective on their lives.[10]

Following this logic of our particular Jesuit, Catholic, predominantly white, and male-led institution, we made deliberate choices about the kinds of pedagogy we engaged in even on the days when we remained in the classroom. Among these were the daily roundup of current events for which we asked students to connect the materials we were reading to the world. One week this meant seeing the contemporary relevance and resonance of Michele Wallace's 1991 essay "Storytellers: The Thomas-Hill Affair," which we read during the same week that the Supreme Court hearings for Justice Brett Kavanaugh were taking place in October. As my students watched Christine Blasey Ford testify before the Senate Judiciary Committee, they had just begun to analyze how race, class, and gender figure in public conversations about sexual assault. We established a critical space in the classroom by doing activities such as reading Jordan's "Poem About My Rights" aloud at the beginning of class, or playing clips from performances of *for colored girls who have considered suicide when the rainbow is enough*. Our commitment to being disruptive also led us to center the voices of Black women survivor activists, scholars, creators, and local organizers. We also claimed space on campus by having students participate in a national walkout organized to support survivors and encouraging them to participate in student-led protests. Lastly, we transcended the space of the campus by requiring them to do work with local community organizations. Importantly, we asked that the organizations determine what kind of work the students could do so as to avoid the troubling "savior complex" dynamic that runs rampant on campuses such as ours. We wanted our students to understand that service is about learning, proximity, and solidarity.

Many, if not most, Black feminists grapple with how institutional practices and structures can be destructive spaces that do not work in service of Black feminism. In *Black Feminism Reimagined*, Jennifer Nash writes,

> It is crucial to note that Black feminism—and Black feminists—have long been attached, optimistically or self-destructively (or maybe both)—to the university. Indeed, Black feminist theory has a long history of both tracking the violence the university has inflicted on Black female academics (often by demanding Black women's labor—intellectual, political, and embodied labor) and advocating for institutional visibility and legibility. . . . Black feminism has remained oriented toward the university despite this violence, and has largely retained a faith in the institution's capacity to be remade, reimagined, or reinvented in ways that will do less violence to Black feminist theory and Black feminists' bodies.[11]

Nash refers to the long-standing critique of how the university "disappears" Black women; it is one reason why the Black Feminist Classroom must be a space of disruption in order to transcend racial and gender injustice. As we experienced, teaching a class about rape culture at a Jesuit university was not easy, and the challenges were there from the beginning. For example, we received pushback about naming this course. Originally our title was "Transforming Rape Culture," borrowing from the title of the volume. We were urged to reconsider and find a title that did not include "rape" in it. In another instance we did an activity that intentionally took up and disrupted the campus space by participating in a walkout while classes were in session. On the day of the national walkout in support of survivors organized by Tarana Burke during the Senate Judiciary Hearing, the students who participated were publicly berated by an administrator for being disruptive.

But ours was a vision that always intended to disrupt and expand.

> Black feminist pedagogy aims to develop a mindset of intellectual inclusion and expansion that stands in contradiction to the Western intellectual tradition of exclusivity and chauvinism. It offers the student, instructor, and institution a methodology for promoting equality and multiple visions and perspectives that parallel Black women's attempts to be and become recognized as human beings and citizens rather than as objects and victims.[12]

Describing the urgent necessity of Black feminist pedagogy on college campuses, Omolade names the "need for instructors to struggle with students for a better university."[13] While we did achieve this kind of transformative atmosphere, it was never lost on us that teaching about #BlackLivesMatter and #MeToo meant grappling with painful topics and dealing with traumatic experiences. We had students whose family members were killed by gun violence, students who were survivors of rape and childhood sexual abuse, students who were triggered by the material but uncertain of where their flashbacks were coming from. My understanding that feminist pedagogy alone is inadequate to the barriers facing women, people of color, and queer people in institutions of higher education is why we insisted that students in this class move beyond the classroom as well as the university in order to transform rape culture. Teaching our students to break boundaries and create spaces also meant critiquing the institutional structures that they were a part of and finding ways to move beyond them both literally and figuratively.

We plan to teach our class again in fall 2021, but in very different circumstances. Our world is still in the midst of a pandemic that has disproportionately affected Black and Brown people in this country. Furthermore, our students will come to campus on the heels of the most recent iteration of Black Lives Matter—the 2020 uprisings that began the last weekend of May to protest the deaths of George Floyd, Breonna Taylor, and Ahmaud Arbery. As we prepare to teach our class in this unprecedented atmosphere of 2020, we know that it will be even more important to incorporate the voices and experiences of the first cohort of students from 2018.

I want to give the final words of this essay to those students whose testimonies remind me of Black feminist thinker bell hooks's point that personal testimony helps to chart new theoretical journeys. As bell hooks insightfully notes, "personal testimony, personal experience, is such fertile ground for the production of liberatory feminist theory because it usually forms the basis of our theory making. I am grateful to the many women and men who dare to create theory from the location of pain and struggle, who courageously expose wounds to give us their experience to teach and guide, as a means to chart new theoretical journeys."[14] By way of conclusion, I offer four examples from essays that students who took the class in their first year wrote to apply for the position of junior teaching fellow in their third year. Below are examples of what those students learned from the class in their own words. Their names are Grace Assogba, Latifat Odetunde, Bilguissa Barry, and Taleah Pierre-Louis. I am grateful to these women who are daring to create new theories out of their developing academic expertise and lived experience; they are an example of creating space *and* breaking boundaries that everyone in our community can learn from.

Black Lives to #MeToo was more than just a course. When confronted with how to manifest and fight against enduring injustices I realize that this course is a toolbox. The tools allow us to construct our identities and reinforce oppositional knowledge so that when we go out into the world, and we look to reimagine liberation as storytellers, as frontline responders, as disruptors, as healers, as artists, we can bridge the gap, unapologetically.[15]

Reflecting upon my college experience and analyzing the climate of today's society, I now know that this course has made me more informed in my activism, provided me the tools necessary to help people of multiple marginalized identities, and has helped my interactions in the outside world not only in the US, but the greater African diaspora. The class helped me build my skillset in order to create the change that I want to see in the world. Growing up in a traditional Haitian household, although I was aware of society's injustices and was very inclusive in my beliefs, I was discouraged to engage outwardly in my activism, and was specifically told to not bring the attention towards myself in order to not become a target for hateful or violent acts. Taking this class in the Fall of 2018, however, revealed how passionate I was about being vocal regarding important issues that affect my daily life, such as white supremacy, sexism, and everything that they impact. The confidence that I have gained from this course has allowed me to inform my peers and family, as well as mediate in and empower those whom I share spaces with. I would love to have the opportunity to be a part of the team that allowed me to not only be more informed, but be a better human being as well.[16]

I can honestly say that that course was the most impactful course I've taken during my time at Boston College. Not only did the requirements prepare me to be successful for the rest of my academic career but the subjects discussed, #BlackLivesMatter and #MeToo, forever inform my politics and praxis. Taking this class lit a passionate fire within me that has fueled my devotion to transforming rape culture and intersectional approaches to violence and healing overall; it's one of the reasons I was unafraid to become a Bystander Education Trainer. I am excited at the prospect of working as a Junior Teaching Assistant for a class that has meant so much to me, so that I could help others through the sometimes isolating feeling of imposter syndrome and navigating the depth and heaviness of the content that we face.[17]

This course taught me how to use my sociological imagination where I combine both history and my biography to understand the vectors of oppression that my intersections face, and its impact on my position in society. One of the readings from the class that resonated with me was Angela Davis's *Women, Race, and Class*, where I learned about the trap of loyalty, and how Black women have been socialized to trump their race over their gender in efforts to keep the movement for Black liberation moving. Before this course, I did not consider my gender and the ways in which both race and patriarchy played a role in my experiences. Therefore, the course merging both activism and education accelerated my journey of self-love, and has evolved me into a Black feminist that is conscious of the rape culture society we breathe in.[18]

Notes

1. June Jordan, "Poem About My Rights," in *Directed by Desire: The Collected Poems of June Jordan* (Port Townsend, Wash.: Copper Canyon Press, 2005).

2. It should be noted that the poem first appeared in *Essence* magazine, a popular magazine by and for Black women.

3. Barbara Ransby, Keynote address for Breaking Boundaries, Created Spaces conference at Georgetown University, January 2019.

4. See Frances Maher, ed., *The Feminist Classroom: Dynamics of Gender, Race, and Privilege* (Lanham, Md.: Rowman and Littlefield, 2001).

5. Emilie Buchwald et al., *Transforming Rape Culture* (Minneapolis: Milkweed, 1993), preamble.

6. Ashon Crawley, *Blackpentecostal Breath: The Aesthetics of Possibility* (New York: Fordham University Press, 2016).

7. Full disclosure: I have been involved in A Long Walk Home as board member, performer, and lecturer since the organization was founded in the early 2000s.

8. Lynn A. Higgins and Brenda R. Silver, eds., *Rape and Representation* (New York: Columbia University Press, 1991), 2.

9. Higgins and Silver, 2.

10. Cheryl Clarke, "Black, Brave, and Woman, Too," *Sinister Wisdom* 20 (1982); 92.

11. Jennifer Nash, *Black Feminism Reimagined: After Intersectionality* (Durham, N.C., Duke University Press, 2019). Nash defines the "Black feminist" approach as one that "centers analyses of racialized sexisms and homophobia, and that foregrounds Black women as intellectual producers, as creative agents, as political subjects, and as 'freedom dreamers' even as the content and contours of those dreams vary" (13). Similarly, for us the Black feminist classroom meant taking the structure dictated to us by the university and imagining a different architecture of the class. By Black feminist architecture, I am signaling our attentive design of the class, which, though

dictated by the university Dr. Shawn McGuffey and I had to work hard to make our own and serve our purposes.

12. Barbara Omolade, "A Black Feminist Pedagogy," *Women's Studies Quarterly* 15, no. 3/4, *Feminist Pedagogy* (1987): 32–39. Published by:The Feminist Press at the City University of New York. Stable URL: https://www.jstor.org/stable/40003434. Accessed 1/22/2019.

13. Ibid.

14. bell hooks, *Teaching to Transgress: Education as the Practice of Freedom* (New York: Routledge, 1994), 74.

15. Grace Assogba (Boston College MCAS 2022), *Junior Teaching Fellow Application Essay*, July 2020.

16. Taleah Pierre-Louis (Boston College MCAS 2022), *Junior Teaching Fellow Application Essay*, July 2020.

17. Bilguissa Barry (Boston College MCAS 2022), *Junior Teaching Fellow Application Essay*, July 2020.

18. Latifat Odetunde (Boston College MCAS 2022), *Junior Teaching Fellow Application Essay*, July 2020.

Truth-Telling in History and Literature

Constructive Uncertainty

Allison Adair and Sylvia Sellers-García

Truth-Telling as Theoretical Concept

Allison and I went to college together, and there's no doubt that common train-ing forms common thinking. We both studied literature as undergraduates, but we were also both part of Brown University's Writing Fellows program, an approach to peer mentoring that stressed methodology and self-critical aware-ness in the teaching of writing. I remember absorbing early on that it was al-ways better, if I could, to write a comment in the margin phrased as a question, not an assessment or even a suggestion.

Some habits die hard. We still think in questions, and this was starkly evident when Allison and I first discussed compatible classes several years ago. Common interests easily rose to the surface—travelers, marginal characters, subversive texts, and unreliable narrators—but we settled on a common question that we felt occupied the central place, directly or indirectly, in many of the texts we found most compelling: Is it possible to tell the truth about the past?

We liked many things about this question. We liked its simplicity. We liked that in the phrase "telling the truth about the past," there was equally room for both literature and history. We liked the feel of universality, since describ-ing the past is something we all do, every day, on the scale of the trivial and the scale of the national. At the time, pre-2016 election, the topic seemed broadly accessible but not politically urgent in the way that it has since be-come; now, the question of truth-telling seems even more explosive. Fine with us, since we've always been convinced of its vital importance.

In keeping with the central approach, which takes its direction from a question, we organized our syllabi around questions. "Can we trust historical documents?"

"Is all writing about the past a form of fiction?" "How can one be truthful in telling another's story?" "What is the relationship between moral truth and fact?" These questions, along with others, provide signposts that guide us loosely through a series of discoveries, problems, and concluding questions. There's room for plenty of detours, but we do have a general route in mind.

The question "Is it possible to tell the truth about the past?" works so well partly because students already think they know the answer. Although they vary in their intellectual sophistication, just about every student we've seen comes to us from high school with neatly packaged assumptions about who tells the truth (teachers, textbooks) and how to acquire it (digest and memorize). A first part of the arc involves shaking these assumptions, and it is one of the most satisfying aspects of teaching this course. I have watched, with delight, how startled and even vexed students appear when they realize that they cannot trust a history book to tell the truth. Indeed, they are not sure they can trust me, either. Am I not also a historian, with my own axe to grind? It is powerful to undermine one's own authority in the classroom, and to pass on to students the burden of wondering and scrutinizing and disbelieving. It's a mode of thinking that will far outlast their memory of an individual text. In my course, shaking these assumptions begins with study of the so-called "conquest" of Mesoamerica, and we read Hernán Cortés and Bernal Díaz del Castillo, sixteenth-century Spaniards, along with historical renderings by William Prescott (a nineteenth-century Bostonian) and Inga Clendinnen (a twentieth-century Australian). Through these readings, the students see clearly how the skewed perceptions, cultural blindnesses, and self-aggrandizement of historical actors get sewn into the fabric of historical tellings. We read Prescott, who stuffed himself with these tales of grand men like so much cotton candy, and then we read Clendinnen, who eviscerates the myth of the cunning conquistador, presenting instead a complex lesson about the untranslatability of war and the insatiable human desire to make stories with meaning. By week three, the students are skeptics.

The question "Is it possible to tell the truth about the past?" also works well because it highlights both tensions and points of congruence between history and literature. Both history and literature, in the most basic sense, are in the business of telling the truth about the past. It's what they exist to do. But they do it in different ways. (Or do they?) We've resisted a facile debate on which does it better, since there would be little to gain from any conclusion, but the comparison yields other, more interesting problems. History often gets it wrong, or adopts so many conventions of literature that it becomes indistinguishable from its cousin. And literature may make claims to invention, but it also manifestly offers compelling truths. How are we to understand these seeming contradictions? In my course, we read some fiction (like W. G. Sebald's *Austerlitz* and Laura Esquivel's

Malinche), along with historical texts that push the boundaries, like Simon Schama's *Dead Certainties* and Howard Getz's *Abina and the Important Men*. For a large middle portion of the course, we spend time dissolving what had seemed like differences, only to find and clarify new differences. With the aid of books like Natalie Zemon Davis's *The Return of Martin Guerre*, we discover that the meaningful fissures are not between history and fiction, or between fact and invention, but rather appear in more unexpected (and subtle) places: between the careful use of context and its absence; between the conscious acknowledgment of the author's positionality and blithe unawareness; between the intent to satisfy readers and the willingness to leave them with doubts.

Lastly, the question "Is it possible to tell the truth about the past?" works because it makes an effortless connection between the personal and the scholarly, political, and abstract. The analogy is always there by implication. But in my course the students are invited explicitly to reflect on their own pasts in a final project (which they are also welcome to execute as a traditional paper). Applying some of the methods observed in the course, students must grapple with their own forms of truth-telling. I've seen some remarkable pieces in response to this invitation. And even the ones that aren't as remarkable in the rendering nonetheless contend with complicated issues: problems of memory, difficulties of portraying a loved one, and the persistent wish to depict oneself well.

At the end of the course, I don't expect students to be able to answer the question, "Is it possible to tell the truth about the past?" I do hope they have a renewed sense of how to engage claims to truth in a world that is unreliable and that deals in deliberate untruths. I also hope, especially in this day and age, that they have a clearer sense of what one colleague described as the difference between neutrality and objectivity. Surely we are none of us neutral, but we can agree on the parameters for the seeking of truth. We can agree on the nature of evidence, and on what makes a good claim or a bad claim. We can agree that in the absence of neutrality, something else must be established as common ground. I also hope that the students leave the course with more questions, with a sense of being somewhat comfortable with uncertainty, with a desire to push on things that seem too simple, and with a healthy suspicion of grand claims.

Pedagogical Strategies

Selecting and Organizing Texts

As Sylvia mentioned, we have been lucky in that our pedagogical impulses tend to overlap, even when it comes to selecting course texts: Our initial, independently drafted reading lists featured both Italo Calvino's *Invisible Cities* and the diaries of Christopher Columbus. Primo Levi's repatriation memoir *The Reawakening* (*La tregua*) is a cornerstone of the literature class, and the history section's discussion of Inga Clendinnen's *Reading the Holocaust* complements and complicates the literary analysis of Levi. In developing paired courses, we sought to prioritize considerations of genre theory and of disciplines as constructions, and to interrogate the supposed hard line between narrative truth and historical truth. To accomplish these goals, however, we passively allowed as well as actively engineered *proximate* rather than *parallel* relationships among course materials. In other words, it's important that our sections are cousins, not twins.

To throw into relief the history section's discussion of celebrated Guatemalan autobiography/manifesto *I, Rigoberta Menchú*, the literature section takes up James Frey's discredited addiction memoir *A Million Little Pieces*. Frey's book shares many of the structural experiments that energize Menchú's own genre-bending memoir; however, Frey's undisclosed fictionalizations led him not to Stockholm but to the blacklist. Students are usually unaware of controversy related to the book, and despite the syllabus questions framing this unit ("What makes a narrator/an account reliable or unreliable?," "How do we sort/rank inconsistent or unreliable accounts?," "Is there any value in deception?"), they tend to become consumed by Frey's narrative intensity and aggressive irreverence. Upon learning that parts of the book are fictionalized, students express a crisis of categorization, one that quickly translates to a crisis of confidence: How could Frey's book have been catalogued as memoir? Who decides how a text is classified, and what else have we consumed that has been so (gulp) egregiously misclassified? What is the line between fiction and non-fiction, anyhow, and (why) do we rank these two categories differently? Why is it that (after-the-fact and commercially motivated) classifications of the *same exact text* should provoke in us such radically distinct reading experiences, and such charged personal responses?

Initially, the conversation surrounds Frey's text, but it quickly transitions into a discussion about literary culture and about us as readers: how our premises and expectations (personal, collective, cultural) complete a text and determine its essential meaning, at least in part; and how basic enjoyment of a good story can impact the degree to which we find it "credible." When we move on to Tim O'Brien's beguiling fiction-masked-as-nonfiction/nonfiction-enabled-by-fiction in "On a Rainy River"—for, as O'Brien says, "[Fiction is] for getting at the truth when the truth isn't sufficient for the truth"—students must confront the discrepancies in their own responses to Menchú's vs. O'Brien's vs. Frey's so-called fictionalizations. At first, the line seems clear: Some changes are acceptable, some are not. But why? The students must account for shifting (read: nuanced) standards. Pushing this realization a step further, more explicitly into issues of identity and equity, readings from contemporary poet Eduardo C. Corral are always met with great enthusiasm, especially his poem "In Colorado, My Father Scoured and Stacked Dishes," from *Slow Lightning*. Even after the warning lights of Frey and O'Brien earlier in the unit, students assume autobiography in Corral's poetry—partly, they ultimately articulate, because it's poetry, and partly because the narrative "I" in Corral's poem suits a preformed vision of "the" Mexican American experience. Conversations about the line between fiction and nonfiction invariably circle back to unarticulated premises about what students find "believable" or "relatable." It's useful to deconstruct such terms. The suffix "-able" has rarely been examined at age eighteen, but it should be: Is it the text that is able to be believed, or the reader who is able to believe? Where does the ability (power) lie? These terms might obscure how much the processes of *believing* or *relating* are contingent on *the reader* rather than *the text*.

The readings detailed so far might seem theme-specific, but the transferrable goal comes in selecting texts that encourage metacognition and that catalyze earnest (and sometimes uncomfortable) debate: Why was Menchú met with a Nobel Prize for Peace, whereas Doubleday offered refunds to those who bought Frey's book? How can it be that O'Brien's imaginative and psychological experiences of being drafted should take precedence over his temporal one? What is at stake for each writer, as a person and as a protagonist? For which objective facts are alterations acceptable, even illuminating, and for which are changes unethical? What does it mean to "dramatize" or "fictionalize" a true event—and could a fictionalization ever get us closer to the essential truth of a situation? Does essential truth itself change, relative to the political expediencies of the moment? What is the difference between autobiography and memoir, nonfiction and literary nonfiction? Because these are earnest, ongoing questions—enduring questions—the text sequence in the literature section and the pairings relative to the history section reveal themselves to be less directive and dogmatic, and more provocative, more generative, more real.

Such pairings do not necessarily require the friction of different genres; at least, with some discussion, students come to see that, frequently, genre or classification becomes a code for perspectives that have been authenticated versus those that remain unauthenticated and are therefore at risk of being devalued or even erased. Toward the end of Amitav Ghosh's brilliant historiography/ethnography/travel memoir *In an Antique Land*, the narrator struggles to locate research related to Sidi Abu-Hasira, a religious figure who remains significant in rural Egypt—a local holy man who defied what Ghosh considers to be decidedly modern divisions between various spiritual traditions, a prophet of sorts whom villagers still celebrate with an annual festival. Ghosh combs through the history and religion sections of libraries on four continents, only to come up short. Finally, in a crushing realization, he finds a wealth of information about the holy man, filed away under "folklore." Active classification thus turns this real-life, documented paragon of religious pluralism into a unicorn, a myth, the imaginative coping mechanism of a taxed peasant psychology. Regardless of the discipline, students can and should be sensitized to the ways in which genre and other disciplinary classifications actively determine significance, assign value, and not always after the fact.

Often these revelations occur spontaneously and in a deeply personal way, as in a recent Truth-Telling in Literature session on reliable and unreliable narrators. We had finished reading Poe's short story "The Tell-Tale Heart," Robert Frost's "The Road Not Taken," and John Neihardt's heavily edited *Black Elk Speaks*, the last of which was paired with *Encyclopedia Britannica* entries related to the Battle at Wounded Knee. For each of these texts, there are easy/obvious ways to engage issues of reliability, and there are more complex/thorough ways. Professor Sellers-García and I operate on the premise that students should be invited to rise to the occasion of complexity.

In "The Tell-Tale Heart," for example, it's not wrong, but it's simplistic to come to rest on the notion that the speaker is an example of an "unreliable narrator"—the story's ironies are too multidimensional. More helpful, perhaps, is to analyze why we, as readers, tend to reject immediately as "crazy" certain aspects of the narrator's tale (e.g., his insistence that he is "not mad," the notion of the evil eye, the throbbing floorboards) but accept some details practically without question (the narrator's sense of time as he approaches the eye, the policemen's supposed ignorance as to the narrator's guilt, even the very idea that the speaker has, in fact, committed murder).

Students come to see that perhaps no story lacks an alternative perspective—instead, the reader steps in to offer that alternative perspective. In other words, in the absence of a reasonable character to serve as proxy, we ourselves enter the text to evaluate "evidence," but often in highly specific, narrow, even uninformed ways, based on something like instinct. During the discussion in question, a young woman offered her personal yardstick for assessing reliability, insisting that in order to be deemed credible, a narrator's (and by extension, any person's) behaviors and reactions would need to reflect "what [the student] would do, how [she] would react" in a similar situation. In other words, narrators are reliable if they are just like us. With the slightest bit of pushback, the student recognized with some horror how wildly that approach could backfire: Reactions predicated on difference of any sort risk being rendered "unreliable" or, as the student put it, "suspect." This young scholar reflected on her own identity as a woman and as a person of color, and noted how un- justly such subjective indices have been applied in her own life. (We ended class that day by viewing video clips from the George Zimmerman trial, spe- cifically testimony from Trayvon Martin's friend Rachel Jeantel, whose ver- nacular and whose experiential touchstones were seemingly incompatible with the very language of institutional justice.) Students' realizations about their— our—own roles in co-authoring narratives can introduce a note of despair; however, that despair can fairly easily be redirected toward empowerment. Awareness leads to clarity, and clarity brings us closer to truth.

In the spirit of "constructive uncertainty," the point here is to be careful not to replace rote classifications of a high school variety with rote classifica- tions of a college variety. If we want students to think about how truths are fairly and unfairly constructed, we need to encourage them, to model for them, and to interrogate for ourselves how we participate in that process, even as read- ers, students, instructors. Selecting texts that require some struggle, texts that offer earnest and enduring questions, is an important first step in the process of asking students to engage issues related to truth-telling. Some material might be new, but texts that are familiar should be actively defamiliarized, not only for the students, but also for us, the instructors. If we're asking students to re- think what they believe they know already, to reconsider ideas or methods that have become ossified by too much direction or by thoughtless practice, then we need to do the same, even—especially—with our clearest and dearest material.

Extracurricular Activities

A concept I find helpful in much of my teaching is the strange and powerful feeling of standing on a moving subway train, without holding on to anything— the absolute and cellular preparedness it requires: body strong, stable but re- sponsive, absorbing and counterbalancing the various forces at work, knees bent, a muscular centeredness that allows the core to remain anchored, even as the spine, the shoulders, the limbs ripple and swell like a great balance scale. This stance, in my view, is a great metaphor for a limber intellect, and most activities in Truth-Telling have been designed with a similar interplay of cer- tainty and uncertainty as the goal.

Getting out of the classroom is especially valuable in this sense, for a few reasons. Community events offer the possibility of a training ground for stu- dents' work as public intellectuals: Undergraduates can practice in real time their skills of digesting new material, synthesizing that material with or differ- entiating it from classroom content, and (often) engaging with that material through Q & A scenarios. Social cues allow students to sense immediately the precision and delicacy required to ask a productive question of good-faith presenters. And considering the speakers' ideas after having encountered them in the flesh offers an opportunity for students to practice empathy and connection even as they deconstruct a conceptual argument or premise—it reminds the students that concepts (like narrative accounts) are ultimately housed in human beings. In terms of truth-telling, so much is learned at public events, and—importantly—the process occurs with little to no direct instruction.

A few years ago, our group attended a campus talk on the politics of narrative itself. Panelists debated poetry's use of the first-person plural "we," mused about how to craft complete narratives without stunting ongoing conversations, and argued about literary research versus cultural appropriation. At the end, a few of the Truth-Telling students posed intelligent questions that they struggled to phrase precisely. When the cohort reconvened afterward to debrief in a separate seminar room, we discussed the panel itself, as well as what's hard about entering the conversation. We broke down the questions the students had posed and those they hadn't, their interest in challenging and simultaneous reluctance to challenge guests' perspectives, how they might have phrased points of inquiry that seemed risky, narrow, or otherwise inappropriate, and more. Students left with a blueprint for future engagement. Recently, the cohort attended a more controversial event, part of a transitional justice conference exploring institutional abuses in Ireland. Survivors of the notorious Magdalene laundries—mothers separated from their children and children forcibly adopted, sometimes out of the country—shared emotional testimony about highly personal *ongoing* injustices and discussed possible paths to action. The students were clearly moved, but perhaps dangerously so, moved to an overwhelming inaction: How, they wondered, could they advance beyond the role of mere spectators, toward a more active participation in the restorative justice process? Similar concerns arose at a poetry reading and panel discussion with war veterans. How to ensure that wide eyes don't obscure clear sight?

Such questions go beyond a single-semester course. After previous work considering the reader's implicit co-authorship of a narrative, however, students were prepared to reflect on their own roles as audience members. How should one behave in a situation of intimate public disclosure? What posture, what types of questions, what signifiers of attention might an audience member offer that say clearly, "We hear you" and "We believe you" and "This was wrong"—that, in effect, complete the bid made by the truth-teller? On the other hand, what responses hijack the truth-telling process? The unscripted nature of public events offers useful opportunity to consider reductive questions. After listening to a feminist legal scholar discuss options related to reparations for historical institutional violence, students expressed dismay when one audience member stood to ask the guest if "so many women become nurses because they're predisposed to caring for others." Weeks later, when reading Calvino's *Invisible Cities*, a student recalled this constellation of conversations after encountering the line "It is not the voice that commands the story: it is the ear." In other words, listening is a critical component of truth-telling. Students left the class with a more mature sense of their own power and accountability as active recipients of others' disclosures. It is instructive that many students over the years have cited these extracurricular experiences as a useful "boot camp" for future independent engagement with community speakers, training that seems essential in any democracy.

In-Class Exercises

The interplay of close textual analysis and open discussion—with a spirit of radical devil's-advocacy—is the cornerstone of the Truth-Telling in History/Truth-Telling in Literature course pair. Some guided in-class exercises have, however, proven especially helpful in advancing and anchoring those skills.

In the literature section, a fundamental shift in students' understanding of narrative theory occurs (with no need to photocopy Derrida!) through a simple *storyboarding exercise*. Print out 3–5 complete copies of the following sentences (or your own versions), with one complete set for each group.

Joe and Denise bump into each other at a street festival

Joe and Denise share a kiss.

Joe drives to a bridge, parks his car, and sits on one of the cables overlooking the canyon below.

Joe receives bad news from home.

Denise sees someone in a coffee shop and feels as if she's fallen in love at first sight.

Denise is fired from her job as an accountant.

Denise receives an important call, but she misses it—the call goes to voicemail.

A child runs into the street.

Someone is driving while trying to light a cigarette and send a text.

The rain turns to snow.

After printing, cut each set into strips, so that one sentence appears per strip, then shuffle each set, making sure that a different "main character" frames each pile (e.g., Set 1, a sentence about Denise; Set 2, one about Joe; Set 3, the child; Set 4, the driver; Set 5, Joe and Denise as a couple). Give a shuffled set of sentences to each group with the simple instruction to "put these in order." They will quickly build a narrative, almost always using the sentence that appears on top as the one that dominates (e.g., if "Joe receives bad news" comes first, the rest of the story tends to be oriented around Joe). Either tell the students that they need to use all of the sentences, or allow only those groups that ask if they can eliminate a few to do so. (They tend to want to eliminate any narrative inconveniences, a tendency which you can ask them to reflect upon in the exercise postmortem; this is also a good time to introduce the idea of teleology.) When students see how the exact same sentences can tell various, unrelated, even contradictory stories—and how their own work to "put the sentences in order" is contingent on their learned or inherited set of pre-existing narrative options—they begin to reflect more deeply on many fields: not just literature and history, but journalism, diagnostic medicine, criminal justice, and more.

A logistically more complex—but equally revealing exercise—involves playing with students' disciplinary associations. In short, *swapping lectures* reveals the biases readers bring to a text and its related discipline. After teaching the Truth-Telling course a few times, Sylvia and I noticed students' tendency—despite our best efforts—to persist in receiving historical narratives as "real stuff" and literature as "made-up stuff." So we decided to shake things up a bit. We have run this exercise several times now, often toward the end of the term, and are always surprised (and somewhat disconcerted) by students' quick descent into our trap. The exercise works as follows: We tell the students that we want them to work on perceiving explicit signifiers of historical versus literary narrative—in other words, how can we distinguish "real stuff" from "made-up stuff"? We provide excerpts of two first-person narratives: the contemporary novel *Dreaming in Cuban* (Cristina García, Ballantine) and the diary of Carrie Berry, a ten-year-old living in 1864 Atlanta. Critically, Professor Sellers-García hands out the (fictional) passage from *Dreaming in Cuban*, while I offer the (non-fiction) passage from Carrie Berry's diary, both of us insisting vaguely but passionately on the texts' "historical significance." Make a list, we suggest, of the ways these texts reveal themselves as fact versus fiction, as reality versus artifice. Within minutes, students are dutifully dismissing young Carrie Berry's misspellings as literary affectation, her fear over Sherman's approach into Atlanta as hyperbole, even stereotype, and the heightened drama as obvious writerly manipulation. "People don't talk like that, even kids," one student noted during last year's exercise. *Dreaming in Cuban*, however, is clearly authentic, with its use of direct quotation, its tonal restraint, its unmediated stream of consciousness. This passage "sounds more realistic," the students say, loose code for "this experience is more in line with my own"—or, better yet, with what most students *imagine* their experiences *might be* during, say, the U.S. Civil War or the Cuban Revolution. "Constructive uncertainty" is a great way to describe the sheepishness students exhibit once we reveal our ruse and reflect, again, on how such framing is at work all around us.

Sylvia mentioned earlier that, under so much pressure to consider and to reconsider positions and positionality, students quickly become skeptics. It is important to us, however, to toe the line between a healthy skepticism and the dead end of cynicism. College students are astute, and they quickly catch on to our slippery games. The risk becomes one of retreat into what might be called "it-depends syndrome"—a diplomatic but ultimately fruitless end point. Class exercises should be designed to resist any carefully disguised version of opting-out. One that works well is the *elementary school lesson plan*. At the end of a unit that involves a sensitive topic (such as Columbus's "New World" conquest, encounters between colonists and Native Americans, gender inequality, or Jim Crow laws), task students to prepare a related lesson plan for an elementary school classroom. One semester, I brought in my own six-year-old and asked students to teach her about Thanksgiving. Students struggled mightily, but in instructive ways: How could they tell the truth about Thanksgiving, its history and its enduring mythology, while simultaneously negotiating civic, cultural, and intellectual objectives? What documents and images would they use, and how would they frame those sources' reliability and completeness? How might students revise their lesson plans for ten-year-olds, fifteen-year-olds, their peers? It's certainly necessary to engage in critique in a Truth-Telling or similar course, but it's equally important to struggle with correcting, restoring, rewriting, and generating.

Monument design similarly requires students to navigate and to overcome intellectual and ethical obstacles. This exercise can be done quickly in class, or it can be assigned as an extended individual or group project. Students select or are assigned a text; they then design a monument inspired by one or more of the text's central complexities. Our class engaged poems from Vietnam veteran Bruce Weigl, but anything that resists easy binaries would work. What should the monument memorialize or honor? What materials might be appropriate, and why? How should the monument be integrated into the natural landscape? (How) will the monument guide a visitor's experience? Will the monument be interactive, and if so, how can the design reduce risk of misinterpretation or desecration? Students might opt to create a visual mock-up of some sort, but all should offer verbally or in writing a detailed analysis of process. (Critical texts that supplement this exercise well are Cathy Park Hong's essay "Against Witness" and the introduction from *The Art of Truth-Telling about Authoritarian Rule* by Ksenija Bilbija et al.) Inspired by Bruce Weigl's poem "Surrounding Blues on the Way Down" from *Song of Napalm*, in which a young draftee despairs to witness military abuse of a Vietnamese civilian, one recent group designed a monument to honor civilian women who suffered during the war. The monument's final stage involved distributing a fresh-cut flower to each visitor. What the visitor decided to do with that flower upon exiting the monument was intended to prompt contemplation. Would it be cared for, grafted, cultivated; or thrown away, tossed aside, forgotten? For this exercise, if a text has sufficient complexity, capturing its essence should offer a useful challenge. Monuments are so often predicated on straightforward notions of victors, victims, and martyrs, but good literature resists such categories. Struggling to reconcile these two approaches can generate new ways of thinking about the past, and about truth, myth, and memory as active constructions.

Offering opportunities for students to make decisions or to determine a best course of action helps them transcend the seductive ease of cynicism, whether personal, intellectual, or political. Paired with final readings that rebuild and redefine their sense of purpose and possibility, such as Plato's Allegory of the Cave and Colum McCann's excellent speech "In Defense of Optimism," such provocative in-class and extracurricular experiences model for students true and rigorous intellectual inquiry, and grant them the permission to relish the ongoing work of constructive uncertainty.

Covid Core Lessons

Elizabeth H. Shlala

As the Covid-19 pandemic made an impact on teaching on campus in the spring, summer, and fall of 2020, we faced a historically unprecedented need to de-densify Boston College's campus while still maintaining high standards of learning and teaching in the University Core Curriculum. We sought to engage and reinforce the two distinctive goals of: (1) *intellectual rigor in pursuit of truth and growth in knowledge of the whole reality* and (2) *the humanist formative ideal of developing the habits of mind, heart, and imagination that will equip students to contribute to the common good and live meaningful lives in service to others.* The university's united efforts in the face of pandemic challenges drew the community closer together, and heightened the important and unique role of the University Core Curriculum.

This chapter addresses how the Complex Problem (CP) and Enduring Question (EQ) courses responded to the Covid-19 pandemic as faculty faced the challenges of academic teaching whether teaching in person, online, or in a hybrid form. The chapter is divided into three sections: the Covid-pivot in spring 2020; preparing the faculty in summer 2020; and creative engagement with in-person, hybrid, and online teaching in fall 2020 with pertinent examples from Complex Problem and Enduring Question courses.

Supporting Pedagogy during the Covid-19 Pivot

Lifelong learning is a hallmark of a Catholic, Jesuit education, and the Course Design Workshops for new CP and EQ faculty fit into this paradigm. Each year new Enduring Question and Complex Problem faculty attend Course Design Workshops the spring before the academic year in which they will offer a course. The goals of the workshops include introducing Ignatian pedagogy, creating syllabi, building faculty relationships across disciplines, and sharing best practices. In response to the Covid-19 pivot, the Course Design Workshops in spring 2020 were quickly shifted almost entirely online. As the assistant dean and associate professor of the practice in the University Core Curriculum, I created, and curated, an online Canvas site for the workshops. The Canvas site enhanced not only accessibility and ongoing faculty support but also created a permanent archive for the Core with modules including sample syllabi and information about budgets and logistics that faculty could go back and refer to over time.

The Canvas Course Design Workshops offered four main modules: Catholic, Jesuit pedagogy in the Core Curriculum; Core Learning Goals; Reflection and Formation; and Joint Assessment. There is also a module specifically for Core Fellows, which includes resources related to pandemic teaching, diversity and social justice, and orientation materials. As one returning Enduring Question faculty member stated about the Canvas site, "It's a terrific resource—nice to have things all in one place and looks like there are pieces that will be 'in progress' permanently with adding resources." Faculty feedback for the Course Design Workshops was positive despite the disruption and the move online; it reflected what was happening in classes across campus. One faculty member, Joe Nugent in English, who taught an EQ for the first time that semester, said that it was the most rewarding teaching that he had ever done and that the Course Design Workshops had changed all of his teaching for the better. Although a seasoned and successful teacher, he learned many useful things that he applied to all of his classes even beyond the Core. Course Design Workshops allow faculty to take innovative pedagogical training in a warm and collegial environment even years into their teaching that they find beneficial.

The provost's office reached out to the Core in spring 2020 to inquire about changes or adaptations made in the delivery of formative education during the Covid-19 pivot. Formative education is often associated with physical and spiritual proximity. I wondered what was happening as our community of learners dispersed from campus. How had the faculty reenvisioned the reflection sessions that are a core design element of the CP and EQ courses?

In reflection sessions, students connect the content of the course materials with their lives beyond the classroom and to the larger world. Reflection is intimately tied to the Core learning goal designed to teach students how to "examine their values and experiences and integrate what they learn with the principles that guide their lives." Reflection sessions can provide a space for discussion for the ethical implications of material covered in the course and help students process their reactions to challenging course materials. I questioned whether that could happen in a meaningful way in a virtual space and if faculty had the time to reimagine their previously planned reflection sessions that often included museum trips, film viewings, guest speakers, class dinners, meditative walks, yoga sessions, and library visits.

With those questions in mind, I conducted a survey of all CP and EQ faculty teaching in the spring 2020 and received useful feedback. I was primarily interested in how reflection sessions were translated from in-person to online activities, especially by faculty who were responding to a once-in-a-lifetime, global pandemic without much prior experience in online course design. Here are some specific examples from the survey:

1. Enduring Question courses "The American Divide: The Economics of Inequality and The American Divide: Philosophy of Inequality" (Geoffrey Sanzenbacher, Social Science core credit, and Cherie McGill, Philosophy core credit). "We did an online trip to the Isabella Gardner Museum. We toured various rooms through their online virtual tour on Zoom, and then looked at eight paintings in detail. We discussed each painting during the Zoom meeting, and then students filled out Canvas discussion board questions to further discuss the experience. I think that the event was solid overall, and the discussion results suggest they saw many of the things we hoped they would see in person. They picked up on issues related to the accumulation of wealth, to privilege and inequality of opportunity, and to how wealth is depicted."

2. Enduring Question courses "Being Human: Secularist-Humanist Perspective" and "Being Human: Theological Perspective" (Marcus Breen, Social Science core credit and Matt Petillo, Theology). Students were asked to engage with other students on Zoom about the way Artificial Intelligence innovations may be regulated. This seemed to be an effective way to encourage the investigation of new approaches to reflection. Much more time is needed to engage students in reflection about Jesuit principles and BC Mission, such as peace and the common good.

3. Complex Problem course "#Shop-Apocalypse: Consumer Culture and the Fate of the Planet" (Julie Schor, Social Science, and Robin Fleming, History II). Film showing including with filmmaker via Zoom leading to discussions of how Covid-19 is affecting students and consumption patterns.

4. Enduring Question courses "Law and Adolescence: Children of Immigrants" and "Law and Adolescence: History of Childhood"

(Daniel Ovado-Milan, Social Science, and Carlos Zúñiga-Nieto, History II, Core Fellows). "First-year students submitted reflective journals where they narrated their reactions to readings in class. The journals allowed them to connect the readings in course but also to make intellectual connections across the social sciences. Before the pandemic, these were physical journals, but after the pandemic, these journals were digital. After the pandemic, students shared their reflections in class during discussions and received feedback from their colleagues. Reflective journaling also allowed students to record their own anxieties and worries during such difficult times. Reflection in digital journals during remote learning enabled students to reflect on the readings but also to integrate contemporary news related to the crisis at the local level. In their hand-written journals, students highlighted noteworthy articles while relating the course material to historical examples from class. The students also shared these journals with colleagues during Zoom meetings and received feedback from each other. The reflective journaling was a central component in the intellectual development during the course as students had the opportunity to further explain how their notions of childhood and youth had changed during the ongoing crisis."

To further gauge how successful faculty were in transitioning from in-person to online learning, we added specific questions with a Likert response scale about the Covid-19 pivot in CP and EQ student course evaluations. Of the more than 500 student respondents, 46.37 percent agreed strongly and 33.99 percent agreed that compared to their other courses that semester, his or her Complex Problem or Enduring Question course made an exemplary transition from on-campus to online learning; a mere 1.77 percent disagreed strongly. In the same format, 48.54 percent of respondents strongly agreed and 32.62 percent of respondents agreed with the statement that "The reflection sessions gave me the opportunity to evaluate and connect course material to my entire life and broader community." The results demonstrate the broadly successful efforts of the faculty to translate in-person reflection practices into an online format.

Reimagining Course Preparations in Summer 2020

In order to prepare faculty to teach in fall 2020, the summer of 2020 was like no other. The traditional faculty summer of research and writing during the lull of teaching undergraduates simply disappeared. In the Core, we spent the summer of 2020 holding Core conversations online to generate ideas with faculty for teaching adaptations, technological innovations, and accessing university resources to deliver excellent teaching to all students wherever they would be in the fall. We listened to spring 2020 Complex Problem and Enduring Question faculty who had experienced the pivot to share best practices about lessons learned for teaching lectures, labs, and reflection sessions during the transition to online education.

There were a number of recommendations that came out of our listening and preparatory sessions held in June 2020, and we shared them widely with faculty. Whether teaching in person, online, or in a hybrid form, faculty were advised to create a comprehensive and inclusive Canvas site. Faculty had to use Canvas and other online tools like Perusall for assignments and Proctorio for exams and quizzes, and course readings on liquid syllabi. They used Panopto to record lectures and have them accessible to students who might be unable to attend class synchronously due to Covid-19 quarantine, illness, or inadequate Wi-Fi. They had to plan reflection sessions and create labs for CP courses accessible to all students wherever they were. I encouraged faculty to access university resources on behalf of students as they worked on their Canvas sites and syllabi including: the Center for Teaching Excellence, the Center for Digital Innovation in Learning, the libraries, the Office of Health Promotion, University Counseling Services, and the Connors Family Learning Center. All of these campus partners provided useful resources for Core faculty.

In fall 2020, we offered thirteen Enduring Question and Complex Problem courses with thirty faculty members for 475 first-year students. Each of the four Complex Problem courses employed a different modality: one Complex Problem course ran fully online; one Complex Problem course gave lectures in person and held their labs online; one Complex Problem course delivered lectures online and held their labs in person; and one Complex Problem course taught all components in person. The Core had three EQ pairs fully online. Three EQ pairs were hybrid with one course taught in person and the other paired course taught online. Three EQ courses were taught fully in person. CP and EQ faculty had to be innovative and collaborative; it is likely that more was asked of these faculty perhaps than any other teaching group at Boston College given the complexity of these courses and the need to make them accessible in multiple modalities.

In order to teach with excellence in my own online courses in fall 2020, and to share my knowledge with interested Core Fellows and faculty, I attended a six-week summer course training in online course design and pedagogy with the Online Learning Toolkit group. Camp Operation Online Learning (COOL) was a course design program that guided educators through the process of developing online courses. Led by dynamic facilitators such as Karen Costa and Judith Dutill, COOL was dedicated to making the course design process accessible and enjoyable for higher educators at every level of experience and technology fluency. My Core colleagues and I worked all summer to make sure that faculty felt comfortable and supported in their fall 2020 teaching arrangements.

In fall 2019 and fall 2020, Natana Delong-Bas, associate professor of the practice in Theology, and I taught our Enduring Question pair "Geographies of Imperialism: Theology of Colonization" and "Geographies of Imperialism: History of Colonization," respectively. Our enduring question linking the pair is: *The age of empires is past—or is it?* To showcase our EQ courses to incoming and prospective students, we presented with three of our past students in the Liberal Arts Advantage series moderated by the vice provost of Enrollment Management, John Mahoney and associate dean of the Core, Brian Gareau in summer 2020. Three EQ and CP courses were featured in each of the one-hour webinars: the EQ course "Life, Liberty and Health" taught by Tracy Regan, associate professor of the practice in Economics and Mary Ann Chirba, Boston College Law School; the CP course "Citizenship, Immigration, and Belonging in the U.S." taught by Gabrielle Oliveira, assistant professor of Teaching, Curriculum, and Society and Andrés Castro Samayoa, assistant professor of Educational Leadership and Higher Education, Lynch School of Education and Human Development; and our course mentioned above. The Liberal Arts Advantage webinars reached more than 1,000 prospective students in summer 2020. Our webinar took place on August 12, 2020, with 676 registered and 362 in attendance. All of the webinars remain on YouTube for additional views.

Engaging with New Core Course Formats in Fall 2020

In response to a concern that there might not be enough seats for international freshmen unable to attend in person, Natana Delong-Bas and I volunteered to teach our EQ pair online in the early morning to be accessible to students abroad in Europe and Asia as well as on campus. Other faculty teaching CP and EQ courses also made accommodations for international students given the global travel bans in place. Core courses had to be accessible to BC students who were unable to return to campus. We spent many hours revising our courses making sure that all of the course material would be accessible online, uploading video content, and creating new assignments for assessment. We had all five of our guest speakers attend via Zoom link over the course of the semester. For one reflection session, instead of a trip to the Museum of Fine Arts in Boston, which we had taken the year before, our students took a virtual trip to the British Museum to consider the collections there related to the British and Ottoman Empires. I invited filmmakers Awa Farah and Alice Aedy, physically located in the UK, to talk to our students about their groundbreaking documentary *Somalinimo*, about attending Cambridge as Black, Muslim, Somali women. To create a purposeful, formative educational experience on the theology side of the course pairing, Natana Delong-Bas incorporated a new series of examen for students to engage. Some of her students described them as "the most important" part of the class because the process included life skills they needed for mental health and personal reflection in the midst of the pandemic; they figured out that they could use them broadly, not just for her classes.

The director of Initiatives for Formative Education, Margaret Laurence, produced formative education panels in summer and fall 2020. In the second webinar, faculty shared their experiences and thoughts on what worked and what did not work during the Covid-19 pivot. I moderated a session with Rafael Luna, associate dean, Morrissey College of Arts and Sciences, director, Pre-Health Program, director, Gateways Scholars Program in STEM on Core and formative education within the sciences on Thursday, September 17, 2020. The panelists were Michael Naughton, Evelyn J. and Robert A. Ferris Professor and Chair, Physics Department; Heather Olins, assistant professor of the practice, Biology Department; and Holly VandeWall, associate professor of the practice, Philosophy Department. Heather Olins, who would teach a Complex Problem course in spring 2021, noted that "deformative" educational practices include putting up walls that exclude certain identities and shut down the natural curiosity of learners. Mike Naughton shared that he encouraged his freshmen classes to open up their minds to think for themselves, to challenge their assumptions, and to take responsibility for their own education. Rafael Luna concluded that all the colors of nature and its diversity open the door for students to be inspired to study science and to learn more about our world and their place in it.

There was creative engagement with in-person, hybrid, and online teaching in fall 2020. One excellent example was the new Complex Problem course "Making the Modern World: Design, Ethics, and Engineering" taught by Core Fellows/ Visiting Assistant Professors Jenna Tonn, Jonathan Krones, and Russell Powell. The freshman-only course fulfilled Core requirements in Natural Science and History II; it also served as a pilot course for BC's new Department of Human-Centered Engineering. The faculty held an online Design Conference on December 6, 2020. Over the fall 2020 semester, nineteen student teams worked creatively and intensively, both in person and remotely, to identify a design problem on campus, to conduct user research, and to prototype a design solution. The conference offered the students the opportunity to present their solutions in five-minute pitches to the BC community and to a panel of guest judges. The competition had two sessions. Over 150 students, faculty, parents, and community members attended the conference. The judges for the first round were Elizabeth Shlala, assistant dean of the Core; Yasmin Zaepoor, visiting assistant professor of Environmental Studies and Core Fellow; and Lyel Resner, social entrepreneur and ethical technology advocate. The winners were "Locked and LOADed," *Remedy Ramps*, with Ben Wakim, Charlotte Rauscher, Corinne Heidloff, and Morgan Brooke. The judges for the second session were Nora Gross, visiting assistant professor of sociology and Core Fellow, Boston College; Pheobe Kuo, artist, woodworker, and design ethnographer; and Brian Rodriguez, director of People & Culture, Hopelab. The winners were "Call Me a Woman in STEM," *EagleLift*, with Veronica Garza, Ellie Sullivan, Aly Steichen, and Helga Tsymbal. The feedback was overwhelmingly positive. Mark Francesconi, a parent of a current student wrote, "As a parent I was extremely impressed—the thought, diligence and professionalism was outstanding. Thank you for inviting us!"

Sunand Battacharya, Boston College, associate vice provost of Design and Innovation Strategies, exclaimed, "Congrats on a very impressive high quality session. Great job by students and faculty. The three of you, as faculty and facilitators, should be very proud. The pilot seems to have yielded great results. Congrats!"

Glenn Gaudette, chair of the Engineering Department, was equally enthusiastic, "Great work by all teams. Congratulations."

Upon reflection on the vast effort the Core launched to support faculty during the Covid-19 pivot and to continue to adapt to changing conditions in the university, three things come to mind. First, the central place of the University Core Curriculum as a site of historical continuity and excellence made the Core the ideal headquarters for reimagining what instruction would look like in a Covid-19 era. Core courses connect to all disciplines and departments, bring in new and established faculty, and offer a remarkable institutional place for sharing best practices; we simply drew upon the heart of the university in 2020. Second, the Core was able to see how the multiple modalities of learning shaped student experiences while supporting faculty experiences in challenging, yes, but unexpectedly fruitful, ways. The online Course Design Workshops and Canvas site, virtual journaling, remote opportunities for examen and retreats, and virtual guest speakers are just a few examples. Finally, the Core's documentation of creative course formats, assessment, and adept adaptations serves not only as a record of teaching during the Covid-19 pandemic but also as some lessons learned for programming future in-person courses for faculty and students in creative and inclusive ways.

Acknowledgments

It isn't possible to mention every person who has contributed to the renewal of the Core curriculum at Boston College over the past ten years. The success of our Enduring Question and Complex Problem courses has come through the hard work of thousands of people: faculty, staff, administrators, and students. We would like to thank some of the people who made key contributions to the effort.

Former Provost Cutberto Garza set the process in motion in 2011 when he asked Mary Crane to begin a conversation about renewing the Core at Boston College. Andy Boynton interrupted that conversation with the crazy idea that a design consulting firm could help, and he, David Quigley, and Mary Crane were soon joined by faculty members Thomas Chiles (biology) and Juliet Schor (sociology), who saw the possibilities that human-centered design could offer to our renewal process.

The work of Core renewal in the 2012–2013 academic year was led by a team composed of people from Boston College and Continuum. The Continuum team was remarkably creative and flexible, inventing a process as we proceeded. Harry West and Gianfranco Zaccai helped set up the team, which was led by Anthony Pannozzo, and included Naomi Korn Gold, Chad Callaghan, Kristin Sjo-Gaber, and Daniel Sobol. Andy, David, Mary, Tom, and Julie were joined on the team by BC faculty members Gail Kineke (earth and environmental sciences), the late Richard Cobb-Stevens (philosophy), and by then Associate Dean Akua Sarr. Journalist Bill Bole was embedded with the team, took copious notes, and helped with communications, as did Sarah Shaughnessy of the Carroll School of Management dean's office.

Whenever the leadership team came up with a plan or proposal, it was first vetted by an advisory committee made up of BC faculty, administrators, and students. These proposals were greatly improved by the critical eyes of this committee, which included Treseanne Ainsworth (English), George Arey (then director of Residential Life), Jeffrey Bloechl (philosophy), Julian Bourg (history), M. Shawn Copeland (theology), Donald Hafner (political science, then associate vice provost for Undergraduate Education), Judith Gordon (management and organization), Burt Howell (mission and ministry), Gregory Kalscheur, S.J. (then associate dean of arts and sciences), Richard Keeley (Carroll School of Management), Siobhan Kelly (student, '15), Jeremiah McGrann (music), Patrick McQuillan (teacher education, special education, curriculum and instruction), Arthur Madigan, S.J. (philosophy), Michael J Naughton (physics), Robert Newton (special assistant to the president), Joseph Quinn (economics), Catherine Read (Connell School of Nursing), Nicholas Reposa (student, '14), and Thomas Wall (university librarian).

Boston College President William P. Leahy, S.J., had the vision to approve our proposal to bring Continuum to campus when it must have seemed to come out of left field. He then had the wisdom to scale down our initial proposal. Jack Butler, S.J., vice president for mission and ministry, supported our efforts all along the way. He believed in the project from the beginning and provided crucial encouragement at moments when our confidence in the possibility of success was flagging. Jack Dunn, associate vice president for university communications, helped us get the word out about the new courses. Gregory Kalscheur, S.J., dean of the Morrissey College of Arts and Sciences, has provided crucial leadership and support.

The work of implementing the Enduring Question and Complex Problem courses and continuing the renewal of the rest of the Core has been ably taken on by a new Core office and new Core Renewal Committee. The first associate dean for the Core, Julian Bourg, made something from nothing and began implementing the new courses from scratch with little help. He was later joined by an assistant director, Charles Keenan. Brian Gareau took over as associate dean and has continued to renew the Core with the help of assistant dean Elizabeth Shlala and administrative assistants Samantha Beard and Fotini Karabinas. A number of faculty have served on the Core Renewal Committee and carried on the work of approving and assessing courses and the program as a whole. As a member of that committee, Celeste Wells has led a very successful assessment initiative.

The success of these courses has also been facilitated by administrators from all over the university. Former Director of Institutional Research, Planning, and Assessment Kelli Armstrong provided crucial encouragement and support, aided by IRPA staff including Jessica Greene, Kathryn Mackintosh, Margaret Ryan, and Emily Carey. Katherine O'Dair, then associate vice president for student affairs, and Michael Sacco of mission and ministry helped us figure out what the reflection portion of the courses might be. Joy Moore, former vice president for student affairs, helped along the way. Staff in Student Services, including former Executive Director Louise Lonabacker, University Registrar Kathy McGuinness, Ursula DellaPorta, and Terry Riordan, crucially helped us find the rooms to teach the new courses in and get them on the schedule. Other Boston College staff, including Julie Devi, Helen Ha, Joe Cella, Tim Mulvey, Alison Bane, and Susan Migliorisi, have provided crucial support. Dean of Undergraduate Admission John Mahoney and Director of Undergraduate Admission Grant Gosselin have made sure that families who apply to Boston College know about our Renewed Core.

We also thank the faculty and administrators who agreed to contribute to this book and have borne with a lengthy process of bringing it to print. Nita Sembrowich copyedited the very rough first draft, and Fredric Nachbaur at Fordham University Press was a patient and encouraging editor. Two anonymous readers provided feedback that greatly improved the book.

The editors also thank each other for sticking together through thick and thin and for embracing our motto "irrational persistence." Core renewal at Boston College has succeeded because of people working together across disciplinary and status divisions. A business school dean, dean of arts and sciences, and an English professor are probably not natural partners for leading a project of this kind. We have been a team in every sense of the word, and we have persevered.

Finally, though, the success of Core renewal at Boston College has come about through the creativity and dedication of faculty across all schools and ranks and the students who bring curiosity and commitment into the Core classroom every day. This book is dedicated to them.

Appendix A

The Vision Animating the Boston College Core Curriculum

2014

I. The Core Curriculum and the Mission of Boston College

Boston College seeks to foster the rigorous intellectual development and the religious, ethical, and personal formation of its students. The Core Curriculum broadens the intellectual horizons of students, introduces them to the best of contemporary pedagogy, research, and teaching, promotes their integration of knowledge, beliefs, and actions, and prepares them for lives of freedom, integrity, leadership, and service.

II. The Core's Foundation in the Jesuit Educational Tradition

The Jesuit, Catholic character of Boston College gives direction to the Core Curriculum by shaping both what is taught and how it is taught. The world in which Jesuits first founded schools was marked by two competing educational ideals: the intellectual rigor and disciplinary professionalism of the university and the humanistic schools' desire to form students' characters for meaningful lives oriented toward the common good. The *Spiritual Exercises* of St. Ignatius also had a profound influence on Jesuit education. The *Exercises* aim to help people, under the direction of an experienced guide, to attain the inner freedom that will allow them to live their lives in ways that satisfy the deepest yearnings of their hearts.[1]

The Jesuit method of education that provides direction to the Core integrates those two educational ideals: (1) the university ideal of intellectual rigor in pursuit of truth and growth in knowledge of the whole of reality, and (2) the humanistic ideal of developing the habits of mind, heart, and imagination that will equip students to contribute to the common good and live meaningful lives. The *Spiritual Exercises* provide a model of how teachers and students interact in Core courses. "[T]he *quality* of the relationship between the guide of the *Spiritual Exercises* and the person making them is the model for the relationship between teacher and student. Like the guide of the *Exercises*, the teacher is at the service of the student, alert to detect special gifts or special difficulties, personally concerned, and assisting in the development of the inner potential of each student."[2]

The *Exercises* also present a spirituality that seeks to find God in all things. For those who see the world in this way, it is possible to encounter God at work in creation and human activity, and especially in the search for truth, the desire to learn, and the call to live justly together. A university inspired by this worldview is necessarily diverse, pluralistic, and inclusive. In the Catholic understanding, God's Word has taken on our humanity, and thus whatever makes us more authentically human brings us closer to God: "Whatever humanizes, divinizes."[3] Accordingly, all who are committed to the pursuit of the truth, whatever their beliefs, are invited to share their expertise, intelligence, and imagination as full participants in introducing students to the search for truth and meaning that animates the Core Curriculum.

III. The Core Curriculum as a Distinctive Component of the Boston College Undergraduate Experience

Boston College's commitment to liberal education demands the highest quality scholarship that integrates the development of new knowledge, reflection on enduring questions, and creativity in responding to contemporary problems. At Boston College, this commitment has four primary components: (1) a Core Curriculum that establishes a common intellectual foundation for all undergraduates, (2) a major that provides a curricular sequence for intense exploration of a particular discipline, (3) electives that allow the pursuit of particular interests outside of the Core and the major, and (4) campus community life that offers opportunities for personal, religious, and social growth outside the classroom setting.

In providing a common intellectual foundation for all undergraduates, the Core introduces students to serious academic and personal exploration. It invites them into a conversation about questions that have long concerned reflective people and to enter into a dialogue of faith and reason in pursuit of truth. The

Core provides information and perspective and encourages sound judgment and the beginning of wisdom. It counteracts the contemporary danger of superficiality stemming from quick access to vast amounts of information and the expression of opinions without the "laborious, painstaking work" of serious inquiry and reflection.[4] Faculty teaching in the Core, in partnership with colleagues from the offices of Mission and Ministry and Student Affairs, are encouraged to enable students to explore beyond the classroom, engaging them in experiences and service opportunities on and off campus, connecting what is learned with the world around the university. The Core Curriculum thus furthers the development of the intellectual, reflective, ethical, and creative habits of mind that will enable students to become lifelong learners, to seek meaning in their lives, and to work toward constructing a more just and human world.

Individual Core courses work together to contribute to the Core's shared goals of opening the mind and heart, encouraging character formation, deepening human sympathy, inspiring creativity, enriching understanding of human diversity, and stimulating clear thought and persuasive expression. Students are expected to develop an adroitness of mind in meeting new questions and to lay a foundation for exploring questions they will encounter not only in their more specialized studies but also throughout their lives.[5]

IV. The Substance of the Boston College Core

The first Jesuit colleges sought to introduce students to the best of what was known at the time. Today, the disciplinary breadth of the Core reflects the same conviction: faculty experts introduce students to the foundational ideas and methods of inquiry in the major disciplines in the university. Becoming educated requires careful and conscientious study in fields from theology and history to philosophy and literature, from mathematics and physics to the arts to political science and beyond. The humanities and natural and social sciences help ground our understanding of who we are, what it means to be human, how the world works, where we come from, and where we are going.

Disciplinary specificity provides a necessary, but not sufficient, depth of inquiry: The desire to know aspires to understand how things might be connected into a more meaningful whole. Through engagement with the distinctive ways of searching for truth in the disciplines, the Core Curriculum invites students and faculty to see how the various disciplines, with all their specificity, differentiation, and limitations, might work together to construct an integrated understanding of reality. Just as true knowledge is not mere information, genuine wisdom requires attention to the wholeness we desire and to the development of a moral compass that unites the mind, heart, and imagination in reflective action.

The solutions to twenty-first-century problems require both disciplinary specificity and depth and a broader perspective. Intellectually satisfactory efforts to explore enduring questions and complex problems today benefit from a range of disciplinary perspectives. The Core Curriculum, therefore, works to promote interdisciplinary inquiry and expression.

As a Jesuit, Catholic university, Boston College is grounded in a "faith that seeks understanding" and in the proposition that thinking is an essential part of believing. The Core embodies that principle, not only in theology's scholarly exploration of faith, but in the conviction that the search for truth in any discipline is part of the search for God.

V. The Distinctive Role of Faculty Who Teach in the Core

The Jesuit educational tradition was founded on the premise that teaching the best of what was known should be combined with character formation in service of the common good. While many modern universities have de-emphasized the latter, Jesuit colleges and universities today have refused to abandon this commitment and envision a special role for the teacher: caring for students as whole persons and helping them to integrate what they learn with how they live.

Faculty teaching in the Core should be attentive to the context of their students' lives, striving *to teach these students*, rather than simply a body of material, helping students to see why their Core courses matter in their lives. To care *about*—to become reflectively engaged—is to care *for*. A meaningful life is found neither solely in knowledge nor in action, but in the reflective interplay of what one understands and believes and how one acts, especially in the service of others: *Why* does studying this material contribute to better understanding what it is to be a person? *Who am I becoming* as I engage this material? *How* does my study of this material contribute to my better understanding of the world in its wholeness?

Finally, faculty who teach in the Core share with their students the passions that have guided them in their own vocations, helping students to care about learning as a fundamental starting point for becoming citizens, leaders, and human beings of depth of thought, creative imagination, and compassion. To care about learning, therefore, is to care for one another and for our world. Faculty who share their love of learning with their students can change students' interests and lives and open up possibilities for the mutually enriching encounters, conversations, reflection, and discernment that lead to wisdom.

VI. Core Curriculum Learning Outcomes

Guided by this vision, students completing the Boston College Core Curriculum will:

1. Demonstrate the critical, mathematical, informational, analytic, expressive, and creative skills that are essential tools of the educated person well prepared for a meaningful life and vocation.
2. Understand the major ideas and methods of inquiry of the scholarly disciplines found in the university and be able to use those methods of inquiry as beginning practitioners to address complex contemporary problems.
3. Be able to identify and articulate the strengths and limitations of the disciplines and the relationship of the disciplines to one another, and demonstrate an understanding of the breadth and diversity of human knowledge as well as its openness to integration in more comprehensive wholes.
4. Be conversant with and able to discuss intelligently enduring questions and issues that are fundamental to human inquiry and that have shaped the traditions from which the university has emerged.
5. Demonstrate the ability to apply more than one disciplinary perspective to the same enduring question or complex contemporary problem.
6. Be familiar with the scholarly exploration of religious faith and understand how faith and reason are related in the search for truth.
7. Demonstrate the ability to examine their values and experiences and integrate what they learn with the principles that guide their lives.
8. Be prepared and disposed to use their talents and education as engaged global citizens and responsible leaders in service of the common good.

Notes

1. John W. O'Malley, S.J., "How the First Jesuits Became Involved in Education," in *The Jesuit* Ratio Studiorum: *400th Anniversary Perspectives*, ed. Vincent J. Duminuco, S.J. (New York: Fordham University Press, 2000), 58–59, 61, 68.

2. "The Characteristics of Jesuit Education: Some Characteristics of Jesuit Pedagogy," in *The Jesuit* Ratio Studiorum, *supra* n. 1, at 212.

3. Michael Himes, "Living Conversation: Higher Education in a Catholic Context," *Conversation on Jesuit Higher Education* (Fall 1995): 25.

4. Adolfo Nicolás, S.J., "Depth, Universality, and Learned Ministry: Challenges to Jesuit Higher Education Today," remarks for "Networking Jesuit Higher Education: Shaping the Future for a Humane, Just, Sustainable Globe," Mexico City, April 23, 2010.

5. *See* "Jesuits and Jesuit Education: A Primer" (from *Jesuits and Boston College: A Working Paper for Discussion*, prepared by the Boston College Jesuit Community, 1994), in *A Jesuit Education Reader*, ed. George W. Traub, S.J. (Chicago: Loyola Press, 2008): 41.

Appendix B

Boston College Core Curriculum Required Courses

1 Course in Arts
2 Courses in History (History I: pre-1800, History II: post-1800
1 Course in Literature
1 Course in Mathematics
2 Courses in Natural Science
2 Courses in Philosophy
2 Courses in Theology
1 Course in Writing
1 Course in Cultural Diversity (may be fulfilled by another Core course, may be fulfilled through a Cultural Diversity, Difference Justice and the Common Good, or Engaging Difference and Justice course)

Appendix C

Complex Problem and Enduring Question Courses, 2015–2021

New Courses Have an Asterisk before the Course Title

Fall 2015

*Complex Problem | SOCY1501/EESC1501
Global Implications of Climate Change
Brian Gareau, Sociology, and Tara Pisani Gareau, Earth
and Environmental Sciences
1 Social Science + 1 Natural Science

*Complex Problem | HIST1503/SOCY1503
Understanding Race, Gender, and Violence
Marilynn Johnson, History, and Shawn McGuffey, Sociology
1 History + 1 Social Science

*Enduring Question | SOCY1702 - ENGL1702
The Body in Sickness and Health
Jane Ashley, Nursing
Reading the Body
Laura Tanner, English
1 Social Science + 1 Literature

Spring 2016

*Complex Problem | HIST1501/ENGL1501
Genocide and Crimes Against Humanity

Devin Pendas, History, and Maxim D. Shrayer, Slavic
and Eastern Languages and Literatures
1 History + 1 Literature

Enduring Question | BIOL1701 - THTR1701
Epidemics, Disease, and Humanity
Mary Kathleen Dunn, Biology
Devising Theater: Illness as Metaphor
Scott Cummings, Theater
1 Natural Science + 1 Arts

Enduring Question | ENGL1703 - PHIL1703
Humans, Nature, and Creativity
Min Song, English
Inquiring about Humans and Nature
Holly VandeWall, Philosophy
1 Literature + 1 Philosophy

Enduring Question | ENGL1701 - HIST1701
Truth-telling in Literature
Allison Adair, English
Truth-telling in History
Sylvia Sellers-García, History
1 Literature + 1 History

Enduring Question | PHIL1702 - POLI1701
Power, Justice, War: The Ancients
Robert Bartlett, Political Science
Power, Justice, War: The Moderns
Aspen Brinton, Philosophy
1 Social Science + 1 Philosophy

Enduring Question | THEO1701 - MUSA1701
Spiritual Exercises: Engagement, Empathy, Ethics
Brian Robinette, Theology
Aesthetic Exercises: Engagement, Empathy, Ethics
Daniel Callahan, Music
1 Theology + 1 Arts

Fall 2016

Complex Problem | SOCY1507/THTR1501
Can Creativity Save the World?

Spencer Harrison, CSOM, and Crystal Tiala, Theatre
1 Social Science + 1 Art

Complex Problem | HIST1505/SOCY1509
Planet in Peril: The History and Future of Human Impacts on the Planet
Prasannan Parthasarathi, History, and Juliet Schor, Sociology
1 History II + 1 Social Science

Enduring Question | ENGL1701 - HIST1701
Truth-Telling in Literature
Allison Adair, English
Truth-Telling in History
Sylvia Sellers-García, History
1 Literature + 1 History I

Enduring Question | MUSA1701 - THEO1701
Aesthetic Exercises: Engagement, Empathy, Ethics
Daniel Callahan, Music
Spiritual Exercises: Engagement, Empathy, Ethics
Brian Robinette, Theology
1 Arts + 1 Theology I

Enduring Question | ENGL1703 - PHIL1703
Humans, Nature, and Creativity
Min Song, English
Inquiring about Humans and Nature
Holly VandeWall, Philosophy
1 Literature + 1 Philosophy I

Enduring Question | HIST1702 - ENGL1710
Family Matters: Histories of Adoption and Kinship
Arissa Oh, History
Family Matters: Stories of Adoption and Kinship
James Smith, English
1 History II + 1 Literature

Enduring Question | BIOL1702 - ECON1701
Human Diseases: Plagues, Pathogens, and Chronic Disorders
Kathy Dunn, Biology
Human Diseases: Health, the Economy, and Society
Sam Richardson, Economics
1 Natural Science + 1 Social Science

Spring 2017

Complex Problem | *PHIL1501/EESC1505*
A Perfect Moral Storm: The Science and Ethics of Climate Change
David Storey, Philosophy, and Corinne Wong, Earth and
    Environmental Sciences
1 Philosophy II + 1 Natural Science

Complex Problem | *THTR1503/POLI1031*
Performing Politics
Luke Jorgensen, Theatre, and Jennie Purnell, Political Science
1 Arts + 1 Social Science

Complex Problem | *HIST1507/FILM1501*
Social Problems on the Silver Screen
Lynn Lyerly, History, and John Michalczyk, Fine Arts
1 History II + 1 Arts

Enduring Question | *EESC1701 - THEO1703*
**Building a Habitable Planet—Origins and Evolution of the Earth:
    Geoscience Perspectives**
Ethan Baxter, Earth and Environmental Sciences
**Building a Habitable Planet—Origins and Evolution of the Earth:
    Theological Perspectives**
Natana Delong-Bas, Theology
1 Natural Science + 1 Theology II

Enduring Question | *SLAV1161 - THEO1702*
What Is the Good Life? Tolstoy to Chekov
Thomas Epstein, Slavic & Eastern Languages and Literatures
God and the Good Life
Stephen Pope, Theology
1 Literature + 1 Theology II

Enduring Question | *ENGL1705 - SOCY1703*
Reading and Writing Health, Illness, and Disability
Amy Boesky, English
The Social Construction of Health and Illness
Sara Moorman, Sociology
1 Literature + 1 Social Science

Enduring Question | *ENGL1704 - RLRL3373*
Love, Gender, and Marriage: Writing & Rewriting the Tradition
Treseanne Ainsworth, English

Love, Gender, and Marriage: The Western Literary Tradition
Franco Mormando, Romance Languages & Literatures
1 Writing + 1 Literature

Enduring Question | ENGL1708 - SOCY1704
Narrating Black Intimacies
Rhonda Frederick, English
Black Intimacy and Intersectionality in the U.S.
Shawn McGuffey, Sociology
1 Literature + 1 Social Science

Enduring Question | ENGL1709 - CHEM1701
Living in the Material World
Elizabeth Kowaleski Wallace, English
Living in the Material World
Dunwei Wang, Chemistry
1 Literature + 1 Natural Science

Fall 2017

Complex Problem | SOCY150101 + EESC150101
Global Implications of Climate Change
Brian Gareau, Sociology, and Tara Pisani Gareau, Earth
    and Environmental Sciences
1 Social Science + 1 Natural Science

Complex Problem | HIST151101 + BIOL150301
Science and Technology in American Society
Andrew Jewett, History, and Christopher Kenaley, Biology
1 History II + 1 Natural Science

Enduring Question | ENGL170301 + PHIL170301
Humans, Nature, and Creativity
Min Song, English
Inquiring about Humans and Nature
Holly VandeWall, Philosophy
1 Literature + 1 Philosophy I

Enduring Question | MUSA170101 + THEO170101
Aesthetic Exercises: Engagement, Empathy, Ethics
Daniel Callahan, Music
Spiritual Exercises: Engagement, Empathy, Ethics
Brian Robinette, Theology
1 Arts + 1 Theology I

Enduring Question | SOCY170201 + ENGL170201
The Body in Sickness and Health
Jane Ashley, Nursing
Reading the Body
Laura Tanner, English
1 Social Science + 1 Literature

*Enduring Questions | EESC170201 + ARTH170101
Living on the Water: Costs, Development, and Sea Level Change from Venice to Boston
Gail Kineke, Earth and Environmental Sciences
Living on the Water: Venetian Art, Architecture, and the Environment
Stephanie Leone, Art History

*Enduring Question | PHIL170501 + MATH170101
Being Human: The Philosophical Problem of Nature and Mathematical Knowledge
Colin Connors, Philosophy
Understanding Mathematics: Its Philosophical Origins, Evolution, and Humanity
Ellen Goldstein, Mathematics
1 Philosophy I + 1 Mathematics

*Enduring Question | BIOL170301 + THTR170201
Your Brain on Theatre: On Stage and Off
Daniel Kirschner, Biology
This Is Your Brain on Theatre: Neuroscience and the Actor
Patricia Riggin, Theatre
1 Natural Science + 1 Arts

*Enduring Question | CLAS170101 + SLAV116401
Death in Ancient Greece: Achilles to Alexander the Great
Hanne Einsfeld, Classical Studies
Death in Russian Literature: Heroes, Cowards, Humans
Thomas Epstein, Slavic and Eastern Languages and Literatures
1 History I + 1 Literature

*Enduring Question | POLI104801 + HIST170601
How Democracies Die: A Political Postmortem
Matthew Berry, Political Science
How Democracies Die: A Historical Postmortem
Jesse Tumblin, History
1 Social Science + 1 History II

Enduring Question | ENGL171201 + ENGL171301
  Roots & Routes: Writing Identity, Migration, and Culture
  Lynne Anderson, English
  Roots & Routes: Reading Identity, Migration, and Culture
  Elizabeth Graver, English
  1 Literature + 1 Writing

Spring 2018

Complex Problem | SOCY150901 + HIST150501
  **Planet in Peril: The History and Future of Human Impacts
    on the Plant**
  Juliet Schor, Sociology, and Prasannan Parthasarathi, History
  1 Social Science + History II

*Complex Problem | HIST150901 + POLI104301
  The History and Politics of Terrorism
  Julian Bourg, History, and Peter Krause, Political Science
  History II + 1 Social Science

Complex Problem | ECON150101 + ENGL150301
  Beyond Price: Markets, Cultures, Values
  Can Erbil, Economics, and Kalpana Sheshadri, English
  1 Social Science + Literature

Enduring Question | BIOL170201 + ECON170101
  **Human Diseases: Plagues, Pathogens, and Chronic
    Disorders**
  Kathy Dunn, Biology
  Human Disease: Health, the Economy, and Society
  Samuel Richardson, Economics
  1 Natural Science + 1 Social Science

*Enduring Question | POLI104501 + HIST170301
  **Religion in a Secular World: Separating Church,
    Mosque, State**
  Jonathan Laurence, Political Science
  Religious Diversity in a Muslim World
  Dana Sajdi, History
  1 Social Science + History I

*Enduring Question | ENGL171401 + HIST170401
  Reading Man, God, and the Whale in Melville's *Moby-Dick*
  Michael Martin, Honors

Worlds of *Moby-Dick*: What Historical Forces Shape
a Book's Greatness?
David Quigley, History
Literature + History II

Enduring Question | HIST170501 + ENGL171501
Revolutionary Media: How Books Changed History
Virginia Reinburg, History
Revolutionary Media: How Reading Changes Us
Mary Crane, English
History I + Literature

Enduring Question | ENGL170901 + CHEM170101
Living in the Material World
Elizabeth Kowaleski Wallace, English
Living in the Material World
Dunwei Wang, Chemistry
Literature + 1 Natural Science

Enduring Question | POLI104601 + SOCY170601
Politics of Human Rights
Jennie Purnell, Political Science
Human Rights and Social Welfare
Margaret Lombe, Social Work
1 Social Science + History II

Enduring Question | BIOL170401 + ENGL171601
Metamorphosis: Evolution and the Genetics of Change
Welkin Johnson, Biology
Metamorphosis: Storytelling as an Attempt to Manage Change
Dayton Haskin, English
1 Natural Science + Literature

Enduring Question | SOCY170701 + ENGL171701
Passion, Power, and Purpose: Adolescence in a Digital Age
Belle Liang, Lynch School of Education
Fictions of Development: Adolescence in Historical Context
Maia McAleavey, English
1 Social Science + Literature

Enduring Question | ENGL171801 + ENGL171901
**Reading In/Justice: Literature as Activism from Abolition to
#BlackLivesMatter**
Lori Harrison-Kahan, English

Writing In/Justice: The Power of Response
Eileen Donovan-Kranz, English
Literature + Writing

Enduring Question | POLI104701 + ENGL172001
Creating the Modern State: Power, Politics, and Propaganda
from the Renaissance to the 21st Century
Hiroshi Nakazato, International Studies
Creating the Modern Identity: Power, Politics, and Propaganda
from the Renaissance to the 21st Century
Susan Michalczyk, Honors
1 Social Science + Literature

Enduring Question | SOCY170501 + SOCY170801
Growing Up Gendered: Contemporary Media
Representations
Lisa Cuklanz, Communications
Growing Up Gendered: Socio-Cultural Perspectives
on Gender in Contemporary Society
Sharlene Hesse-Biber, Sociology
Literature + 1 Social Science

Enduring Question | SOCY170901 + HIST170701
In Search of Human Rights: Health and Healthcare
Lauren Diamond-Brown, Sociology
In Search of Human Rights: U.S. Foreign Relations
Amanda Demmer, History
1 Social Science + History II

Enduring Question | HIST170801 + EESC170301
Nature on Exhibit: From Sea Monsters to Sea World
Jenna Tonn, History
Through the Looking Glass: Business and the Natural
Environment
Lucy McAllister, Environmental Studies
History II + 1 Natural Science

Fall 2018

Complex Problem | HIST151101 + BIOL150301
Science and Technology in American Society
Andrew Jewett, History, and Christopher Kenaley, Biology
1 History II + 1 Natural Science

Complex Problem | SOCY151101+AADS150101
From #BlackLivesMatter to #MeToo: Violence and Representation in the African Diaspora
Régine Jean-Charles, Romance Languages and Literatures, and
    Shawn McGuffey, Sociology
1 Social Science+1 Literature

Enduring Question | UNAS170401+UNAS170501
When Life Happens: Disability and the Stories We Tell
Clare Dunsford, English
When Life Happens: Psychology Views Disability
Penny Hauser-Cram, Lynch School of Education
1 Literature+1 Social Science

Enduring Question | ENGL172201+UNAS170101
Oppression and Change in the Contemporary United States: Writing as Social Action
Paula Mathieu, English
Oppression and Change in the Contemporary United States: Sociocultural and Psychological Perspectives
Lisa Goodman, Lynch School of Education
1 Writing+1 Social Science

Enduring Question | PSYC109101+ENGL172301
Thinking about Feelings: The Psychology of Emotion
Andrea Heberlein, Psychology
Feeling Like Ourselves: How and Why Literature Moves Us
Andrew Sofer, English
1 Social Science+1 Literature

Enduring Question | UNAS170301+PSYC109201
Humans and Other Animals: Changing Perceptions of Humankind's Place in Nature
Rory Browne, Morrissey College of Arts & Sciences
Humans and Other Animals: The Mental Life of Animals
Jeffrey Lamoureaux, Psychology
1 History II+1 Social Science

Enduring Questions | ECON170201+UNAS170201
Life, Money, and Health: The Economics of Health Care
Tracy Regan, Economics
Life, Liberty, and Health: Policy, Politics, and Law
Mary Ann Chirba, Law
1 Social Science+1 History II

Enduring Question | SLAV116601 + CLAS170201
St. Petersburg: Dream & Reality
Thomas Epstein, Slavic and Eastern Languages and Literatures
Rome: Art, Regime & Renaissance
Christopher Polt, Classical Studies
1 Literature + 1 History 1

Enduring Questions | ENGL172101 + HIST170901
Finding the Animal: Beasts and Boundaries in Literature
Robert Stanton, English
From Weevils to Wolves: How Animals Made the World
Zachary Matus, History
1 Literature + History I

Enduring Question | POLI102601 + PHIL170701
**Taking Power/Seeking Justice: On the Causes and Consequences
of Social Change Movements**
Paul Christensen, Political Science
**Seeking Justice/Taking Power: The Philosophy of Radical Social
Change**
Eileen Sweeney, Philosophy
1 Social Science + 1 Philosophy

Enduring Question | ENGL170401 + RLRL337301
Love, Gender, and Marriage: Writing & Rewriting the Tradition
Treseanne Ainsworth, English
Love, Gender, and Marriage: The Western Literary Tradition
Franco Mormando, Romance Languages and Literatures
1 Writing + 1 Literature

Enduring Question | ENGL170101 + HIST170101
Truth-Telling in Literature
Allison Adair, English
Truth-Telling in History
Sylvia Sellers-García, History
1 Literature + 1 History I

Enduring Question | EESC170201 + ARTH170101
**Living on the Water: Coasts, Development, and Sea Level Change
from Venice to Boston**
Gail Kineke, Earth and Environmental Sciences
Living on the Water: Venetian Art, Architecture, and the Environment
Stephanie Leone, Art History
1 Natural Science + 1 Arts

Enduring Question | BIOL170301 + THTR170201
Your Brain on Theatre: On Stage and Off
Daniel Kirschner, Biology
This Is Your Brain on Theatre: Neuroscience and the Actor
Patricia Riggin, Theatre
1 Natural Science + 1 Arts

Enduring Question | POLI1048 + HIST1706
How Democracies Die: A Political Postmortem
Matthew Berry, Political Science
How Democracies Die: A Historical Postmortem
Jesse Tumblin, History
1 Social Science + 1 History II

*Enduring Question | HIST171301 + UNAS170901
**Environmental Crisis: How Past Disasters Shape
    the Present**
Evan Hepler-Smith, History
**Environmental Crisis: Sustainability, Resources, and
    the Future**
Jonathan Krones, Environmental Studies
1 History II + 1 Natural Science

*Enduring Question | Theology Core BIOL170501 + THEO170401
In the Beginning: Scientific Explorations of Our Origins
Michelle Meyer, Biology
In the Beginning: Biblical Explorations of Our Origins
Jeffrey Cooley, Theology
1 Natural Science + 1 Theology 1

*Enduring Question | Theology Core THEO170501 + RLRL335001
The Pursuit of Happiness in Theology and Spirituality
Andrew Prevot, Theology
The Pursuit of Happiness in Literature and Film
Laurie Shepard, Romance Languages and Literatures
1 Theology I + 1 Literature

Enduring Question | Theology Core THEO170201 + SLAV116101
The Good Life
Stephen Pope, Theology
Tolstoy, Dostoevsky, and Chekhov: What is the Good Life?
Thomas Epstein, Slavic and Eastern Languages and Literatures
1 Theology I + 1 Literature

Enduring Question | Theology Core THEO1700.01
Theological Inquiry: Origins and Evolution of the Earth
Natana Delong-Bas, Theology
1 Theology 1

Enduring Question | Theology Core THEO1700.02
Theological Inquiry: Artificial Intelligence
Matthew Petillo, Theology
1 Theology I

Spring 2019

Complex Problem | EESC150701 + HIST151301
Powering America: Energy, Tech, Environment
John Ebel, Earth and Environmental Sciences, and Conevery
    Valencius, History
1 History II + 1 Natural Science

Complex Problem | POLI103101 + THTR150301
Performing Politics
Luke Jorgensens, Theatres, and Jennie Purnell, Political
    Science
1 Arts + 1 Social Science

Enduring Question | POLI102801 + UNAS170601
God and Politics
Alice Behnegar, Political Science
God and Love
Christopher Constas, Honors Program
1 Social Science + 1 Philosophy

Enduring Question | BIOL170201 + ECON170101
Human Disease: Plagues, Pathogens, and Chronic Disorder
Mary Kathleen Dunn, Biology
Human Disease: Health, the Economy, and Society
Samuel Richardson, Economics
1 Natural Science + 1 Social Science

Enduring Question | BIOL170401 + ENGL171601
Metamorphosis: Evolution and the Genetics of Change
Welkin Johnson, Biology
Metamorphosis: Storytelling
Dayton Haskin, English
1 Natural Science + 1 Literature

Enduring Question | ENGL170901 + CHEM170101
Living in the Material World
Elizabeth Kowaleski Wallace, English
Living in the Material World
Dunwei Wang, Chemistry
1 Literature + 1 Natural Science

Enduring Question | EESC170101 + THEO170301
Building a Habitable Planet, Geoscience Perspectives
Ethan Baxter, Earth and Environmental Sciences
Building a Habitable Planet, Theological Perspectives
Natana Delong-Bas, Theology
1 Natural Science + 1 Theology

*Enduring Question | COMM170101 + ENGL172501
Social Norms and Values: Disney
Rita Rosenthal, Communication
Narrative and Myth in American Culture: Disney
Bonnie Rudner, English
1 Social Science + 1 Literature

*Enduring Question | ENGL172401 + HIST171001
Nature and Power: Reading the American Place
Suzanne Matson, English
Nature and Power: Making the Modern World
Ling Zhang, History
1 Literature + 1 History II

*Enduring Question | ARTS170101 + PHIL170901
Arts of Creativity: Buzzword to Artwork
Sheila Gallagher, Studio Art
Art of Creativity: Crisis and Transformation
Richard Kearney, Philosophy
1 Arts + 1 Philosophy

*Enduring Question | UNAS170701 + PHIL171001
Modern Science and Ancient Faith: Neuroscientific
Jessica Black, Social Work
Modern Science and Ancient Faith: Philosophical
Daniel Mckaughan, Philosophy
1 Social Science + 1 Philosophy

*Enduring Question | FILM170101 + UNAS170801
Coming of Age: Film
John Michalczyk, Honors

Coming of Age: Literature
Susan Michalczyk, Honors
1 Arts + 1 Literature

Enduring Question | PHYS170101 + ENGL172601
Inspiration in Imagination
Michael Naughton, Physics
Reading the Impossible Universe
Joseph Nugent, English
1 Natural Science + 1 Literature

Enduring Question | POLI102501 + HIST171101
Human Rights in International Politics
Ali Banuazizi, Political Science
Human Rights in History
Devin Pendas, History
1 Social Science + 1 History II

Enduring Question | COMM170201 + THEO170601
Being Human: Secular-Humanist Perspective
Marcus Breen, Communication
Being Human: Theological Perspective
Louis Petillo, Theology
1 Social Science + 1 Theology

Fall 2019

Complex Problem | HIST150501 - SOCY150901
**Planet in Peril: The History and Future of Human Impacts
    on the Planet**
Juliet Schor, Sociology
Prasannan Parthasarathi, History
Fulfills 1 Social Science + 1 History II

Complex Problem | ECON150101 - ENGL150301
Beyond Price: Markets, Cultures, Values
Can Erbil, Economics
Kalpana Seshadri, English
1 Social Science + 1 Literature

Complex Problem | HIST171501 - SOCY171301
**Citizenship, Immigration & Belonging in the United States:
    Can Education Save Us?**
Andrés Castro Samayoa, Lynch School of Education

Gabrielle Oliveira, Lynch School of Education
1 Social Science + 1 History II + Cultural Diversity through DJCG

Complex Problem | *SOCY150101 - EESC150101*
Global Implications of Climate Change
Brian Gareau, Sociology and International Studies
Tara Pisani Gareau, Earth and Environmental Sciences
1 Social Science + 1 Natural Science + Cultural Diversity through EDJ

Enduring Question | *HIST170501 - ENGL171501*
Revolutionary Media: How Books Changed History
Virginia Reinburg, History
Revolutionary Media: How Reading Changes Us
Mary Crane, English
1 History I + 1 Literature

Enduring Question | *ENGL171901 - ENGL171801*
Writing in/ Justice: The Power of Response
Eileen Donovan-Kranz, English
**Reading in/ Justice: Literature as Activism from Abolition to
    #BlackLivesMatter**
Lori Harrison-Kahan, English
1 Writing + 1 Literature+ Cultural Diversity through DJCG

Enduring Questios | *ENGL171701 - SOCY170701*
Fictions of Development: Adolescence in Historical Context
Maia McAleavey, English
Passion, Power, and Purpose: Adolescence in a Digital Age
Belle Liang, Lynch School of Education
1 Literature + 1 Social Science

Enduring Question | *UNAS170101 - ENGL172201*
Oppression & Change in US: Sociocultural & Psych
Lisa Goodman, Lynch School of Education
Oppression & Change in US: Writing
Paula Mathieu, English
1 Social Science + 1 Writing + Cultural Diversity through DJCG

Enduring Question | *ENGL171301 - ENGL171201*
Roots & Routes: Writing Identity
Lynne Anderson, English
Roots & Routes: Reading Identity
Elizabeth Graver, English
1 Writing + 1 Literature

Enduring Question | HIST170401 - ENGL171401
Worlds of Moby-Dick: What Historical Forces Shape a Book's Greatness?
David Quigley, History
Reading Man, God, and the Whale in Melville's Moby-Dick
Michael Martin, Honors
1 History II + 1 Literature

Enduring Question | ECON170201 - UNAS170201
Life, Money & Health: The Economics of Healthcare
Tracy Regan, Economics
Life, Liberty & Health: Policy, Politics & Law
Mary Ann Chirba, BC Law
1 Social Science + 1 History II + Cultural Diversity through EDJ

*Enduring Question | UNAS171001 - CSCI170101
Privacy, Fairness, and Law
Alfred Yen, BC Law
Privacy, Fairness, and the Digital World
Howard Straubing, Computer Science
1 Social Science + 1 Mathematics

Enduring Question | UNAS170501 - UNAS170401
When Life Happens: Psychology Views Disability
Penny Hauser-Cram, Lynch School of Education
When Life Happens: Disability and the Stories We Tell
Clare Dunsford, English
1 Social Science + 1 Literature

*Enduring Question | UNAS154001 - UNAS154101
Trash Talking: Political Ecology of Waste and Resources
Jessica Worl, Sociology
Talking Trash: Industrial Ecology of Waste and Resources
Jonathan Krones, Environmental Studies
1 Social Science + 1 Natural Science

*Enduring Question | HIST171601 - THEO170701
Geographies of Imperialism: History of Colonization
Elizabeth Shlala, History
Geographies of Imperialism: Theology of Colonization
Natana DeLong-Bas, Theology
1 History II + 1 Theology (Sacred Texts & Traditions)
+ Cultural Diversity through EDJ and DJCG

Enduring Question | *HIST170601-02 - UNAS154201-02*
  How Democracies Die: A Historical Postmortem
  Jesse Tumblin, History
  How Democracies Die: The Politicization of Emotions
  Carlos Zúñiga Nieto, History
  1 Social Science + 1 History II

Spring 2020

Complex Problem | *HIST151301 - EESC150701*
  Powering America: The Past and Future of Energy, Technology, and the Environment
  John Ebel, Earth and Environmental Sciences
  Conevery Valencius, History
  1 History II + 1 Natural Science

Complex Problem | *SOCY171401 - HIST171701*
  #Shop-Apocalypse: Consumer Culture's Past and the Fate of the Planet
  Juliet Schor, Sociology
  Robin Fleming, History
  1 Social Science + 1 History II

Complex Problem | *HIST151101 + BIOL150301*
  Science and Technology in American Society
  Andrew Jewett, History
  Christopher Kenaley, Biology
  1 History II + 1 Natural Science

Enduring Question | *COMM170201 - THEO170601*
  Being Human: Secular-Humanist Perspective
  Marcus Breen, Communication
  Being Human: Theological Perspective
  Louis Petillo, Theology
  1 Social Science + 1 Theology (Christian Theology)

Enduring Question | *HIST171001 - ENGL172401*
  Nature and Power: Making the Modern World
  Ling Zhang, History
  Nature and Power: Reading the American Place
  Suzanne Matson, English
  1 Literature + 1 History II

Enduring Question | *ECON170301 - PHIL171101*
The American Divide: The Economics of Inequality
Geoffrey Sanzenbacher, Economics
The American Divide: The Philosophy of Inequality
Cherie McGill, Philosophy
1 Philosophy + 1 Social Science + Cultural Diversity through EDJ

Enduring Question | *UNAS170801 - FILM170101*
Coming of Age: Literature
Susan Michalczyk, Honors
Coming of Age: Film
John Michalczyk, Art, Art History & Film
1 Art + 1 Literature

Enduring Question | *SOCY171101 - COMM170301*
Social Inequality in America
Eve Spangler, Sociology
Rhetoric of Social Inequality in America
Celeste Wells, Communication
1 Social Science, 1 Literature + 1 Cultural Diversity (Difference, Justice & the Common Good)

Enduring Question | *ENGL171001 - SOCY171501*
Family Matters: Stories of Adoption and Kinship
James Smith, English
Family Matters: Psychology and Adoption
Oh Myo Kim, Lynch School of Education
1 Social Science + 1 Literature

Enduring Question | *BIOL170501 - THEO170401*
In the Beginning: Scientific Explorations of Our Origins
Michelle Meyer, Biology
In the Beginning: Biblical Explorations of Our Origins
Jeffery Cooley, Theology
1 Natural Science + 1 Theology (Sacred Texts and Traditions)

Enduring Question | *PSYC109201 - ENGL172101*
Humans and Other Animals: The Mental Life of Animals
Jeffrey Lamoureux, Psychology
Finding the Animal: Beasts and Boundaries in Literature
Robert Stanton, English
1 Literature + 1 Social Science
1 Social Science + 1 History II

Fall 2020

Complex Problem | AADS150101 - SOCY151101
**Where #Black Lives Matter meets #Me Too: Violence &
Representation in the African Diaspora**
Régine Jean-Charles, Romance Languages and Literatures
Shawn McGuffey, Sociology
Lab instructor: Nora Gross, Core Fellow (Sociology)
1 Literature + 1 Social Science + Cultural Diversity through
Engaging Difference & Justice

Complex Problem | ENGL150301 - ECON150101
Beyond Price: Markets, Cultures, Values
Kalpana Sheshadri, English
Can Erbil, Economics
1 Literature + 1 Social Science

Complex Problem | SOCY150901 - HIST150501
**Planet in Peril: The History and Future of Human Impacts
on the Planet**
Juliet Schor, Sociology
Prasannan Parthasarathi, History
Lab Instructor: John Brooks, Core Fellow (English)
1 History II + 1 Social Science

*Complex Problems | EESC171701 - HIST1617
Making the Modern World: Ethics & Engineering
Jonathan Krones, Core Fellow, Environmental
   Studies
Jenna Tonn, Core Fellow, History
Lab Instructor: Russ Powell, Core Fellow (Theology)

Enduring Question | UNAS170201 - ECON170201
Life, Liberty & Health: Policy, Politics and Law
Mary Ann Chirba, Law
Life, Money & Health: The Economics of Healthcare
Tracy Regan, Economics
1 History II + 1 Social Science + Cultural Diversity through
Engaging Difference & Justice

Enduring Question | ENGL1723 - PSYC1091
Thinking about Feelings: The Psychology of Emotion
Andrea Heberlein, Psychology

Feeling Like Ourselves: How and Why Literature Moves Us
Andrew Sofer, English
1 Social Science + 1 Literature

Enduring Question | EESC170201 - ARTH170101
Living on the Water: Coasts, Development, and Sea Level Change from Venice to Boston
Gail Kineke, Earth and Environmental Sciences
Living on the Water: Venetian Art, Architecture, and the Environment
Stephanie Leone, Art History
1 Natural Science + 1 Arts

Enduring Question | MUSA170101 - THEO170101
Aesthetic Exercises: Engagement, Empathy, Ethics
Daniel Callahan, Music
Spiritual Exercises: Engagement, Empathy, Ethics
Brian Robinette, Theology
1 Arts + 1 Theology (Christian Theology)

Enduring Question | COMM170101 - ENGL172501
Social Norms and Values: Disney
Rita Rosenthal, Communication
Narrative and Myth in American Culture: Disney
Bonnie Rudner, English
1 Literature + 1 Social Science

Enduring Question | COMM221601 - SOCY170801
Growing Up Gendered: Contemporary Media Representations
Lisa Cuklanz, Communications
Growing Up Gendered: Socio-Cultural Perspectives on Gender in Contemporary Society
Sharlene Hesse-Biber, Sociology
1 Literature + 1 Social Science

Enduring Question | HIST171601 - THEO170701
Geographies of Imperialism: History of Colonization
Elizabeth Shlala, History
Geographies of Imperialism: Theology of Colonization
Natana DeLong-Bas, Theology
Fulfills 1 History II + 1 Theology (Sacred Texts & Traditions) + Cultural Diversity (THEO1701 through DJCG & HIST1716 through EDJ)

Enduring Question | POLI105101 - THEO171001
Flawed Founders: George Washington and the Mythology of a Heroic President
Marc Landy, Political Science
Flawed Founders: King David and the Theology of a Political Hero
David Vanderhooft, Theology
1 Social Science + 1 Theology (Sacred Texts & Traditions)

Enduring Question | ENVS107701 - HIST107601
Environmental Migration: Climate Change
Yasmin Zaerpoor, Environmental Studies
Environmental Migration: Asylum Seekers
Carlos Zúñiga Nieto, History
1 Social Science + 1 History II

Spring 2021

Complex Problem | HIST1503 - SOCY1503
Understanding Race, Gender, and Violence
Marilynn Johnson, History
Shawn McGuffey, Sociology
Lab Instructor: Daniel Millán, Core Fellow (Sociology)
1 History II + 1 Social Science + Cultural Diversity through Engaging Difference & Justice

Complex Problem | BIOL170601 - ENVS107501
Understanding & Protecting Our Oceans in the Wake of Climate Change
Heather Olins, Biology
Yasmin Bijani Zaerpoor, Environmental Studies
Lab Instructor: John Brooks, Core Fellow (English)
1 Natural Science + 1 Social Science

Complex Problem | UNAS171101 - THEO171101
Neuroscience and Religion: Conflict, Coexistence or Collaboration
Jessica Black, School of Social Work
Mellisa Kelley, School of Theology & Ministry
Lab Instructor: Russ Powell, Core Fellow (Theology)
1 Natural Science + 1 Theology (Christian Theology)

Complex Problem | HIST1513 - EESC1507
Powering America: The Past and Future of Energy, Technology, and the Environment
John Ebel, Earth and Environmental Sciences
Conevery Valencius, History
Lab Instructor: Jonathan Krones, Core Fellow (Environmental Studies)
1 History II + 1 Natural Science

*Complex Problem | SOCY171401 - HIST171701
Consumer Culture: Past, Present, and the Fate of the Planet
Juliet Schor, Sociology
Robin Fleming, History
Lab Instructor: Carlos Zúñiga Nieto, Core Fellow (History)
1 Social Science + 1 History II

*Enduring Question | ECON170301 - PHIL171101
The American Divide: The Economics of Inequality
Geoffrey Sanzenbacher, Economics
The American Divide: The Philosophy of Inequality
Cherie McGill, Philosophy
1 Philosophy + 1 Social Science

*Enduring Question | SOCY171101 - COMM170301
Social Inequality in America
Eve Spangler, Sociology
Rhetoric of Social Inequality in America
Celeste Wells, Communication
1 Social Science + 1 Literature + Cultural Diversity through
    Engaging Difference & Justice

Enduring Question | CLAS170101 - SLAV116401
Death in Ancient Greece: Achilles to Alexander the Great
Hanne Eisenfeld, Classical Studies
Death in Russian Literature: Heroes, Cowards, Humans
Thomas Epstein, Classical Studies
1 History I + 1 Literature

Enduring Question | FILM170101 - UNAS170801
*Coming of Age: Film (FILM170101)
Eileen Donovan Kranz,
Coming of Age: Literature (UNAS170801)
Susan Michalczyk, Honors
1 Arts + 1 Literature

Enduring Question | ARTH172001 - PHIL172001
Animals in the Moral Imagination: Art and Empathy
Jennifer Burns, Art History
Animals in the Moral Imagination: Beyond Human Justice
Melissa Fitzpatrick, Carroll School of Management
1 Philosophy + 1 Arts

Enduring Question | THEO170301 - EESC170101
Building a Habitable Planet, Geoscience Perspectives
Ethan Baxter, Earth and Environmental Sciences
Building a Habitable Planet, Theological Perspectives
Natana Delong-Bas, Theology
1 Natural Science + 1 Theology (Sacred Texts & Traditions)

Enduring Question | HIST172501 - SOCY172501
Who Are You? The Science of Self
Jenna Tonn, Core Fellow (History)
Who Are You? The Sociology of Self
Nora Gross, Core Fellow (Sociology)
1 History II + Social Science

Contributors

Allison Adair is associate professor of the practice in the English Department at Boston College and specializes in creative writing, with a focus on poetry and flash fiction and a special interest in digital humanities. She is the author of poems published in many venues, including *North American Review, Southwest Review, American Poetry Review, Pushcart Prize XLIII,* and of prose in *Grub Daily.* She taught the Enduring Question course "Truth-telling in Literature."

Lynne Anderson is the director of English Language Learning at Boston College. Trained in applied linguistics, she teaches writing, literature, and oral language production courses. She is the author of *Breaking Bread: Recipes and Stories from Immigrant Kitchens.* She is interested in the intersections among language, culture, identity, and food. She teaches narrative nonfiction writing workshops on the topic of food and culture, including a course abroad in Paris each spring for BC's Office of International Programs. She taught the Enduring Question course titled "Roots and Routes: Writing Identity, Migration, and Culture."

Robert C. Bartlett serves as the Behrakis Professor in Hellenic Political Studies at Boston College. He is the author or editor of eight books, including *Sophistry and Political Philosophy: Protagoras' Challenge to Socrates* (2016) and an edition of Aristotle's *Art of Rhetoric* (2019), both published by the University of Chicago Press. His principal area of research is classical political philosophy. In conjunction with Aspen Brinton, he taught an Enduring Question seminar titled "Justice and War: The Ancients," which was largely devoted to a study of Thucydides' *War of the Peloponnesians and the Athenians.*

William Bole is the director of Content Development at Boston College's Carroll School of Management. He is co-author of several books, including (with Bob Abernethy) *The Life of Meaning: Reflections on Faith, Doubt, and Repairing the World.* His writing has focused on religion, politics, business, and higher education, and has appeared in the

Washington Post, New York Times, and *Los Angeles Times,* as well as *America, Commonweal, Christian Century, Forbes, Utne Reader,* and other outlets. He spent fifteen years as a reporter for wire services sponsored or syndicated by the *New York Times,* Associated Press, Newhouse, and Knight Ridder, and for nearly a decade as a research and writing fellow at Georgetown University's Woodstock Theological Center.

Toby Bottorf leads the Client Engagement team at EPAM Continuum. He previously spent nine years leading project teams to design solutions for complex human and technical systems. His service design work builds on a career in graphic design, and interface and interaction design. Toby's passion is understanding where people find connection in their everyday interactions with products, services, and complex systems. He takes a systematic, consilient approach to identifying the right ideas and their emotional and functional criteria for success. He wants to build new systems that in addition to being very smart, also have great emotional intelligence, or at least good manners. Most new technology is plenty smart but very rude. Toby holds a Master's degree in communications design from the Institute of Design at IIT and a B.A. in art from Yale University. He is a frequent writer, guest lecturer, conference speaker, competition judge, and critic.

Andy Boynton is the John and Linda Powers Family Dean of the Carroll School of Management at Boston College. He is the author of *The Idea Hunter: How to Find the Best Ideas and Make them Happen* and has a blog on leadership and innovation on Forbes.com.

Jack Butler, S.J., is a member of the East Coast Province of Jesuits and the Haub Vice President for University Mission and Ministry at Boston College. He received his Ph.D. from Loyola University, Maryland, and has been a member of the community for twenty years.

Daniel Callahan is an associate professor of music at Boston College. His first book manuscript, *The Dancer from the Music,* explores the use of music in American modern dance. His article on John Cage and Merce Cunningham, "The Gay Divorce of Music and Dance," appears in the *Journal of the American Musicological Society.* He previously taught at Columbia University, where he received his Ph.D., and the University of Chicago, where he was a Mellon Postdoctoral Fellow. He will work on his second book project, *Conducting Oneself,* exploring the choreographies and identities of orchestra conductors who challenge the maestro stereotype as a 2019–2020 Fellow at the Radcliffe Institute of Advanced Study at Harvard University.

Mary Thomas Crane is the Thomas F. Rattigan Professor of English and director of the Institute for the Liberal Arts at Boston College. She works on early modern English literature and is the author of *Framing Authority: Sayings, Self, and Society in Sixteenth-Century England* (Princeton University Press, 1993), *Shakespeare's Brain: Reading with Cognitive Theory* (Princeton University Press, 2000), and *Losing Touch with Nature: Literature and the New Science in Sixteenth-Century England* (Johns Hopkins University

Press, 2014). She has taught the Enduring Question course "Revolutionary Media: How Reading Changes Us."

Hanne Eisenfeld is Behrakis Assistant Professor in Hellenic Studies at Boston College. She specializes in archaic and classical Greek poetry and Greek religion and myth. Her current project focuses on a set of mythical figures in Pindar's victory odes who challenge the boundaries between mortality and immortality. She teaches the Enduring Question course "Life and Death in Ancient Greece."

Thomas Epstein is associate professor of the practice of the humanities at Boston College. He specializes in modern and contemporary Russian culture, especially poetry and cinema. His most recent publications include "Time Out: Dead End as Exit in Viktor Krivulin's novel *Shmon*" (*Novoe literaturnaia obozrenie*, 2018), and "Russian Beat: Wilderness of Mirrors," in *The Routledge Handbook of International Beat Literature* (Routledge, 2018). He is currently preparing for publication a book of annotated translations by the contemporary Russian poet Elena Shvarts, titled *After Paradise*. He taught the Enduring Question course "Life and Death in Russian Literature."

Brian J. Gareau is an associate professor of sociology at Boston College. He was named associate dean for the Core in 2018 and is responsible for overseeing the University Core Curriculum. As associate dean, he chairs the University Core Renewal Committee and works with faculty and academic departments on their engagement with the Core Curriculum. His scholarship focuses on the sociology of global environmental governance, especially the governance of ozone layer depletion and global climate change. He also publishes on theorizations of society/nature relations, alternative development, and agrifood systems. His latest book, *Organic Futures* (Yale University Press, 2017), co-authored with former BC undergraduate Connor J. Fitzmaurice, was translated into Japanese in 2018. Gareau's latest project involves conducting research on the links between cranberry production in Massachusetts and global climate change. He has co-taught the Complex Problem course "Global Implications of Climate Change" with Tara Pisani Gareau.

Tara Pisani Gareau is associate professor of the practice at Boston College and the director of the Environmental Studies Program. Her research aims to apply ecological principles to restore ecological function and resiliency to agricultural landscapes. Her research projects include examining the effect of native plant hedgerows on biological control services in California, investigating the effects of tillage and cover crops on epigeal arthropod communities in Pennsylvania forage and feed systems, studying dragonflies and damselflies for their potential to regulate pest populations in cranberry bog systems, and assessing the impact of climate change on the sustainability of cranberry bogs in Massachusetts. She has co-taught the Complex Problem course "Global Implications of Climate Change" with Brian Gareau.

Elizabeth Graver is a professor of English at Boston College and is the author of four novels: *The Honey Thief, Unravelling, Awake,* and *The End of the Point*. Her work has appeared in *Best American Short Stories* and *Best American Essays,* and she has received fellowships from the Guggenheim Foundation and the National Endowment for the Arts. She is currently at work on a novel inspired by the migration story of her Sephardic Turkish grandmother. Her Enduring Question course is titled "Roots and Routes: Reading Identity, Migration, and Culture."

Stacy Grooters is the executive director of the Center for Teaching Excellence at Boston College. Her research examines roles of instructor and student identities in the classroom, as well as questions of diversity in higher education. Her most recent publication examines the POD Network's scholarly engagement with diversity in its publications and conference. She received a Ph.D. in English from University of Washington in Seattle.

Régine Michelle Jean-Charles is a Black feminist literary scholar and cultural critic specializing in francophone studies. She is the director of Africana studies, Dean's Professor of Culture and Social Justice, and professor of Africana studies and women's, gender, and sexuality studies at Northeastern University. The focus of her scholarship and teaching on world literatures in French is on Black France, Sub-Saharan Africa, Haiti, and the Haitian Diaspora. She is the author of *Conflict Bodies: The Politics of Rape Representation in the Francophone Imaginary* (Ohio State Universiry Press, 2014), *Martin Luther King and The Trumpet of Conscience Today* (Orbis Books, 2021), and *Looking for Other Worlds: Black Feminism and Haitian Fiction* (University of Virginia Press, 2022).

Gregory Kalscheur, S.J., joined the faculty of the Boston College Law School in 2003. Since 2014 he has served as the dean of the Morrissey College of Arts and Sciences at Boston College. He received his A.B. in 1985 from Georgetown University, and his J.D. in 1988 from the University of Michigan, where he served on the editorial board of the *Michigan Law Review*. After law school, he clerked for Judge Kenneth F. Ripple, U.S. Court of Appeals for the Seventh Circuit, and worked as a litigator at Hogan & Hartson in Washington, D.C. He received his M.Div. and S.T.L. from the Weston Jesuit School of Theology and an LL.M. from Columbia University. Father Kalscheur's primary teaching and research interests include law and religion, constitutional law, civil procedure, Catholic social thought and the law, Ignatian spirituality and legal education, and the connection between the Catholic intellectual tradition and the academic mission of the contemporary, Jesuit, Catholic university.

Elizabeth Kowaleski Wallace is a professor emeritus of English at Boston College. She specializes in British eighteenth-century literature and culture and feminist and cultural theory. She is also interested in contemporary British culture, including drama, the novel, and film. She has published on eighteenth-century women writers, eighteenth-century consumer culture, and on the way that the British slave trade has been remembered and represented in the popular imagination (*The British Slave Trade and Public Memory* [Columbia University Press, 2006]). She taught the Enduring Question course "Living in the Material World" with Dunwei Wang.

Prasannan Parthasarathi is a professor of South Asian history at Boston College. He is the author of *The Transition to a Colonial Economy: Weavers, Merchants, and Kings in*

South India, 1720–1800 (Cambridge University Press, 2001), *The Spinning World: A Global History of Cotton Textiles* (Oxford University Press, 2009), and *Why Europe Grew Rich and Asia Did Not: Global Economic Divergence, 1600–1850* (Cambridge University Press, 2011), which received the Jerry Bentley Book Prize of the World History Association. He is now working on a study of agriculture and the environment in nineteenth-century South India. His articles have appeared in *Past and Present*, the *Journal of Social History*, *Modern Asian Studies*, and *International Labor and Working-Class History*. He is a senior editor of *International Labor and Working-Class History* and served on the editorial board of the *American Historical Review*. He teaches with Juliet Schor a Complex Problem course titled "Planet in Peril."

David Quigley is the provost and dean of faculties and a professor of history at Boston College. He was previously dean of the Morrissey College of Arts and Sciences at BC. He is the author of *Second Founding: New York City, Reconstruction, and the Making of American Democracy* (2004). He has taught the Enduring Question course "Worlds of *Moby-Dick*: What Historical Forces Shape a Book's Greatness."

Brian D. Robinette is an associate professor of theology at Boston College. He researches and teaches in the areas of systematic, philosophical, and spiritual theology, with special interests in anthropology, secularity, and contemplative theory/practice. He is the author of the award-winning *Grammars of Resurrection: A Christian Theology of Presence and Absence* (Crossroad, 2009) and is currently working on a theology of creation, tentatively titled *The Difference Nothing Makes: Creation, Christ, Contemplation*.

Juliet B. Schor is a professor of sociology at Boston College. Her books include the *New York Times* best seller *The Overworked American*. She is also the author of *The Overspent American*, *Sustainable Lifestyles and the Quest for Plenitude*, and *True Wealth*. Schor has written extensively on issues of working time, consumption, and environmental sustainability. Since 2011 Schor has been studying the "sharing economy," including both large platforms and smaller community initiatives. Schor is a former Guggenheim Fellow, Radcliffe Fellow, and Brookings Institution Fellow, and in 2014 she received the American Sociological Association's award for Public Understanding of Sociology. Schor is the chair of the board of directors of the Better Future Project, the parent organization of 350MA, a large climate activist organization in Massachusetts. She co-teaches "Planet in Peril: The History and Future of Human Impacts on the Planet."

Sylvia Sellers-García is a professor of history at Boston College. She is a historian of colonial Latin America, focusing on documentation, archival studies, and marginality. Her book *Distance and Documents at the Spanish Empire's Periphery* (Stanford University Press, 2013), considers the relationship between documents and distance in the Spanish Empire. *The Woman on the Windowsill: A Tale of Mystery in Several Parts* (Yale University Press, 2020), tells the story of a sensational crime that took place in Guatemala City in 1800. Sellers-García also writes fiction for adults and young readers, several of which examine the intersection of the fantastical and the historical. An enduring interest for Sellers-García is the meeting point of fiction and history, the related meeting point of academic writing and popular writing, and what we can learn from them about ways of knowing. With Allison Adair, she teaches the Enduring Question course "Truth-Telling in History."

Elizabeth H. Shlala is the assistant dean of the Core and associate professor of the practice at Boston College. She is a historian of the Middle East and North Africa and is also a visiting scholar at the FXB Center for Health and Human Rights at the T. H. Chan School of Public Health at Harvard University. Her work explores the nexus of modern migration and law in the Middle East. Her main research areas are twofold: legal imperialism and colonial hybridity in the late Ottoman period and the social and economic impact of contemporary global migration. Her most recent book is titled *The Late Ottoman Empire and Egypt: Hybridity, Law, and Gender.*

Min Hyoung Song is a professor of English at Boston College, where he is chair of the English Department and directs the Asian American Studies Program. He is a participating faculty member in the Environmental Studies Program and an affiliated faculty member of the African and African Diaspora Studies Program. His teaching and research have increasingly become focused on the intersections of race, ecology, and aesthetics. He is completing a book manuscript tentatively titled "Everyday Denial and Climate Lyricism." He is the author of *The Children of 1964: On Writing, and Not Writing, as an Asian American* (which won several awards) and *Strange Future: Pessimism and the 1992 Los Angeles Riots*. He is the co-editor of *The Cambridge History of Asian American Literature*, and is general co-editor of the four-volume Cambridge University Press series Asian American Literature in Transition. He taught the Enduring Question course "Humans, Nature, and Culture."

Jenna Tonn is an assistant professor of the practice and director of undergraduate studies for the human-centered engineering program at Boston College. Dr. Tonn received her Ph.D. in the history of science from Harvard University and taught in the Program in Studies of Women, Gender, and Sexuality at Harvard before arriving at BC as one of the first cohort of Core Fellows. Her research centers on the social and cultural history of scientific knowledge, with a specific focus on women and gender in STEM. She is currently working on a book about masculinity and experimental biology in the nineteenth-century United States. Her next project is a history of radical feminist biology. Dr. Tonn holds a B.A. and M.A. from Stanford University. She designed and taught the hands-on experiential laboratory practicum (STEM Lab) for the Complex Problem course "Science and Technology in American Society."

Holly VandeWall is associate professor of the practice in the Philosophy Department at Boston College. She received her Ph.D. in the history and philosophy of science at the University of Notre Dame and also holds a Master's degree in science and ethics from the Graduate Theological Union in Berkeley, California. Her research includes work on the provision of scientific advice for environmental policy, the history of U.S. water policy, environmental ethics, and the use of history and philosophy of science in the improvement of scientific literacy. She is co-author of a textbook in the history and philosophy of science with Bloomsbury Press. Her Enduring Question course was titled "Inquiring about Humans and Nature."

Dunwei Wang is a professor of chemistry and chair of the chemistry department at Boston College. He graduated from the University of Science and Technology of China with a bachelor of science degree in 2000. He continued his education at Stanford until 2005, where he earned his Ph.D. in chemistry. After two years of postdoctoral research at Caltech, he joined Boston College in 2007, serving as assistant, associate, and full professor of chemistry. He leads a team researching on solar energy conservation and storage. He is also the chair of the Chemistry Department at Boston College.

Index

CPSIA information can be obtained
at www.ICGtesting.com
Printed in the USA
JSHW021049260423
40844JS00001B/6